It Kept Me Off The Streets

The Sleepless Nights of an Ultra Runner

Martin Thomerson

Published by: Martin Thomerson
itkeptmeoffthestreets@outlook.com

ISBN: 978-1-5262-0323-6

Cover photograph:
The author ascending Pillar during the 10 Peaks race, Lake District (2011)
(photo by Brandon Webb)

Rear cover photograph:
The author in a snowstorm on the summit of Bowfell, Lake District (2012)

Papers used in this book are natural, renewable and recyclable products sourced from well-managed forests.

Typeset in Times, designed and produced by Gilmour Print
www.self-publish-books.co.uk

For Clair, Kieran and Harry

Contents

	Preface	*vii*
1.	Yr Wyddfa	*1*
2.	Storm: Welsh 1,000-metre Peaks Fell Race *(June 2009)*	*9*
3.	Where and When	*18*
4.	Heat: Old County Tops Fell Race *(May 2010)*	*25*
5.	End to End	*35*
6.	First Hundred: South Downs Way Race *(September 2010)*	*51*
7.	There and Back	*62*
8.	Perfect Day: 10 Peaks *(July 2011)*	*67*
9.	Cycling to a Number	*75*
10.	Hard Graft: OMM Elite *(October 2011)*	*82*
11.	Gearing Up	*95*
12.	Gaining Confidence: South Downs Way 100 *(June 2012)*	*105*
13.	Training	*113*
14.	Trip to the Afterlife: Lakeland 100 *(July 2012)*	*121*
15.	Motivation	*131*
16.	Frozen: High Peak Marathon *(March 2013)*	*139*
17.	Peak Bagging	*148*
18.	Running Flat: Thames Path 100 *(March 2013)*	*164*
19.	It's not about the Bling	*173*
20.	Big Mountains: Courmayeur Champex Chamonix *(August 2013)*	*180*
21.	The Road to Hell	*190*
22.	Grind: Fellsman *(April 2014)*	206

23. A Marathon's a Sprint 216

24. Once More: Lakeland 100 *(July 2014)* 223

25. An Occupational Hazard 233

26. Three out of Three: Lakeland 100 *(July 2015)* 239

27. Stress Fracture 249

28. The Big One: Ultra Trail du Mont Blanc 260
    (August 2016)

29. Why? 276

30. Past, Present and Future 281

Acknowledgements 284

About the Author 285

Appendix: List of Races 286

Preface

I'm not a runner. I'm definitely not a road runner. Everyone thinks I am but I'm not. Granted, I've run a lot of miles in my time but I just don't see myself as a runner.

I'm a mountain man, an outdoor guy, a cyclist, a fellsman, a hill walker, a peak bagger, a husband, father, brother, son and uncle. I'm someone who likes to challenge myself to set goals and achieve them.

Is my primary focus to lace up my running shoes and just go running to rack up the miles? No. Running is something I do that enables me to achieve my goals. I like running but I would never call myself a runner.

I've done a lot of endurance challenges in my time and dedicated huge amounts of my life towards them. This book is about some of my adventures as a fell and ultra runner, interspersed with my approach to endurance activities and tales of other challenges. I think it shows a breadth to what I've done over the last 25 years and that's what's important to me.

I'm proud to say that I've never run a race less than a marathon or category A fell race. I never will. This led me to generate an alternative title for this book which I eventually rejected:

'I Didn't do it by Halves.'

It's a good title and completely relevant but the road running reference isn't where my focus lies. My primary love is the hills and if running on them keeps me off the streets, then that's just fine by me.

Hopefully this book will explain that.

Martin Thomerson, 2016

1   Yr Wyddfa

'Find something you like doing and do a lot of it.' (Anon)

Friday 6th May 2016. Llanberis, Gwynedd, North Wales.

I've been here before. The Snowdonia Marathon starts and ends here. The Snowdon fell race too. Between the two, I've run them twelve times. I've run from Llanberis on my own, on many, many occasions. After a run, I sometimes have a pint at The Heights or the Padarn Lake Hotel. At other times, I'll eat at Pete's Eats. I have what I see as my own parking space in the car park adjacent to the Electric Mountain visitor centre. I feel at home here.

In winter, Llanberis is a dreary, run-down little village with the vast, grey slate quarries on the opposite side of Llyn Padarn dominating. In summer, it's full of tourists heading for the Mountain Railway, the Electric Mountain, the National Slate Museum or the Lake Railway. On marathon and fell race days it positively buzzes.

Five miles south of Llanberis lies the mighty mountain of Yr Wyddfa, more commonly known as Snowdon. Standing 1,085m above sea level, it's the highest peak in England and Wales, topped only in Britain by the mountains of the Scottish Highlands. It's a fine, triangular-shaped mountain with rocky outcrops, dizzying precipices and sharp ridges heading away from its summit. It has good paths to the top from all directions, each different in character and offering a different challenge. In the summer months, the railway from Llanberis ferries tourists to the top where the 2009 visitor centre sits resplendent, with unsurpassed views as far as Ireland and Scotland. It was used by Edmund Hillary for training before the successful 1953 expedition to conquer Everest. In summary, it's a fine mountain.

Today I'm in Llanberis to run up it.

It's 5 pm on a clear, cool, Friday evening. I'm in my running gear, with full leg cover and two layers on my top. This will

1

probably be too warm on the lower slopes but it will be cooler once I get high up and this will save me stopping to add a layer on the way up. I have a buff wrapped round my wrist to use as a hat if I need it. I've got a rucksack with my waterproofs, a thin fleece, a headtorch, a few bits to eat and a bottle of water. I probably won't need much of this but I'm always prepared. My car keys, phone and wallet are just unusable weight for this trip, trappings from a materialistic world that seem so important every day, yet in the activity I love most are completely useless. Putting them into the bottom of a rucksack always serves as a simple reminder of why I love heading into the hills. It will be just me and the mountain for the next couple of hours, a great way to end the week and forget about the stresses of day-to-day life.

I head out of the car park and jog gently up the road, past the mountain railway station and turn right into the long, straight road that leads to the bottom of the incline. This will be the last flat running for the next hour or so. I always love running along this road, with terraced houses on the left and the road rising steeply up ahead. It reminds me of the Snowdon fell race and feels like I'm about to exit civilisation for a mini-adventure in the hills. At the end of this road is a gate and then it heads upwards. It's a mile up the road until the exit onto the fellside but it's a very steep mile. I'm not properly warmed up yet and my legs feel heavy. The incline is severe, quickly taking me to the limit of my ability. Very soon, I'm breathing hard, the backs of my legs are straining badly and I'm fighting to keep going. I'm overheating so have pushed my sleeves up but just concentrate on taking small, running steps until the slope eases after the first few bends. I recover slightly but know that there's a second kick coming around the next corner. This section's shorter but very steep again and now I've got sweat pouring into my eyes. Soon enough, I can turn off the road, through the gate and onto the good path where the gradient will be easier until I climb much higher.

The path on the lower slopes is good underfoot, very wide

and well maintained. However, it's still a challenge to run on, hopping up rocks, picking little lines through the rougher sections and avoiding any loose stones. I'm running with my head down, constantly scanning the ground a few metres ahead of me to avoid difficulties. When running on the hills, this is so often the way, concentrating on each footstep, rather than the effortless striding out that all road runners are used to doing.

There are a few walkers heading down and I get the usual comments: 'You must be fit', 'Are you running all the way up?' and 'Have you missed the train?' I tend to nod an acknowledgement but it's hard work running uphill so I don't have any spare energy for conversation.

The gradient on the path is steady, nice to run along and I slowly make progress up to the little bridge under the railway track. The views across to the right are fantastic, with the peaks of Moel Eilio, Foel Gron and Moel Cynghorion standing as sentinels across the valley. These are great hills but so little frequented with Snowdon drawing all the attention.

It's getting cooler as I climb higher, with a gentle breeze blowing across the hillside so I've pulled my sleeves back down. The Halfway House comes and goes, then shortly afterwards the path heads steeply up the rocky staircase leading to Clogwyn station. Once again, I'm working very hard to maintain my running, just concentrating on watching my feet on the rocks. My legs still feel heavy and I've got lots of aches and pains: both achilles tendons, the arch of my right foot, right knee and left shin. This always seems to be the way these days, nothing too bad but constant reminders that I've had some big days out recently and my legs know about it. I can't rest just yet though.

I head under the railway for a second time, emerging high above the Llanberis Pass. The few cars on the road look tiny, far, far below. I haven't seen any other walkers for a while now, so feel as if I've got the mountain all to myself.

The path now heads up steeply and rockily towards the upper reaches of the mountain. On a good day I can run all the way up here. Today, however, I'm feeling sluggish and soon hit the point at which my running pace is the same as a fast walk. I switch styles, moving to a brisk walk, hands on thighs, to push myself along. I'm still moving upwards rapidly but now more comfortably with less energy being expended. I can look around to take in the views. The Glyderau mountains are fantastic to the left, severe rocky peaks across the valley. As the path swings right, I can see across the hills to the west, all the way to the Llyn Peninsular and the Irish Sea.

The gradient eases and I start running again, trundling upwards around the slopes of Snowdon's sister peak, Garnedd Ugain. I reach the famous obelisk where the Pyg, Miners and Ranger paths all converge for the final ridge. The path runs adjacent to the railway now and I'm into the last few minutes of pushing upwards, the mountain dropping steeply away to both sides. The visitor centre comes into view, there's another walker just departing the summit with his dog, then I have the final few steps up onto the summit. I jog slowly up the steps and touch the large stone trig point at the very top.

I have the summit to myself which is rare for Snowdon. The views in all directions are incredible, although restricted by a slight haze. I take a few minutes to look around and enjoy the peace and tranquillity. It's absolutely silent up here and feels detached from the land below. It's amazing.

After a few minutes, I'm starting to get cold so head back the way I came. The running is much easier now with gravity assisting. A quarter of the way back to Llanberis, I head off the path to run across the grassy slopes of the mountain's shoulder for a mile or so. The silence of the evening, with no one within miles of me, is invigorating. It's just me, trundling across a grassy hillside, with everything I need on my back. I love times like this, trotting along in the hills, with great views and all alone. Just me, my thoughts and my ability to navigate myself around the hills. It's very simple but, for me, it's life's greatest pleasure.

Soon enough, I'm back in Llanberis after two and a half

hours of running. It's been a short trip to the hills for me but a very special one.

This was my 100th ascent of Snowdon.

A day later, I returned to walk up it again with my wife, Clair, and our two boys, Kieran and Harry. It felt right to run it solo to rack up my 100th ascent because this is how I usually spend my time in the hills. It equally felt right to return the next day and walk it for number 101, as a celebration with my family.

Snowdon is the mountain I've climbed more than any other. I've climbed 570 different peaks, making 2,133 ascents, which gives an average of 3.7 ascents for each peak. Snowdon is a long way above this 3.7 average because it's such a great mountain to climb and has so much variety.

I first climbed it back in 1994 with a group of university friends as the final peak on the National Three Peaks Challenge. This is a recognised challenge to climb the highest mountains of Scotland, England and Wales in under 24 hours. I recall it being a fairly grim undertaking, with many hours of driving, broken by a quick assault on a peak and then back to the driving. We climbed Snowdon from Pen-y-Pass, going straight up and down the Miners' track. It was an uneventful walk in typical conditions of low cloud with no views. Little did I know at the time just how often I'd return to this fine mountain over the years to come.

Since then I've climbed Snowdon from all directions and on all routes. I've run up it 73 times and walked 28. I've climbed solo 84 times, climbed with someone else eleven and as part of a race six. I've been up the Llanberis path 57 times, Ranger eighteen, Miners eleven, Pyg seven, Watkin four, South Ridge three and Crib Goch once. I've even climbed it four times in a single day when training for a race in the Alps.

I have many great memories on Snowdon. I've seen all number of crazy things on its slopes which you just don't see on any other mountain. I've seen sedan chairs being carried up, wheelchairs being hauled up, people in fancy dress and charity t-shirts with collection buckets, tourists in flip-flops who have come up on the train, children enjoying the climb and mountain bikers lugging their bikes up. Snowdon attracts people during the summer like no other mountain. This is fine during good weather but the weather is often poor. On these occasions, I've so often seen people inappropriately dressed and ill-equipped for conditions that can be very challenging. This isn't just in winter but in summer too. Summer storms can batter its summit, with high winds, poor visibility and low temperatures that you just wouldn't believe when down in the safety of the valleys far below. In winter, I've been horrified at how unprepared people are when trying to climb it. Snowdon kills people most winters because it has some perilous drops and steep slopes, so you need the right equipment to tackle it when it's covered in snow and ice.

Then there's the train. So many dislike the train because it drags tourists effortlessly to the summit while others have ascended under their own efforts. I must say that I rather like it. The feat of engineering to actually build a track to the highest point in England and Wales is impressive. As is seeing, hearing and smelling the little steam trains labouring upwards towards the summit. Seeing the track unusable in winter, covered in snow drifts and thick ice near the summit, also serves to remind me how nature is far more powerful than ourselves, preventing the train from running during the winter months. Personally, I think the train and the visitor centre add something to Snowdon that no other English or Welsh mountain has, although I don't ever go inside the visitor centre unless I'm with someone else. I like the way the train makes the mountain accessible to those who otherwise wouldn't be able to experience what it's like to stand on a mountain top and admire the views (when there are some) or experience the bad weather (when there are none).

I've experienced extremes of weather on the mountain. One memorable day saw me climbing up the Pyg track in the dark in thick snow. Towards the top, the path was completely obliterated and was just a steeply raked snow slope. As I climbed diagonally across it, carefully planting my crampons and ice axe for security, my headtorch picked out crags in front of me, blocking my way. I was looking for the exit onto the summit ridge but must have gone wrong across the slope despite having done the route many times before. Fairly quickly I realised that I must be too low, so by climbing just twenty metres or so directly upwards I managed to rectify the situation. Admittedly, it was dark but mist creates similar circumstances even if it's light. When I emerged onto the summit ridge, I was almost swept straight off it again as the wind was blowing at gale force with driving snow. I'd been sheltered in the lee of it on my climb up. I made it to the summit but only by walking very carefully, bent double and placing every footstep with caution. Visibility was practically zero, even as daylight emerged on that ridge. Conditions were a complete white-out, with the cloud, driving snow and ground all indistinguishable from each other. If I hadn't known the summit ridge so well, I would have turned back. This was a good example of how difficult conditions can be in winter and why Snowdon and other mountains need respect. The summer tourists on the train would never believe it was the same place.

The best day to be on Snowdon is on fell race day each July. The atmosphere in Llanberis is amazing, as 500 runners run a helter-skelter five miles to the summit, climbing 3,000 feet upwards, before plunging straight back down the way they came to lose all that height. I've done the fell race four times and every one was a great day out. My personal best of 1:39:43 pales into insignificance against the course record of 1:02:29. This record has stood for 31 years and will probably never be beaten. It's about the same my best time to the summit, only the halfway point of the race. The mountain is lined with walkers and spectators, all applauding and cheering. The television helicopter buzzes overhead and you get to see the front runners coming back down as you ascend. This is worth the entry fee alone, to see first-hand these supermen as they hurtle back towards Llanberis at speeds that defy logic.

The saddest sight I've seen on any mountain was on Snowdon in the 2009 fell race. As I ran down the steepest section, still high on the mountain, I was warned of an injured runner ahead. I then saw a fellow runner being given CPR by a Mountain Rescue team at the side of the path. As I dropped out of the cloud, the RAF rescue helicopter was hovering just above the path waiting to come in and assist. Tragically, the runner died, which put the whole race into perspective. He'd been very fit and healthy, had done the race multiple times but suffered a heart attack on the ascent. The image of him at the side of the path will always remain with me and always serve as a reminder of how dangerous and physically exerting our mountains are.

On a happier note, Clair and I climbed Snowdon on New Year's Day 2000, the first day of the new Millennium. There can't be a finer way to have seen in the next one thousand years.

Snowdon has both happy and sad memories for me. There's no other place that I've travelled to so often, where I've exerted myself so strenuously and have experienced such extreme conditions. This mountain has taught me a lot about myself, about mountain running and about my ability to deal with testing situations. It's a fantastic mountain and my favourite.

Hills and mountains have played a large part in my life. I've spent many thousands of hours walking or running over them. They define who I am, what I love doing and what I want to be remembered for. Snowdon more so than any other. Completing my 100th ascent of this great mountain has fulfilled one of my life's ambitions and is something of which I'm very proud.

However, it wasn't my only ambition. I've done a few other outdoor things in my time. The tales that follow are all part of the greater whole, my adventures in working towards other goals or simply just enjoying myself in the great outdoors.

2 Storm: Welsh 1,000-metre Peaks Fell Race
(June 2009)

'The full race from Aber is a gruelling event, even in fine weather. It is a test of fitness, endurance and orienteering skills and the terrain is wild and remote. The A Class Fell Race is considered to be one of the most arduous events in the UK fell running calendar.' (Race Organiser)

The Welsh 1,000-metre Peaks fell race is a long-established race on the annual fell running calendar. It's derived from the recognised challenge of walking or running the fifteen 3,000-feet peaks in Snowdonia but is a variant devised by the army. Starting at Aber on the North Wales coast, it covers 22 miles with 8,000 feet of climbing through the Carneddau and Glyderau mountains, before a final ascent to the finish on the summit of Snowdon. The classic route, which was run until 2012, takes in the four Welsh summits above 1,000 metres in altitude, these being Carnedd Llewelyn, Carnedd Dafydd, Garnedd Ugain and Snowdon. In 2013, a fifth peak was added, Glyder Fawr, after it was re-surveyed and elevated above the 1,000 metre height.

The race was the original four-peak route when I ran it in 2009 and 2010. It's the kind of race that suits me and that I love. It's a long journey with a purpose, running from the coast to the highest point in Wales. Navigation skills are essential, as is the ability to move across rough mountain terrain quickly, with the Carneddau being wild and remote, the Glyderau being steep and rough, and the race finishing with a big climb up to Garnedd Ugain, before heading to Snowdon's summit for the finish. After finishing, there's then a five-mile walk down the mountain to return to your car in Llanberis. This is unique from any other race that I've done, in having such a remote finishing place.

The week prior to the race, in June 2009, I'd been on holiday in Porthmadog on the edge of Snowdonia. It was the May bank holiday week and we'd got lucky with the weather which had been perfect with sunshine all week and temperatures of 25 to 30 degrees. This broke on Friday evening with a sudden drop in temperature and a storm on the way in from the Atlantic.

On Saturday morning the weather was wild. I parked up in Llanberis to catch the event bus to the start at Aber. I'd arrived early and was waiting in the car. It was rocking in the wind, with the rain lashing off the windscreen. I had limited kit with me and was planning to run in shorts with a large bumbag but was reconsidering my decision as it appeared so awful and would be a lot worse higher up. I concluded that I'd stick with my plan as I knew the terrain well and knew that I'd be up and then down from the high ground quickly. I was going to run in sufficient layers on my top half and with a decent waterproof so experience said that I'd be fine.

We all got the bus to the start and it was a subdued journey with everyone wondering how bad conditions would be and whether they'd got the right gear, especially as it was off the back of the hottest week of the year. The bad weather had come as a bit of a surprise after a week of sustained good weather. I was confident in my ability but never look forward to climbing up high in bad weather, as it's always testing and much harder work than when the weather's good.

The start was from a field by the coast, where we all registered and then, to a man, huddled under a large tree to shelter from the wind and rain. There were 82 of us starting the fell race. We would be chasing down 196 people entered as walkers or from the armed services who'd set off an hour and a half before us. There was a real sense of Dunkirk-spirit under that tree, chatting about what lay ahead and with jokes being cracked. It was a fantastic twenty minutes or so, a time when we just wanted to get on with things but also didn't want to leave the safety and camaraderie of that tree. A few minutes before the start, we were called over to the start line on the other side of the field. We were checked to ensure that we had a map and compass and then given a very straight briefing. The organiser told us to expect zero visibility and winds of over eighty miles per hour on the tops. Reports from the marshals were that it was sleeting up there.

He told us simply, 'If there's anyone who's not comfortable in those conditions or not properly equipped then you should not leave this field.'

The message was very clear and not one competitor would have been in any doubt about the severity of the conditions that were awaiting us on the hills. Once he'd confirmed that we were all starting, he uttered the best words that I've ever heard at any race start: 'Right lads, we're taking this seriously and I want no messing about. When I say "Go" you bloody well go!'

A minute later, we were on our way, running through the lanes of Aber and onto the tourist track towards the famous waterfalls. The route then headed off through the woods, climbing steadily, across a rocky scree section and into a narrow, technical little valley above the mighty waterfalls. These were in spate and a cacophony of noise with all the night's rainfall cascading over them. We then emerged onto the open fellside, already in the cloud, climbing up to the first checkpoint on the side of Yr Aryg. Shortly before arriving, there were two competitors from the earlier races heading back down towards us. This was the first sign that anything was difficult because they'd started a long time before us and I wouldn't have expected to see anyone for a while yet.

We were strung out across the fell already and I was working on a compass bearing in case I lost sight of the line of runners in front, as visibility was poor. The wind was buffeting us about and it was colder than expected but the best approach was to keep trucking as fast as possible to get across the high ground quickly. Once we hit the main ridge, the strength of the wind was apparent and it was howling. Progress was difficult due to being blown about and the rain was horizontal. Conditions were extreme but I'd been out in worse before so I just kept moving and concentrating on my navigation. I wasn't with anyone but runners were ahead and behind me. I reached the summit of Carnedd Llewelyn which was the first of the high 1,000-metre peaks. The wind was screaming across the summit, the marshals were hunkered down and I just checked in at the control and got out of there as fast as I could. Just before arriving at the summit, I'd taken a new bearing to exit the summit on, so I could move off very quickly.

I picked my way carefully down the scree, moving on and off the path and struggling to stay upright in the wind. I was conscious that I needed to keep moving because, although I had a few layers on my top, I was only wearing shorts and needed to keep generating heat. I moved very carefully along the narrow ridge that needed crossing to the next peak, picking my way slowly along the slippery rocks which were made far more hazardous by the wind that was howling over the col. I got quite cold across here because I couldn't speed up at all due to the harsh conditions and technical terrain. Once I emerged onto the wider hillside beyond, I could push on harder on the long, steady climb up to Carnedd Dafydd, peak number two.

This was an out-and-back route, so I noted the position of the ruined wall that I'd look for on the return which would be my marker to drop off the path and head straight down the fellside. I reached the summit quickly and checked in with the marshals but didn't hang around and started to retrace my steps. I'd been alone in the mist all the way to the summit but was conscious that I had a very difficult, off-path descent coming up. As I headed down, I passed a number of runners who were a few hundred metres behind me and were still heading up to the summit. I made a decision that will seem alien to pure racers but was very sensible given the conditions. I slowed down to allow them to catch me before I got to the turn-off point at the ruined wall. The descent beyond there is not on a path, navigating down through rough terrain which I didn't know well, there was very little visibility and I could hardly stand up in the howling wind. My thinking was that we'd have safety in numbers if there were three or four of us together over this upcoming difficult section.

This plan worked well and by the time I reached the wall there were four of us together. I was working on a bearing down the hillside, as were the others, and we were all spread out a little bit, shouting out good lines and little routes down through the rocky outcrops and steep grassy sections. We hit the wall that we were aiming for at the bottom of this section, still high in the mountains, and progressed along to the safety checkpoint a bit further on. This checkpoint was introduced a few years beforehand because a competitor had sadly died after falling over a crag on this descent, a little further over on the hillside. The safety control pulled us away from that dangerous area. On this occasion we couldn't find it. A couple of other competitors were in the area and we soon concluded that we were in the right place and had to move on. Afterwards we were told that the control was missing due to the harsh conditions and we were correct to ignore it and proceed.

We all spread out again from here and ran down to the access road at Ffynnon Llugwy reservoir, nestled under the ridge of Carnedd Llewellyn. This was the hardest section of navigation now over with and the wildest, most remote hills completed. As I ran down the road with another runner, we saw the RAF rescue helicopter flying into the hills from which we'd just emerged.

'Somebody's in trouble,' I commented to him and we discussed how testing that section had been. There was a checkpoint at the bottom where we hit the main road through the Ogwen valley. As we went through, the marshal asked, 'Are you continuing?' to which we both replied, 'Yes,' as we ran on. It was a bizarre moment because we both exchanged quizzical looks afterwards and he said, 'Sounds like a lot are pulling out,' but we just kept running.

We ran through the valley, across the road and then onto a long, hard climb up a grassy mountainside with no path. Once again, I was alone up here, heading through the mist and keeping my head down against the swirling wind and rain. This was a proper storm that you get in the mountains, where you're not in control of all of your movements as the force of the wind is so powerful it can literally knock you from your feet. It's difficult to describe unless you've experienced it but when you're alone, with zero visibility, on dangerous ground that you need to navigate over, wind and rain assaulting all your senses, then it's an incredibly intense experience. It's potentially very frightening and unless you know what you're doing and how to get yourself through it and out the other side, then it's a very dangerous position to be in. I was just concentrating on climbing upwards and knowing I had a right turn towards the top to look for, before heading for a small tarn which was close to the next control. This was my last big navigation test. There was no one to follow through here but I hit it all perfectly and then was on a decent track down the other side, to drop down towards Pen-y-Pass and the final section of the race.

I arrived at the Pen-y-Pass checkpoint and the option was again given of retiring, rather than subjecting myself to the onslaught that would await high up on the exposed summit of Snowdon. I said that I was fine, had no issues and pressed on. I headed onto the Pyg track which is one of the main tourist paths up Snowdon. Unsurprisingly, it was deserted, which is unusual for a Saturday in summer. I was cold and tired but pleased to be on the final pull. It was a long slog up the rocky track but I was making good progress and conscious of the need to just keep moving efficiently against the wind, cold and rain. After an hour or so, I emerged at the obelisk on the col where the wind was screaming over the main summit ridge and it was difficult to make any progress against it. I took the right turn and headed up to the summit of Garnedd Ugain, checking in with the cowering marshals. I then headed back to the obelisk for the final ten-minute slog up to Snowdon summit and the finish. It was wild up here but I'd experienced the same many times before and was comfortable in such aggressive conditions. I reached the summit to finish and shouted a few words of thanks to the marshals in the maelstrom while clinging onto the summit rocks. I was handed a medal which I stuffed in my bumbag and then left after less than a minute to get myself off the mountain and down to a safer altitude.

The run off Snowdon back down to Llanberis is one that I've done many times before but it was slow going with the wind screaming across the mountain. Halfway down, I saw the RAF helicopter again and it registered with me that I'd never seen it twice in one day before. Conditions must be bad. I didn't see anyone else on the descent and just kept trucking down as fast as I could with tired legs.

When I reached the car, I realised how cold I was as I struggled to undo my shoelaces and get myself changed into warm clothes. I was shivering badly but at least I was off the mountains and had food and a flask of coffee to revive myself with. It had been a good day out, I'd run well and coped well with the extreme conditions. All my previous experience in bad weather had served me well as I was never close to my limit, never in danger and never had any doubt about my ability to carry on and continue the route. On many other occasions, I've turned back on routes when the weather was too bad and I wasn't comfortable with continuing on. Not so today, as I felt the entire route had been manageable with my mountain-craft skills, physical fitness and previous experience.

We were staying at Clair's parents in North Wales that night so I drove back, showered and relaxed in the knowledge of a job well done. What happened in the early evening was just bizarre.

I was sitting on the sofa with a beer when I got a text from my brother.

'Are you ok?'

I texted back, 'Yes. I finished in 5:59.'

Then a few minutes later my other brother rang me.

'Are you ok?'

'Yes. Kev's just texted asking the same. Why?' I asked.

'Haven't you seen the news?'

'No. What's happened?'

Then it all came out. The BBC had got hold of the story that

15

a fell race was in trouble in Snowdonia due to being hit by an 85 mph storm. The BBC reported that over twenty competitors were rescued by Mountain Rescue and that the race had been abandoned. This then sparked all the usual debate about how irresponsible it was to be up in the mountains in those conditions. Also how irresponsible it was for the organisers to allow the event to continue in the face of such atrocious weather.

My take on the whole thing is that I ran the entire race from start to finish, was never near my survival limit and got myself home safely without even knowing there was a problem. I was so surprised when contacted by my brothers to see if I was ok. Of course I was, why wouldn't I be? Admittedly I'm an experienced mountain runner but if I can run the race and not even know that anything would be amiss, as I've been out in conditions similar or worse on many occasions, then why would it be irresponsible to run the race?

The race organiser was absolutely crystal clear in spelling out the conditions that we'd face on the summits, so no competitor started that race without knowing what they were in for. In my eyes, testing conditions are part of the challenge of being out in the hills and I'm well equipped to deal with them. Admittedly a few competitors got caught out and came down with hypothermia but these were in the minority and the event was at no fault in my view. I love the self-sufficiency and self-responsibility that is an essential part of surviving in the mountains. I would think something has gone very wrong if we start applying restrictions to those who go out in harsh weather, wanting to test and better themselves in such conditions.

All told, I would rate this race as my finest pure fell running achievement due to the speed that I maintained in such harsh conditions. I finished in 5 hours and 59 minutes, which is only five minutes slower than my time a year later when conditions were almost perfect, being warm, full visibility and I knew the course better. Comparing the conditions on the two days, I'd have expected a difference in times of twenty to thirty minutes, not just five.

The Welsh 1,000-metre Peaks is a great race, a great route and a great journey. It doesn't have the draw of the classic long fell races in the Lake District but that's part of its appeal. Long may races such as this continue in our hills, in all weather conditions.

278 started, 92 finished, I came 28th. The race had a 67% drop-out rate.

3   Where and When

'When eating an elephant take one bite at a time.'
(Creighton Abrams)

On any race, you always want to try and predict your finishing time as well as where you'll be at critical points on the course. This becomes more important as the races get longer so you can mentally prepare yourself for how long you're going to be out running. It's also important because ultras always have time cut-offs along the route and if you're at the back end of the field it's good to know how close or not you will be to these cut-offs.

When I run a marathon, I always have a target time and a pace to get to that target time. This is typically 3 hours and 15 minutes which is just under 7.5 minutes per mile. I tend to be a bit faster in the early miles and a bit slower in the later miles but not by much. I can track this using my watch with splits which has become much easier now with a GPS running watch. Prior to this, it was always necessary to take a split time at each mile marker which are not always easy to spot. Either way, you can easily calculate your rough finishing time by knowing how many minutes you're up or down on your target pace and where that will leave you at the race finish.

For an ultra, it's a whole different ball game. There are a lot of variables that affect your running pace that need to be considered and make predicting times much more difficult.

Ultras are generally run over mixed terrain and not on roads. The underfoot conditions can be road, hard trails, grass, mud, rocks, dusty track, moorland, off-path sections and anything else. The ground conditions can vary from bone dry to wet, boggy or even snow and ice depending on the time of year. For a run over the same route, the conditions can vary wildly by season which translates into different times over the same ground. In the 2011 Tour de Helvellyn race in the Lake District, I was wading through waist-deep snow to climb Sticks Pass which was incredibly slow and not even at walking pace, then had skiers coming past me as I ran down the other side. Such are the extreme underfoot conditions that you can have on ultras.

Not only does the terrain underfoot vary but ultras generally involve hills which have uphill, downhill and flat sections. Uphill sections are slower than downhill and speed is difficult to predict depending on how steep the climbs or descents are, coupled with the nature of the ground underfoot.

As well as the ground, there will be obstacles to clear such as gates, stiles and cattle grids. These all slow you down. On a 100-miler, just one per mile will add up. On the South Downs Way there are 95 stiles and gates. If you slow by just ten seconds at each one, then you'll lose sixteen minutes over the full distance. Ten seconds might sound a lot to get over a stile or through a gate but when you're shattered and not moving well, then you soon lose time at these points. I've had times where I could hardly lift my legs to get over a stile.

Another less obvious obstacle that can slow you down is a field of cows, particularly if they're unsettled or gathered at the gate or stile that you need to use. I've experienced this a number of times. When 95 miles into my first 100-miler on the South Downs Way, there were cows that wouldn't move from a gate and blocked our progress. We had to move around them to a suitable point on a fence then carefully climb it, avoiding getting snagged on the barbed wire. It wouldn't have been too much of an issue normally but with 95 miles in the legs it was a slow and difficult manoeuvre. On another race, the Three Rings of Shap, on a very warm and humid day in the Vale of Eden, there were lots of fields of cows. They were all very restless, maybe due to the uncomfortable, hot conditions and being disturbed by lots of runners. Care was needed as they stampeded about, to pick our way around them without aggravating them further. Each field was considerably slower than it would have been if it were empty of cows.

Navigating takes time too. Ultras vary and some are fully marked courses which you just have to follow. However, if it's an event that you need to navigate yourself then you can easily lose time when you have technical or confusing sections to work your way across. If you get it wrong, time must be spent back-tracking and getting yourself back on course. The best way to mitigate the risk of this is to recce sections of the course beforehand to become familiar with it and to walk your way through the route.

Darkness adds another dimension that you don't get on marathons. This compounds the variables as you're generally slower at night. This is for two reasons. Firstly, the reduced visibility makes navigation, route-finding and picking your way across difficult ground more difficult. On open moorland you may be working on a compass bearing and that can be very slow going. On technical, rocky ground you may be picking your way between rocky crags and trying to find a line that would be obvious in daylight. Secondly, the tiredness of the early hours is challenging as your mental capability slows and at times you will struggle to stay awake, generally slowing you down. This makes decision-making and navigation slower, as well as the general progress across the ground.

General fatigue causes a drop-off in pace on an ultra. On a marathon my pace might slow by up to a maximum of 10% during the race. On my most consistently paced marathon, at Manchester in 2014, I ran the second half within 53 seconds of my time for the first half, only a 1% drop-off in pace. On a long ultra your pace slows continually as time progresses. Some people call this a decay curve because your pace simply decays away as the time elapses. This can be as much as a slowing of 70 to 80% on a 100-miler, an incredible reduction in pace that you would never believe possible from running distances up to a marathon. This slowing is hard to predict without experience.

Finally, there are stops. On a marathon you never stop. You will slow to grab a drink at a drink station, occasionally stop for a quick toilet stop but basically you never stop. On an ultra, every checkpoint will take time. Refilling a water bottle and grabbing some food takes two to three minutes, replenishing something from a rucksack and a general sort-out can quickly consume ten minutes, a change of socks or administering to a blister ten to fifteen minutes, then a major sort out and hot food at a halfway checkpoint will take twenty to thirty minutes. On top of this is stopped time on the trail for navigating, putting on or removing layers, re-folding maps and toilet stops. Over a full day this adds up significantly and is all time lost against the clock.

Given all this variability, how can you predict not only a finishing time but also the times that you'll arrive at intermediate checkpoints? It's actually not that difficult and is reasonably straightforward to build an approximate schedule for your race. You just need to apply some logic based on assumptions and experience.

Start by breaking the route down into logical sections, typically five to ten miles long. This may already be done for you by the event being broken down into sections between checkpoints. This will naturally provide sensible sections to focus on. If these sections are too long or not suitable, then simply study a map of the route and measure distances, identifying sections that appear simple and logical. Typical features to break it down with are road crossings, settlements, peaks, passes, valley bottoms, lakes, rivers or other features that will be unmistakable when you arrive at them.

Now that you have your sections, you need to apply a pace at which you will travel over the ground. This can then be converted to give you estimated times. All road runners know their pace in minutes per mile so can apply this to predicting finishing times. For all the reasons given, on ultras over mixed terrain, pace varies wildly. The best way of predicting your pace is simply from experience of running over different types of terrain, under different conditions and over different distances. This can be from similar events or just from training runs. I have all my training runs and event splits logged in spreadsheets so have a vast amount of data to work with from runs of different lengths, over lots of different types of terrain, in many different weather conditions and at different times of the year.

So knowing the length of event and the type of terrain, I can set a start pace based on how fast I'll begin the run. For a long trail ultra I might start at twelve minutes per mile. I will then apply knowledge of how much I'll slow down over the course of the event due to fatigue and reduce my pace accordingly. For a 100-miler, this might slow as far as thirty minutes per mile. Again, the best way of having the knowledge of what this degradation of pace will be is from experience and split times from previous events or long training runs over similar ground. By applying these paces, I now have an approximation for my moving time. I will then go back over the sections and think about any particular factors for each section that would merit adjusting the pace. The most pertinent factors are uphill or downhill sections. If a section is all uphill, then it will be significantly slower than one that is entirely downhill running. I will adjust the schedule accordingly. The other most relevant factors are for ground that's difficult to cross, such as bogs, or overnight sections where the pace will be slower and a small adjustment can be made for this.

Now that you have your moving time, you need to add your stopped time. This is the time that you will lose at each checkpoint. I keep this simple but always add something in. On a 100-miler, I will typically add two minutes for the first couple of checkpoints, then five to ten minutes for each one up to the halfway point. I'll assume thirty minutes at this major checkpoint, then ten minutes for each one from there until the finish. This all adds up considerably but is realistic for the time that you will spend at checkpoints. Again, the best method of knowing how long you'll be stopped for is from experience. I always take a split time when I arrive at a checkpoint and another when I leave so I have all this data from previous events to guide me.

Piecing all of this together gives a full schedule for the event with a realistic pace over the ground and checkpoint time factored in. Now compare this against any cut-off times on the course and check that you have a margin of error. If not, then go back and review it to see if you've been too cautious with your pace anywhere and adjust if necessary.

The best way to check if this schedule is actually realistic is to run timed recces of sections of the course. This may not always be possible due to location and time constraints but is worthwhile if you can. On a recce, I would expect to be quicker than my pace during a race, but this does depend on whether I'm reviewing an early or a late section in the race. This is all useful data gathering and allows the schedule to be sanity-checked against real time spent on the ground.

The first time that I ran the Old County Tops fell race in the Lakes, I went through exactly this planning exercise. This race has a very harsh cut-off after 7 hours and 45 minutes. The whole race is run over very tough ground and with a lot of climbing. I ran quite a few recces of the course through the winter to familiarise myself with the details but could never obtain the pace required to get through the cut-off. It was a huge reality check and meant that I was approaching the event fully aware of how risky it could be. However, I knew that most of the recces had been compromised by the conditions in winter. Five weeks before the race, I finally had good conditions and managed a fast recce of one of the long and difficult sections from Thirlmere through to Scafell Pike via the notorious Wythburn valley containing an area known simply as The Bog. At last, I had the data to be confident that I could clear the cut-off. When the race came, conditions were similar and I cleared the cut-off by twenty minutes.

When you've done a race, you then have no need for this planning exercise as you already have a schedule to run on in subsequent years. This is the best schedule that you will ever have as it contains all your own specific data of your pace over the exact course, at the right time of year, with your own decay rate and realistic stop times.

I always like the schedule to be comfortable and one that I should be able to beat. This is psychologically advantageous when running. It always feels much better to be ahead of schedule rather than behind, even if it is only an arbitrary estimate that you're working on. I always print the schedule out and carry it as a laminated card with my map which I stuff down my rucksack belt so it's easily accessible on the go.

For me, planning a schedule and running recces is all part of preparing for a race. It helps me to prepare mentally and review the route intimately beforehand. It isn't an approach taken by everyone but I believe it's the best approach and one that's served me well over the years. It's all part of the rich and varied experience that is part of running ultras in the hills.

4   Heat: Old County Tops Fell Race *(May 2010)*

*'The Old County Tops fell race is a 37-mile/10,000-feet event
(distance and climb dependent on whether you go the right
way). The race starts in Great Langdale and takes in the tops of
Helvellyn, Scafell Pike and Coniston after which the survivors
are fed and watered.' (Race Organiser)*

In the world of traditional fell running, races in England are
categorised by the Fell Runners Association (FRA) on two
metrics: their distance and their severity. Races are classed as
short (S), medium (M) or long (L), simply based on their
distance. They are also categorised A, B or C, based on the
amount of off-road running and climbing involved. I've only
ever been drawn to the more severe races so have only run
category A events. The most testing races are the AL races
(category A long). The Lake District specialises in these with
an annual calendar of classic long fell races, which reads like a
tour guide of Cumbria from where fell running emerged:
Borrowdale, Wasdale, Buttermere, Ennerdale, Duddon, Three
Shires, and Helvellyn and the Dodds. At this level there is also
the Lake District Mountain Trial, which I've completed twice.
This is an awesome test of navigation and endurance that
follows a different route every year, with competitors setting
off at intervals so there is no mass start and no option of
following.

  Then there is one other race that stands just slightly apart
from all these other super tests of mountain-craft and
endurance: the Old County Tops fell race. It sets the pulse
racing and strikes fear into anyone who knows it. It's a bit
different to the other races, a bit off-the-wall and one that only
attracts a certain type of individual. It's an AL race but run in
pairs for safety. All finishers are awarded the coveted cotton t-
shirt which is worn with pride and respect in any fell running
circles thereafter. To obtain that t-shirt you must cover 37 miles
with 10,000 feet of climbing, over rough ground, taking in the

summits of Helvellyn, Scafell Pike and Coniston Old Man along the way. If you find these three peaks on a map of the Lake District, you'll see how far apart they are and that there are no convenient roads linking them. It's all rough ground. Not only that, you have to be quick. There are two cut-offs en route, the critical one being after 25 miles at Cockley Beck. Your pace needs to be under nineteen minutes per mile to get through this, which might not sound fast, but over that distance and terrain it sees many teams timed out each year. It's a race that I love, always first on my calendar each year and always a fantastic day out.

The first thing that's difficult is it's a pair's race. This means that you have to find a partner who also wants to complete it, which can be difficult in itself. For example, I was running a recce of a section of the course before the 2009 race. As I arrived at Angle Tarn, there were two fell runners standing by the stream.

One of them said, 'You look like you're on a mission. Are you training for something?'

'I'm running a section of the Old County Tops,' I replied.

He told me, 'That's a great race. I've done it three times. I've got a much faster partner this year so could be on for a good time. The trouble is I have to find a new partner each year because no one will ever do it twice.'

It's even more complicated than that. Both you and your partner need to be a similar pace over the type of terrain that you're covering. If the pairing is unbalanced, then the faster partner spends the whole time frustrated because they are constantly slowing or waiting for the other one. Conversely, the slower partner spends the whole time chasing the faster one, working at their limit and basically just hanging on all the way round. Both situations are very frustrating and detract from the enjoyment of the event. Another factor is that you rely on both partners being fit, well and uninjured on the day of the event, which increases the risk of you actually getting to the start in the first place.

I'd completed this race in 2009 with a friend, Brandon, with whom I'd run quite a few mountain marathons which require you to run as a pair. Brandon and I are very equally matched in running pace, both on roads and in the mountains. We've also both come into fell running from a hill walking background, so are strong navigators and have lots of experience in the hills. This meant that we knew we'd be well matched in our ability to make the cut-offs that are the key to success at this race. I've run many big races and challenges with Brandon so we know each other's ability very well.

However, this year I was running with another friend, Greg. Greg was drawn immediately to it when I said I wanted to do it again, as he likes a big challenge. Greg is very fit and has plenty of long hill walking experience, although he was relatively new to running at the time. This was to be his first fell race, which really was a case of diving in at the deep end. However, he's one of the most determined people you'll ever meet and I had no doubt that he'd be able to keep up the pace to make the cut-offs, even though we'd be untested as a pair before the event. It would be a bit of a leap of faith, although it wouldn't be for lack of determination if we weren't to get round.

The days running up to the race had perfect British summer weather. Every day had wall-to-wall sunshine and the temperature got slightly warmer each day. The weather forecast for the day of the race was for temperatures just below thirty degrees and unbroken sun. This would add to the test as running in heat is always draining.

After an early start to drive up to the Lakes, we registered at the New Dungeon Ghyll pub in Great Langdale at 7 am. It was already hot, even at this time. The big priority was to get plenty of sunscreen on and ensure that we were well hydrated before the start. Due to the heat and perfect weather forecast, we were both running with minimum kit. This was shorts and t-shirt, carrying a bumbag with the bare essentials of food, water, waterproofs, hat, gloves, map and compass. The waterproofs, hat and gloves were never going to be used but these are a standard requirement at all FRA races.

We started at 8 am with 84 pairs heading off down the broad track through the middle of the valley. We were towards the back of the field, trotting along nicely and chatting. After barely 200 metres, a competitor just ahead of us turned to his partner and said, 'So far, so good.' Everyone around laughed and it's now something that I often say as I start a long challenge.

After a mile, there's a pinch-point where the whole field has to cram through a small gate to head up onto the fellside. We had to wait for a minute or so to squeeze through, which seems crazy when the field would get so strung out later on in the day. It was then a stiff pull up the hill and onto a path that wound steadily up and around the edge of Silver Howe. We'd only covered a mile or so but already had sweat pouring into our eyes from the heat. Some competitors had their tops off and everyone was drinking loads despite having barely got started. It was quite apparent that the conditions were going to be testing and talk amongst the competitors was of simply surviving the course.

We headed over the shoulder and then down into the beautiful village of Grasmere. There was no time for the tourist sites today as we headed on towards the long climb up Tongue Gill to Grisedale Tarn. There were opportunities to refill our water bottles from streams as we headed up, as well as to cool our feet off and tip cold water over our heads. Blisters are a big problem on hot days and the key is to keep your feet cool. The best way of doing this is to keep your shoes wet by hopping in every stream. This isn't an option on long ultras because your feet will wrinkle up but on a normal day it's the best approach I've found to reducing the risk. This was to be the pattern for every stream we crossed during the rest of the day, cooling off and refilling our bottles.

It was then a big climb from the tarn up onto the Helvellyn ridge and we reached the summit of Helvellyn eight minutes slower than the previous year. This was a worry as we'd lost a third of our time margin for the critical cut-off already. However, we were moving as well as anyone else and had a big, big descent to focus on now. The fastest route to the valley floor is to descend directly south-west down the hillside and follow the line of the stream on an ever-steepening spur of the hill. This is a dizzying descent and hard on the legs as you move quickly downwards, while retaining your balance on the steep grassy slopes. Emerging at the bottom into the car park, after an adrenaline-flowing 28 minutes, we'd completed the first major section.

We drank heavily at the checkpoint, refilled our bottles, then grabbed a quick sandwich and headed off. There was no time to spare and we didn't know how critical every minute could become later on.

We headed into the Wythburn valley and through The Bog. It was 11 am and this valley was like a furnace. There was no shade, no cloud cover and we were all suffering after three hours of hard running. We were drenched in sweat and all the fun of the first few hours had rapidly vanished. We were definitely going to be in survival mode for the rest of the day if it remained like this. It was clear that other runners were struggling too. Everyone was complaining about the heat and some pairs were stopping for a breather. We soldiered up through the valley with another pair and chatted to try and keep our minds off it. One of them wasn't feeling great. His words summed the state of play up nicely, 'I don't know if I want to crap or throw up.'

The upper reaches of Wythburn just got hotter as the sun burned down on us. I was starting to wonder how far we'd get as we were having to push all the time to keep the pace up; the conditions were clearly taking their toll on us and others. The only hope was that as we reached higher ground, there might be a breeze to cool us off. As we crested the rise of Greenup Edge it was clear that there was not.

We covered the next four miles to Angle Tarn in much the same manner, struggling against the heat. We cooled off in the intervening stream at Sticks Pass, drinking, pouring water on our heads and replenishing our bottles yet again. Every runner was straight into every stream all day, whether just standing, sitting or even lying down to fully cool off. The heat was suffocating because there was absolutely no breeze to cool us as we worked so hard.

It was incessant. I've never pushed so much, for so long, in such heat. It just sapped all our energy from us, draining us. Unfortunately, there was no option of easing off as the clock was against us. In the nine miles since Helvellyn, we'd lost another fifteen minutes over my previous time. This was going to leave us very tight at the critical Cockley Beck cut-off if the time losses continued.

Angle Tarn is an obvious bail-out point on the route. From here it's a rough but straightforward walk back down into the Great Langdale valley to the race finish. There were loads of runners retired here. They were in the lake, the stream and generally strewn all over the place. Maybe they were the sensible ones but we weren't done yet and headed on.

Up onto Esk Hause, then around to climb up onto the high ridge near Great End. As we ran across the Hause we came across our two mates from Wythburn. One was sitting on a rock, his partner flat out at his feet, curled up and not moving.

'Is he ok?' we asked.

'He'll be ok in a minute.'

We headed on but it didn't look like their race was going much further.

We moved across the highest ground in England and then it was a murderous final pull up onto the summit of Scafell Pike. The peak was littered with walkers, all enjoying a fantastic day out on the mountain, taking in the scenery and largely adopting a leisurely approach to hill walking. Not so for us. We checked in with the marshals and headed off quickly, checking our watches and registering that we'd lost a couple of minutes more against our schedule. We had very little time in hand for the cut-off so had to keep motoring.

We took ten minutes to retrace our steps to Broad Crag col and then had a steep descent over scree into the depths of Little Narrowcove. On the unstable rocks at the top, Greg came down with cramp in his leg. We were with another pair here; one of them grabbed his foot and helped him stretch against it. Heat depletes your salt levels and cramp can result. Luckily I rarely suffer but Greg had been getting twinges for a while. He recovered and we headed down as fast as we could into the glorious wilds of the Great Moss.

The heat was stifling down in this valley but we just couldn't rest for a second. We skirted the edge of the Moss, observing a pair of runners heading diagonally across and slightly ahead of us. I'd seen this pair on Scafell Pike summit and they had taken the direct descent off Scafell Pike into the Moss. There's a lot of debate over route choice on fell races and this is one of the best examples. From Scafell Pike you have two options to descend. The first is to do as we did, retrace your steps to Broad Crag col and then follow the well-defined valley route down. Although steep and rocky, this is safe, predictable and relatively easy to navigate. The alternative is a more direct line off the summit, through crags and scree slopes to drop directly into the Moss. If you've recced this and know it, then get it right on the day, it might save a couple of minutes. If you haven't and go wrong in the technical ground, you could lose lots and lots of time. I always opt to play safe in the mountains and eliminate all navigation risks. By my observations, the riskier, direct descent was worth a maximum of two minutes' time gain.

We had to keep pushing. We took a few seconds for a good splash and cool down in Lingcove Beck but then it was an eyeballs-out effort down the valley of Mosedale to the Cockley Beck checkpoint. We arrived shattered and were both pretty-much spent, with eleven minutes to spare before the cut-off. However, it wasn't that straightforward. It wasn't the arrival time that mattered, we had to depart before the cut-off. That gave us ten minutes to recuperate.

There were runners sprawled everywhere here. Most were

semi-naked and flaked out. Greg headed straight to the stream for a good sit down to cool off. He said that another runner looked at him in horror, which he hoped wasn't down to his condition. I wasn't quite so bad and concentrated on drinking, eating some sandwiches and flapjack, as well as generally getting myself prepared for the final push. I took a banana and dropped it down my top to eat later, where it would sit quite happily under my t-shirt resting on the strap of my bumbag.

We departed the checkpoint with two minutes to spare and were immediately faced with the notorious Grey Friar climb. This is 1,500 feet of off-path climbing, diagonally up and across the fell. It's a tough climb when fresh but we'd covered 25 miles already with another twelve still to go. It comes at a natural low-point in the race, as we'd pushed like crazy to get through Cockley Beck which, in many ways, felt like finishing. This was a tough climb.

The heat was incessant and we very quickly ran out of steam. It required about an hour of climbing and we were barely ten minutes into it. The time pressure was now off because the time cut-off at the finish was far more generous. We were grinding our way up. Both of us were in our own personal bubbles, not talking much and just concentrating on placing one foot after another. We came across a runner sitting on a large rock looking back the way we'd come. He seemed quite happy to be sitting there, but we couldn't figure out where his partner was. Higher up, other pairs were sitting down resting too. It was carnage. We just kept trucking up that horrible hillside. I was counting down the time to one hour on my watch, which was a long, long hour but eventually we made it.

We emerged to a great view all the way down the ridge to our objective, Coniston Old Man. This was the first point that I knew we'd get to the finish. We'd been on the go for nearly nine hours but it wasn't until we'd got this last big climb done that I thought we should be good to complete the race. This was a big mental lift, although there were still a lot of miles to go and we now had a long out-and-back section to the Old Man.

As we headed out, pairs of runners were heading back, all ahead of us on the course. They were well strung out and everyone looked shattered and drained but they were heading for home.

We reached the checkpoint at Coniston summit and had a quick chat with the marshal. He was hungry but had no food with him. Suddenly I remembered that I'd stuffed a banana down my shirt. I pulled it out. It was hot, sweaty and bruised from nearly two hours down my top. Anyone else would have rejected it. His eyes lit up, he grabbed it and ate it furiously.

We were now on the home leg, seven miles across the tops and through the valleys to the finish. As we headed back on the out-and-back section, we could count how many pairs were behind us. There were just two. We didn't know how many had retired but we knew the fall-out would be significant, as we'd seen the evidence at the checkpoints.

There are no streams up on this section and we were short of water. All we could do was share what we had and ration ourselves until we got to the stream in the valley, about three miles ahead. We made steady progress down to Wrynose Pass, then around Blea Tarn and finally over the crest into the finishing valley. It was a huge relief to be coming home after an epic journey in testing conditions. We dropped down to the road for the final run-in to the finishing field. We checked in with the marshal at the gate and were done, with a finishing time of 11 hours and 32 minutes. A few people clapped our arrival, we shook hands between ourselves and that was it. What a day.

We walked over to the organiser to receive our t-shirts. There was a runner lying prone on the floor with a few others caring for him. We literally stepped over him as the organiser greeted us. He was out cold and muttering deliriously but seemed to be in good hands. It's not the first and certainly won't be the last time I've seen someone in this state after a fell race.

We were handed our t-shirts, a handshake and congratulations from the organiser. We then moved away and slumped down on the floor. We just about had the energy to get cups of tea and some sandwiches but were happy just to be resting and not chasing the clock.

As we sat there, another runner approached Greg, pointed to someone else and said, 'She's a Doctor.'

This was a completely random comment and we were confused but said nothing.

When he moved away, Greg asked me, 'Do I really look that bad?'

We took a while just sitting there, drinking endless tea and trying to recover. Our legs were locked solid and we were both suffering from full-leg cramps. It was a real struggle to even get up from the ground. For a while I wondered how I was going to drive home as the cramps were awful. They'd seize my whole legs and I'd be completely immobile. However, I've learnt over the years that, no matter what condition my legs are in, once I'm sitting in the driving seat I can always drive a car without any issues.

Greg summed the race up nicely with the words, 'It was thirty minutes of realisation, followed by eleven hours of hell.'

This was a very, very hard day. Conditions were perfect for a less arduous day out but we'd been pushing ourselves along the whole way. We'd both been operating at our limits for the full duration of the race. Just finishing was a huge achievement and we were both immensely proud that we'd got through it. Many didn't.

84 pairs started, 57 finished, we came 55th. The race had a 32% drop-out rate.

5   End to End

'The greatest of all victories is to be victorious over yourself.'
(Anon)

Everyone has heard of Lands End and John O'Groats. They are the two extremities of the UK: Lands End at the south-west tip of Cornwall in England and John O'Groats at the extreme north-east of Caithness in Scotland. The shortest distance between the two, using classified roads, is 874 miles. It's a recognised challenge to travel from one to the other, in either direction, by any means of transport, however crazy, such as walking, running, cycling, car, motorbike, horse, wheelchair, skateboard, hitch-hiking or public transport. This is done solo or in groups, over varying timescales, in fancy dress, for charity, as a celebration, a challenge or for any number of other reasons. The traditional name of Lands End to John O'Groats has been popularised to LEJOG (JOGLE if done from north to south) or simply End to End, though I've always preferred the traditional full name.

I've been cycling all my life, ever since riding my first bike as a child. We lived in a cul-de-sac in a village in Essex, so as young children we would spend hours racing up and down our road together. As a teenager, bikes were the best way of getting around the village to meet our friends. I did various paper-rounds in the village, again all using my bicycle. When I was thirteen, I saved up my paper-round money to buy my first racing bike. The quiet country lanes of Essex are ideal for cycling and I loved going out for a ride, as well as my daily mileage doing a paper-round. I've been riding road bikes ever since, only interrupted by a few years of reasonably serious mountain biking while at university. I didn't take to that as much as I did to riding a bike on the road, as it was too technical and too much about skill and balance, rather than straight exercise. Even now, when we visit my parents in Essex, I'll often take my bike with me and head out on the Essex lanes, which remain quiet and free of traffic lights, making ideal cycling country.

In 1992, while at university, I flew to Madrid in Spain with two friends for a cycling holiday. We cycled north from Madrid, through remote Spanish countryside, on a great journey where every day was a simple task of cycling, navigating, finding food, water and a place to camp for the night. We headed up into the Pyrenees, over some incredible mountain passes, before crossing over into France. We finished in Toulouse, three weeks and 900 miles later. This was my first experience of long-distance cycling and the freedom of being out on the open road on a bike. We travelled with minimum kit but our bikes were still well laden down, as we were carrying camping equipment due to the remoteness of the route, as well as our need to minimise all costs. When we finished the journey, we joked that we'd cycled the equivalent of the length of the UK. This sowed a seed in my mind about doing the real thing and cycling Lands End to John O'Groats properly one day.

I'd heard about cycling Lands End to John O'Groats as a child. For some reason it fascinated me, the appeal of travelling from one end of the UK to the other using only a bike. The topic cropped up a few times as I went through university and my early working life, but I didn't ever expect to do it because I'd need a partner and no one else ever wanted to cycle that far. In 1999, I was working in an office in Warrington with another reasonably keen cyclist, named Guy. The challenge of Lands End to John O'Groats came up in discussion and it became clear that Guy also wanted to do it but had never found anyone else to partner him. The opportunity was suddenly there and we started planning.

The average time taken to cycle the route is twelve to fourteen days, fitting it into a two-week holiday. Neither of us could afford that much time from our annual holiday allowance, as it was too big a commitment when we wanted our holidays for other things. I realised that if we could cycle it in nine days, covering 100 miles per day and tag it onto the Easter bank holiday weekend, we could get away with just four days' holiday requirement. Easter was going to be relatively late the next year, which would make it viable, with slightly more daylight and slightly warmer conditions than if it had fallen in March. It was a good proposal, too good an opportunity to miss and was possibly going to be a once-in-a-lifetime chance for us both. We confirmed the proposal with our wives and started planning for Easter 2000.

We split the planning into two parts: I'd plan the logistics and the route, Guy would book all the accommodation. The first problem to solve was the logistics before the start and after the finish. It was a straight-line route and we'd be self-sufficient with no backup, so we needed a plan to get to the start and back again from the finish.

This was actually relatively straightforward. The best cycling route is from south to north, to minimise any headwinds, as the UK's prevailing winds blow from the south-west. This also has the advantage of leaving the most exciting section through Scotland until the end. The best method of travel without support was by train and we could transport our bikes for free in the Guard's van. The outbound leg would be a seven-hour train journey from Warrington to Penzance, with just a single change in Birmingham. There was a convenient train on a Friday lunchtime, getting us to Penzance in the evening, from where it was just a ten-mile cycle ride to Lands End.

For the return journey, we would cycle twenty miles from John O'Groats to Thurso. There was an early train departing Thurso at 6 am on Easter Monday, which would get us back into Warrington eleven hours later, after changing in Inverness and Edinburgh. This gave us the nine days' cycling that we needed and a straightforward method of getting to the start and back from the finish.

I then divided the country up into nine roughly equal segments. Warrington was conveniently located on the route and it became clear that after four days we'd be able to spend a night at home, before another five days on the road to the finish. These were the days before electronic maps, so I spent a lot of time with a road atlas of Great Britain, measuring distance with a map-measuring wheel to find a route that avoided main roads as much as possible. My first draft generated a finishing position for each day, so that Guy could search for Bed and Breakfast accommodation in the local areas. He then rang around and booked us somewhere for every night, with evening meals too if available. After a bit of route adjustment to take the B&B locations into account, we had ourselves a detailed plan. This started and finished at Warrington Bank Quay station, with accommodation booked every night for the trip in advance.

To complete the planning, I detailed the route into small route cards, breaking each day up into smaller segments, with road numbers, critical junctions and towns broken out. I also photocopied the atlas, preparing small map sections with the route highlighted on it. All of this was laminated to survive being outdoors in the wind and rain. This gave us both a small pack of the route details. We both made a small clipboard that attached to our handlebars so that we could keep these handy while moving. We would carry minimum gear in a set of panniers each. Apart from our cycling kit and snacks, we'd carry just a lightweight change of clothes for each evening, wash kit and basic first aid items. It was a minimalist trip.

With three months to go we had everything organised, train tickets and accommodation booked, a detailed route planned and a kit list. We knew exactly what we were doing and were incredibly well organised. We'd taken all the pressure of planning the trip away and now just needed to focus on improving our fitness by getting some long days in the saddle under our belts.

I was doing a lot of hill walking and cycling at the time, so generally had good stamina and plenty of cycling mileage in my legs. In the final three months, I gave up most of my trips to the hills and concentrated on cycling instead. My typical pattern was cycling both days at the weekend, building up the distance each Saturday as a long ride, with Sunday a shorter recovery ride. I'd also run just once midweek to supplement this. By the middle of March, I was comfortably riding eighty to ninety miles each Saturday and then half that on a Sunday. Then with three weeks to go, I suddenly got a sharp pain in my right knee on one of the long rides. It came from nowhere and I was struggling to peddle on it. I had thirty miles left to get home and there was nothing I could do but grit my teeth and get back.

After a few days it hadn't settled down and it continued to be painful to bend my knee. This was a massive worry because we were all set to go and it was an eleventh hour set-back that I hadn't anticipated. I booked a physio appointment and it was diagnosed as a cartilage problem that needed rest. My training was finished and all I could do was take it easy for three weeks before the start. It was incredibly frustrating but I just had to remain positive that it would all work out.

We travelled down to Penzance without any trouble on the train. Guy had booked us a B&B for the first night just outside Lands End, one mile from the end of the road where we'd start. We cycled slowly from the station to the B&B, which was slightly strange as we'd be heading straight back this way the next morning. We were both excited about the journey ahead but also apprehensive as it was an awfully long way. I knew that we'd done everything possible to arrive at this point as organised and as fit as we could be. My only worry was my knee but it had been fine on the slow ride out to Lands End, so the few weeks' rest seemed to have worked. I'd just have to see how it progressed day-by-day.

The next morning, we headed straight down to the end of the road, took photos by the famous distance sign, then lined up on an actual Start line that was painted across the road. A push off on the pedals and we were rolling, on what was undoubtedly going to be a great adventure. The first few miles back to Penzance were great fun, the exhilaration of all the months of preparation coming to fruition. It was hard to believe that we were actually on our way and that, all being well, in nine days we'd achieve a lifetime goal. That all seemed an awfully long way off when we'd only got our own legs to get us there. It was a glorious morning and we had a slight tailwind to add to the sense of ease. The island of St Michael's Mount stood impressive in the bay as we passed back through Penzance and along the coast. It was a nice easy start and felt like a holiday but we were soon to have that knocked out of us, when the roads started heading upwards.

The great thing about cycling is that you experience the countryside far more than you do from a car. Walking and running are similar in this way but you don't cover the same distances as quickly. In any of these, what you get to experience far more than in a motorised form of transport, is how hilly an area is. Cornwall is hilly, not in a gentle way but in a steep, straight-up-and-down way. Neither of us had been to Cornwall for many years and we weren't expecting this. We'd seen the hills from the train the day before but had both sub-consciously chosen to ignore them. Big mistake.

As the day wore on, the roads started heading upwards at an alarming rate. The gradients were steep and it was hard work climbing them. None of the hills were particularly high but they were steep. Once we crested the top we'd go rocketing down the other side and into the next one. This was tiring and we hadn't expected it. This first day was only 83 miles and we were anticipating an easy ride. It was far tougher than we'd imagined.

We cycled across the lower part of Cornwall to Liskeard where we then headed northwards across Bodmin Moor. We'd stopped at a cafe earlier for lunch and to replenish our water. Here we'd purchased some pretty hefty Cornish pasties to eat for our dinner later, as we'd be staying on a remote farm with no food options nearby. These pasties were like bricks in our panniers, as we lugged them up and down the Cornish hills that afternoon.

Most nights we'd eat at the B&B or an adjacent pub but tonight was the one night where we had to sort ourselves out.

Each day we'd eat lunch at a cafe or buy sandwiches and pastries from a bakery to eat outside. We stopped at small shops to replenish our energy supplies of cereal bars, chocolate and cakes to eat while we moved. We kept it very simple.

After ten hours on the road, we arrived at our B&B farm and could both feel the toil of the day in our legs and backs. It had been a big day's cycling but we'd hardly gone anywhere in the grand scheme of the mission and hadn't even left Cornwall yet. The early morning enthusiasm was long gone and it seemed like an awfully long way to the finish.

The second day was one of the longer ones at 108 miles. My legs and back were surprisingly stiff from the first day's hills and it took me the first half an hour of cycling just to free them up and get them moving properly. We headed across to Okehampton, with the steep hills being replaced by more manageable ones, although there was a headwind that was slowing us down. Generally, when you cycle, you do a loop and return to your start point. On a journey such as this, each day is roughly in a straight line. If the wind's behind you then it's great but if, like today, it's in your face, then it becomes the equivalent of cycling uphill all day. The terrain was becoming kinder but the head-wind was negating any benefits of this.

We cycled on to Tiverton, then Taunton, before heading across the Polden Hills to Glastonbury. We ate Chinese take-away sitting in a shop doorway, before cycling on to our next farmhouse B&B. We'd been on the road for eleven hours.

This was the first B&B of many where the owners did a double-take as we walked in. When booking, Guy had told them what we were doing, to make sure we could store our bikes and get an early breakfast to get away promptly. As a result, the B&B's were expecting a couple of prime athletes to come zipping into their yards, before bounding in full of energy and enthusiasm. What they got instead were two thirty-year old cyclists who could hardly walk, hobbled in, made a drama out of climbing or descending stairs and were in bed asleep by 9 pm. It must have been hilarious for them. Every morning we'd depart and then Guy would say, 'I don't think they're confident we're going to finish this.' It kept us amused and in high spirits.

Day three was 88 miles up to Great Malvern in the Welsh borders, via Bath and Gloucester. The wind had changed direction and we had a gentle tail-wind now which was a great help. The only other notable thing about the day was that it snowed during the morning, an unexpected half hour of unpleasantness in an otherwise good day. We turned a corner today, both mentally due to having covered a third of the distance and literally as we were now heading due north. It felt as if we were finally making progress, being north of the River Severn and within a day's cycling of our home stop-off. It was also the shortest day with a little under nine hours on the road. We ate dinner at a pub and for the first time were starting to enjoy the trip.

The next morning, as we mounted our bikes, the lady from the B&B asked Guy, 'What are you going to do next?'

He was completely speechless and muttered, 'Don't know.'

We departed and when out of earshot he let rip, 'What am I going to do next? I haven't finished this yet! Does she know how far we've got left to go?'

It was hilarious. She'd really got to him with a simple question because she hadn't understood the enormity of what we were trying to deal with in our heads. To cycle from one end of the country to the other was frightening. You'd need to plan carefully before driving it and require at least one overnight stop. To pedal our own way was an enormous weight on our shoulders. I felt like I was on a treadmill that I couldn't get off. With six days still ahead of us, the finish was too distant to be able to imagine it.

After clearing some initial hills in the Welsh borders, we headed north to Bridgnorth and Telford. I got a puncture in a country lane and we stopped to change the inner tube. This would be the only puncture that I'd get on the whole trip. As we left Shropshire for Cheshire, the land flattened out and the cycling became easier, so we could keep a good rhythm up. My legs were getting stronger as I was effectively training on the event and I was having no trouble with my knee whatsoever. Once we hit the Cheshire Plain, I led all the way to Warrington, with Guy sat in my slipstream. It was a day where I was very strong and Guy appreciated the tow as he was less so. I was having one of those days where exercise is effortless and I could just power along.

There was a slight climb near Tarporley and I'd left Guy by a few hundred metres as we went up it. I stopped at the top and waited for him, sitting on the grass verge. As he cycled up to me, he stopped but purposely didn't unclip from his pedals and just toppled over sideways onto the soft grass next to me.

'What the hell are we doing?' he asked.

We just sat there laughing at the side of the A49 in the sunshine, contemplating the madness of our journey.

We headed on to my house in Warrington where Guy's dad was waiting to whisk him off home for the night. We'd covered 113 miles today which was the furthest I'd ever cycled in one day. We also had the huge mental boost of being back where we'd started from. This was the point at which it dawned on me how big a challenge it was. Looking at a map, we'd covered an awesome distance, one that had taken over seven hours by train to cover. This in itself was a huge achievement but we still weren't even halfway. I was feeling good but knew that a lot could still go wrong in the days ahead. It was only going to get harder as we headed north.

Spending the night at home was nice but strange. It didn't feel like I belonged there because I was on a mission to get to John O'Groats. Somehow it didn't fit in with the activity of the week and the single-minded focus to keep moving north. I relaxed but was feeling a bit shivery in the evening, so went to bed early to rest. It had been another nine-hour day so I thought it was just fatigue.

Day five was going to be another long one, with 110 miles and ten hours on the road. These were long days coming back-to-back but we were now making significant progress across the map of Great Britain. Guy's dad dropped him back at mine and waved us off. We picked our way up through routes that I knew to Preston, Lancaster and Kendal, before climbing over the pass at Shap on the edge of the Lake District. The weather was fantastic and we were both flying today. The long downhill from Shap summit to Penrith was easy, as we could coast for most of it. From there, it was only a few miles to the village where the B&B was. It had been a straightforward day, although Guy 'blew a gasket', as he put it, a few miles from the finish and struggled in slowly. We'd been on the road for ten hours and the long days were starting to catch up on us. We were over halfway now and would be heading for the Scottish border in the morning.

That evening I felt shivery again, although I hadn't felt anything wrong during the day. During the night, I went to the bathroom and my hands were shaking quite badly. I was worried but all I could do was rest and focus on the last four days.

As we departed on day six we were not in our usual high spirits. I was worried about the shivering, Guy was feeling tired and concerned about hitting the wall the day before. He was also getting some mild knee pain and had asked the owners where we'd be able to find a chemist, to buy a tubigrip support for him and paracetamol for me. As we cycled up the country lanes toward Carlisle, once again we joked that the owners looked like they had no confidence that we'd do this.

As we headed across the Scottish border, just north of Carlisle, we had no option but to cycle on the dual-carriageway for a few miles. This was one of only two short sections of dual-carriageway in the entire 900-mile route that we couldn't avoid without adding significant mileage. This was the main trunk road into Scotland and in the years since has been upgraded to be the M6 motorway. We just put our heads down and were intent on getting across and off it as fast as possible, cycling down the small strip at the edge of the carriageway. Luck wasn't with us though and Guy punctured in the middle of this section, his only puncture of the entire route. Of all the places to happen, it had to happen here. We changed his inner tube on the grass verge, as lorries and cars thundered past at high speed only a few feet away.

We were soon off this though and into Gretna, where a wedding party were having photos taken outside the famous Blacksmith's shop. Guy rang into work to update them on our progress. The comment from the other end was, 'You're on the home stretch now.'

We shook our heads in despair but this really cheered us up. Guy laughed, 'Home stretch? Has he any idea how big Scotland is?'

Little things like this gave us such a shared bond on the trip as it was hard to visualise how great the distances were unless you were covering them under your own steam. It sounds straightforward to ride from Lands End to John O'Groats but it's not until you're actually doing it that you realise how far that distance is.

We headed up a deserted road that runs adjacent to the A74(M) motorway to Moffat, in complete contrast to the busy dual-carriageway, then turned towards Edinburgh. We climbed a pass through the Tweedsmuir Hills, before descending to the village of Walston where our B&B for the night was. It had been a short day at only 93 miles and nine hours.

I'd been fine all day cycling, with no problems eating and drinking to keep my energy levels up and stay hydrated but I felt very shivery that evening. During the night, I was shaking badly in my sleep and struggled to open the door when I needed the bathroom because my hands were shaking uncontrollably. I knew that I was getting ill but had just three more days to last out. I wasn't having this taken away from me after we'd travelled such a long way.

Day seven felt like a holiday, with traffic on the roads heading for the Highlands. It was Good Friday and we cycled for eleven hours, covering 100 miles up to Blair Atholl, crossing the Forth Road Bridge along the way. Two guys on a tandem pulled up next to us as we cycled over the bridge and we got chatting. They were also heading for John O'Groats and had set off the same day as we had. This was one of the strange things about this challenge. We knew that other people might also be doing it this week but how do you know which cyclists are doing it? It was only because we all had panniers on our bikes and were heading over the bridge that we discussed it. We passed these guys a couple of times that day and they passed us back, as we each stopped at different places to rest or eat. We had a feeling of camaraderie with these unknown cyclists and for the first time didn't feel alone on the road; there were some others who knew what we were going through.

My condition was deteriorating now. I could still eat and drink ok but I'd got diarrhoea and had to keep stopping to relieve myself in a convenient spot. Luckily we were in Scotland where the roads were quiet and there were plenty of opportunities to leap over a wall or duck into a wood. On the positive side, I was cycling fine and we covered the distance with no problems, so we were still on track to finish.

The shivering returned in the evening and developed overnight into a full-blown illness. I was cold but sweating through the night. I woke the next day completely drained of energy, feverish and feeling sick. I was pale, sweating and in no condition to do anything, let alone ride a bike through the Scottish mountains. I couldn't face breakfast so lay in bed while Guy ate. He didn't eat much either as he knew it was the end of the road and our dream of finishing had gone. If I couldn't eat, then I was in big trouble because I couldn't get any energy into my body. All our months of preparation were going to end here.

We were both devastated. We'd put so much into this and were on track to finish it but I'd managed to pick up a bug and get ill. We were two days from the finish. This wasn't supposed to happen.

In the end I said to Guy, 'Let's just get going. There's a train station further up the valley. Let's just see how far I can go.'

So that's what we did. It was simple. We headed up the Glen Garry Pass towards Aviemore. Guy took all my gear in his panniers so I had no load. He even took my water. He led the way and I just cycled behind his rear wheel to pick up his slipstream. We simply set off to see how far I could get, whether that be one mile or five.

I cycled for twelve hours, covering 118 miles that day through the Highland mountains. All logic says this was impossible because I ate nothing all day. I could barely sip water, just enough to swallow a few pills. Despite taking paracetamol and diarrhoea tablets, I was shivering the whole time and required frequent toilet stops but we just trundled along. Guy was fantastic, he just sat at the front pedalling away and offering me encouragement every so often.

Another problem that occurred was that my rear tyre was fraying and didn't look like it would last the day but there are no bike shops in the Highlands, except for Inverness. When we got to Inverness it was 5:30 pm and the shops were closing. We managed to find a bike shop and buy a tyre just as he was shutting up for the day. That was another stress factor that we didn't need but at least the bike was sorted now.

Arriving at the B&B in Tain, I just went straight to bed. I was out cold for the night.

The next morning, I was in big trouble and knew the trip was over. I dashed to the bathroom and threw up. This happened a number of times. I was getting worse, not better. This was our last day, with only 88 miles left to John O'Groats but the chances of me getting there were almost zero. I hadn't eaten anything for over a day now and there was no chance of me eating today. I couldn't sip water without retching so I was critically dehydrated too.

All we could do was set off, with Guy leading, carrying all my gear and I would just sit behind him again. We didn't have a plan B, we just set off and cycled. We had no contingency for what to do when I conked out, which surely had to happen before very long. With hindsight, setting off was a foolhardy

47

move but it was what ensured success. I had no other option but to finish.

It was a glorious final day but we had a head-wind. I really, really didn't need this but it was there. We'd also failed to realise how hilly this last day would be as we headed up the coast towards Wick. The road continuously climbed and dropped all the way. We established a pattern for the day. Every time the road climbed, I hadn't got the energy to keep up with Guy. I'd just get into my lowest gear and crawl up, watching him slowly pedalling into the distance. He'd be sitting at the top waiting and we'd then freewheel down the other side together. This was endless, a day spent with my head down trundling up hills at a snail's pace. It must have been incredibly frustrating for Guy too but he didn't say anything. At least we were slowly knocking the miles off.

I was on and off the bike all day for toilet stops. I didn't eat anything and didn't drink anything all day. If I sipped water, I was sick, so there was no point. My tongue was stuck to the roof of my mouth as I was completely dehydrated. I will never, ever be this dehydrated again, unless I get lost in a desert. It set a level and a benchmark that I can always compare against and know that I've had worse. I had no energy whatsoever but I just trundled north. I was at my lowest ebb but life was very, very simple. All I had to do was pedal the bike north.

We cycled for ten hours. In the afternoon we saw our friends with the tandem driving back the other way, waving and hooting at us. This was the only good point of the whole day but it was short-lived. We finally crested the last hill and could see John O'Groats below us, just a mile ahead. This was the point where I knew I'd finish. At no other point in these last two days of hell could I imagine finishing. We coasted down the hill to complete our journey.

We spent some time at the famous signpost, with Guy taking photos and just enjoying the moment. It was the end of an epic journey and I couldn't believe that I'd actually done it. There was no one else around so we just sat there and looked at the sea, content in the knowledge that it was over. It was getting chilly and we had another problem that I hadn't dared to think about all day. It was another twenty miles to our B&B in Thurso. There was no way I could cycle it as I was spent. We were stuck.

We wheeled our bikes over to the hotel and went into the bar to see what we could do. There was a book here that we wrote in and signed to confirm the completion of our ride. I don't know what I wrote but one day I'll have to go back to read it. The barman congratulated us and told us that nine days was a fast time, compared to most cyclists. Guy explained our problem and the barman replied, 'Don't worry. It happens all the time. I'll get Fred with his van, he'll take you.'

It transpired that this happens often, with cyclists completing the journey too tired to continue on to their accommodation. They had a nice little side-line going, running cyclists into Thurso in their van for £20 a ride. Finally, I could relax.

That night should have been a celebration, a night out in Thurso, a few beers and re-living the adventure of the last week. Instead I went straight to bed, with occasional dashes to the bathroom to throw up. Guy went out and returned with fish and chips and a couple of beers for himself. It all just fizzled out which was disappointing for Guy, although I was too ill to care.

The next day's train journey home made for a long day, with some great sights as we travelled through Scotland. I was now on my third day without food and was as dehydrated as I've ever been. I sipped water but my tongue was still sticking to the roof of my mouth. I'd stopped vomiting but was being careful to only drink tiny amounts. Clair met me at the station, Guy sorted my bike out and I went straight home to bed.

Clair had already booked me a doctor's appointment for the next day. It was clear that I was in no fit state to return to work. I told the doctor my symptoms and was diagnosed with flu. He prescribed re-hydration drinks and plenty of rest.

Clair asked whether I'd told him what I'd just done.

'No way. He'd have sent me to hospital.'

I just wanted to be home and recover by myself.

What a week that was. What an incredible journey.

I'd been through the mill but had completed what I'd set out to do. The knee problem that I thought I'd be coping with all week wasn't an issue but then the illness was a bigger one. I learnt a lot about myself that week, a lot about my strength, my determination and my ability to endure very difficult circumstances. It set me a new benchmark of suffering and being able to focus my whole being on achieving an objective. I should not have finished this ride. Physically I wasn't capable of finishing those last two days. If it was an organised event, I'd have been pulled out on medical grounds but I wanted it so badly that I finished it. I don't like to think what would have happened if I'd got ill a day earlier or how I'd have felt if I hadn't completed it. I'd have pushed myself to destruction and been devastated if I'd have failed. This ride took me to a new level and set the foundation for what I'd be able to endure on other long challenges in the future.

We cycled 900 miles, at an average speed of 13 mph. I lost over a stone in weight, more than 10% of my body mass.

6   First Hundred: South Downs Way Race
(September 2010)

'To finish is to win.' (Anon)

In the summer of 2009, I received an email from Brandon. It said, 'I've found this race. What do you think?' There was a link to a website for a race along the full length of the South Downs Way.

My initial reaction was, 'He's gone mad.'

The South Downs Way is a 103-mile hiking trail from Eastbourne to Winchester on the south coast of England, with 13,000 feet of climbing along its length. It follows a more-or-less straight line, over the white cliffs of Beachy Head and the Seven Sisters, before heading inland onto the South Downs escarpment. It has good trails, great scenery and the feeling of being a journey, travelling from one place to another.

It didn't take long for me to be intrigued, then interested, then hooked, then obsessed. This was right up my street. Building up to running 100 miles was the kind of challenge that I could get my teeth into. It was something beyond what I'd done before and that, if I completed it, would define me forever. I replied to let him know that I was definitely in.

We'd both done lots of big endurance challenges before, with some significant time on our feet and distances covered. These days tended to be in the mountains or on a bike, so neither of us had covered more than forty miles on foot in one go before. The race wasn't until September 2010, over a year away, so we had plenty of time. Our first objective was to increase our maximum distance and get ourselves up to about fifty miles. We wanted to have this done and banked before the event entries opened in September. There would only be fifty entries available so we knew that we needed to enter as soon as the event opened if we wanted to guarantee a place.

We decided to run what's known as the Lakes Three Thousanders. This is a recognised challenge to climb the four peaks in the Lake District that are higher than 3,000 feet, in under 24 hours. It's a circular route from Keswick, taking in the summits of Skiddaw, Scafell, Scafell Pike and Helvellyn, a distance of 45 miles, with 11,000 feet of climbing, across rough ground. The fact that it was slightly short of the fifty-mile target didn't matter, as the difficult terrain would more than make up for being a few miles under. We estimated that it would take between sixteen and eighteen hours, so would be a significant day out.

If this went well, then we'd enter the South Downs Way Race, with a full year to build up through a couple of sixty-mile challenges in early 2010. It was a robust plan but we wanted to put ourselves through a tough Lake District challenge first before committing to entering.

In August, we put the plan into action. We day-tripped from my house which added four hours' driving to the day. This wasn't ideal or arguably sensible, but it kept the logistics very simple. We got up at 2 am and I drove us to Keswick. We were running at 4:15 am. The conditions were awful on Skiddaw as we headed straight up from Keswick, with strong wind and driving rain. We quickly made the summit, then descended as day broke and the weather calmed down. We had a long trot through Borrowdale and up onto the Scafell massif, with rough scrambling up onto Scafell itself, then significant descent and re-ascent across to Scafell Pike. These peaks are only a mile apart but it took an hour to travel between them. Then we had a very long slog across rough ground, reversing the route of the Old County Tops race all the way to Helvellyn. A final large climb to the summit, followed by the descent and a soul-destroying run down the main road back to Keswick, finishing at 9 pm. We ate fish and chips outside the Moot Hall, before driving back to Warrington. We were both exhausted and Brandon fell asleep in the car but we were home by midnight. It had been a long and arduous day but we'd been running for over sixteen hours to achieve our objective without too much drama.

52

We entered the South Downs Way Race the next month.

The second step in the plan was to take the distance up to sixty miles and run fully overnight. We'd both done plenty of walking or running in darkness but neither of us had run straight through the night before. We arranged to do an overnight, sixty-mile recce of the middle section of the South Downs Way course from Southease to Queen Elizabeth Country Park at Easter. I drove to Brandon's house in Surrey and we caught a train to Southease. We set off at 4 pm, with a time schedule and plenty of food and warm clothes. Unfortunately, the weather was against us with a headwind for the entire route, which was highly exposed up on the South Downs escarpment. We only had a few hours' running before darkness came and then it was a long night. Brandon had done a lot of walking and running on the Downs so he knew it well. I learnt a lot that night, familiarising myself with a significant section of the route, albeit in darkness. The trail is well marked with a National Trail acorn on the signs, so with maps and watching the signs we had no problems navigating despite the darkness.

Running through the night was much harder than either of us could have imagined. The headwind made it heavy going, the rain lashed in our faces at times and it even hailed at others. In the depths of night, the trail became very muddy and slowed us down considerably. We were sliding around trying to get traction and were reduced to a crawl. This caused us both to get very cold, to keep dozing off momentarily and to be continually banging into each other. We both experienced hallucinations; I saw animals moving to my side at times and roads or fences appearing ahead of us at others. At 4 am there was a thunderstorm with lightning just ahead of us. We should have been worried but I just didn't care anymore. I actually thought, 'Well if it strikes me dead then so be it.' I'd had enough as this was heavy going and an awful experience. Neither of us had been prepared for how tired and disorientated we'd be in the early hours, how the weather and conditions would render us shells of our normal alert and organised selves.

Eventually it got light and I made a conscious effort to eat and drink. We got going more efficiently and made it to the finish, where we caught a train back to Brandon's. We'd run for over sixteen hours.

This recce was a massive learning experience and a huge wake-up call. I'd never imagined that it would be so hard. The weather did us no favours but, even so, it was a huge mental test. There were a number of factors. Conditions underfoot were poor and slowed us down. We were completely unsupported and completely alone. There were no checkpoints, cheery marshals, food stops or anything else to break the route up and offer us encouragement or mental support. It was our first full overnight experience and it was a long night because it was still early in the year. It was very cold, so much so that I was shivering and my teeth were chattering at times. We hadn't eaten enough during the night as we'd been so pre-occupied with all our other problems. Neither of us had run that far before, even in daylight.

We analysed it and learnt from it. We knew that it wouldn't be that bad on race day. If we could run sixty miles unsupported in April in bad weather, then the overnight section of the race could only be better. We'd had a big reality check, our expectations were set and we'd taken a big step towards running 100 miles.

The final step in the plan was to run sixty miles again at the Fellsman. This is a 61-mile race in the Yorkshire Dales with 11,000 feet of climbing, crossing tough ground. It would take longer than the sixty miles on the Downs due to the terrain but was an organised event. It would be our second full overnight run.

We headed up to Yorkshire in May and ran it. It all worked out well, although it was another bitterly cold night on the hills. The terrain was off-path for large sections which made for hard work, the navigation needed care and it took 21 hours. We ran overnight with a tough mountain man called John. Brandon knew him from previous events and introduced me. He was very experienced, very knowledgeable and very good fun to be with. Little did I know it then, but I'd share many more experiences with John over the coming years.

The Fellsman cemented our ability over sixty miles and took our running time beyond twenty hours for the first time. We had now run overnight twice and covered sixty miles twice. In terms of stepping up, we had the solid foundation on which to run our first 100-miler. We were ready.

On the weekend of the race, I took the train to London on Friday afternoon and met Brandon, before we headed down to Eastbourne. We stayed in a hotel on the seafront, which was a short walk from the start. As is often the case before something big, I didn't sleep particularly well but the race didn't start until 10 am so there was no need to get up early. We had a leisurely breakfast and assembled at the bandstand on Eastbourne promenade with the other runners. At registration, I was handed race number thirteen. Lucky thirteen.

Despite there being fifty entries, there were only 34 starters. This usually happens on races because injury or other plans cause drop-outs before the start, although this was a large percentage to fall short by. We had a very small group of us for the briefing, which made this event seem special and close-knit, even though we didn't know anyone else.

At 10 am we were off. We trotted down the prom together as a tight little bunch in the drizzle, covering an easy, flat mile with only a few metres between all the runners. This felt like the start of something special, not only for us on our first 100-miler, but also for the event itself as it was the first time it had been run. We were in at the start of something, both for ourselves and the event organiser.

We headed up onto the trail and climbed towards Beachy Head. It was non-inspiring in the dull, wet weather but we were just starting out on a great adventure so our spirits were high. We chatted to other runners and tried not to think about the vast distance in front of us. After Beachy Head came the Seven Sisters, which is just an undulating series of rolling sea cliffs when you run over the top of them. I'd never been here before and it was, frankly, disappointing in the rain but we weren't here as tourists today. We headed inland to Alfriston, then climbed the first proper hill over Firle Beacon before dropping down into Southease. We'd covered nineteen miles in a little over four hours, completing the first major section of the race. Southease was where Brandon and I had started our overnight recce so it now felt as if we were on familiar ground, which was a huge mental boost. We had a quick stop here to remove stones from our shoes, grab some food and then pressed on.

We climbed over the next hill to Housedean Farm and then headed up onto the main escarpment of the South Downs, which we'd be following for many miles westwards. A couple of mountain bikers came slowly alongside us and asked where we were heading to.

'Winchester,' we replied.

'Over how many days?'

'We're running straight there.'

They nearly fell off.

Along here, we had something to look forward to, as a friend of Brandon's had promised to be at Ditchling Beacon to take some photos and wave us through. Ditchling Beacon is a well-known crossing point of the Downs, where the London to Brighton car and bike races head across the hills. It's feared by many cyclists but for us it was simply a small dip in the hill as we ran across the top.

This was 31 miles into our run. Brandon has told me many times about a friend who says, 'How can you possibly know where you're going to be at a certain time?' We joke about this because we always run with a race schedule and can predict reasonably accurately where we're going to be and when. At Ditchling Beacon we were nine minutes ahead of our schedule after seven hours of running. His friend was waiting. We stopped for a quick chat and some photos, then pressed on.

We ran into the early evening, the weather improved and we were finally able to remove our waterproof jackets. It was getting warmer and looked like being a pleasant evening and night. The time elapsed and the distance covered kept racking up nicely until we were almost halfway, arriving at Washington at 9 pm. Here we took our longest break yet of ten minutes, sitting in a couple of chairs to eat some food. There were a few other competitors and suddenly one of them leapt up, bolted across to the side of the trail and was violently sick in the bushes. It all happened very quickly before he turned and headed back, apologising to the marshals, 'Sorry, it's no reflection on the chef.' The humour at races is always good and this was a fine example.

We left them to it and got on our way, not expecting him to go much further but later we'd heard that he'd got going again just fine. We were heading towards the halfway checkpoint at Amberley where we had drop bags and hot food waiting. We arrived at 11 pm, two minutes down on our schedule which amused the marshals when we apologised for being late. It was a lovely warm evening and we sat in the beer garden of a pub, eating a baked potato, while replenishing food from our drop bags and sorting our gear out. I changed my shoes and socks, with plenty of anti-chafe cream being re-applied. It was very pleasant sitting around chatting to the marshals. After thirty minutes we were on our way and heading into the night.

So far I hadn't experienced any particular problems, although my legs were sore and clothing was rubbing but that's to be expected after nearly sixty miles. We headed into the section where we'd really struggled on our recce due to the mud. Now that it was September, everything was much drier after the summer. We had no problems at all and cruised straight through, wondering what we'd been doing back in April. We hadn't seen any other competitors since the last stop and felt like we had the whole trail to ourselves.

We arrived at the Cocking checkpoint at 3 am, where the two marshals greeted us like old friends. They'd not had anyone through for over an hour and were pleased for the company. We took fifteen minutes here. I was warm and wanted to remove my thermal top from under my t-shirt but couldn't raise my arms properly to pull it off. While I was struggling, the young, female marshal ran over and whipped my top off to help me.

'What's the wife going to say when I tell her about being undressed by a good-looking woman in the middle of the night?' I laughed. We ate profiteroles here which was a real treat. We left in high spirits for the last part of the night.

Our pace slowed as fatigue set in from the distance. We were over two-thirds of the way and had now exceeded our previous longest run of 61 miles. I was starting to struggle as it got light, hitting a massive low patch that I wasn't expecting as we'd now cleared the dark sections. As we ran along a good track on a gentle downhill, the ground opened up beneath me and I took a big jump over a ditch.

'What are you doing?' Brandon asked.

I turned around and there was just trail behind me and certainly no ditch.

'I saw a ditch,' I laughed.

Somehow I'd hallucinated it in broad daylight. I was shattered but we still had thirty miles to go.

We arrived at the Queen Elizabeth Country Park at 7 am, to find a checkpoint at a marquee. It had been eight hours now since we'd seen another competitor so the race was really spread out.

The marshal asked, 'Fancy a bacon butty lads?'

After running all night, we didn't even need to answer. They were gratefully received and were just the ticket to send us on our way. We'd now covered eighty miles with just the last 23 to go. We knew they'd be a very long, incredibly hard 23 miles and take about eight hours but the numbers were getting manageable now.

We headed up onto Butser Hill where an early morning mist had descended. Visibility was low as we ran along the road at the top. We caught up with another runner, the first we'd seen in over thirty miles of running. It was incredible to be running a race and just not see another competitor for that length of time. His name was Dave and he was being supported by a friend who would be meeting him in the next valley.

We left him to it and pushed along. Descending a track through a wood, someone jumped out of the bushes fifty metres ahead of us.

'Have you seen my mate, Dave?' he asked.

'He's not far behind us,' we replied.

He made sure we were ok and asked if we needed anything. He genuinely wanted to help in any way he could. This would set a pattern for the rest of the day. Every time we got near a road, he'd emerge from a corner with the words, 'Have you seen Dave?'

It was brilliant. He was a great guy and it really made our race having him keep popping up on us.

It was a warm day and we climbed over Old Winchester Hill and dropped into Exton at ninety miles. There was a rag-tag checkpoint in a lay-by, which all seemed disorganised but we just stopped and chatted for a few minutes, with Dave trotting in behind us.

The next four miles over Beacon Hill were tough. It was a warm climb on very stiff legs. There were a number of stiles to climb and I was really struggling to lift my legs up to get over them. We just kept plodding along to the final checkpoint at 94 miles. Dave's mate appeared as always, just ahead of the checkpoint, offering us goodies from the boot of his car. We politely declined and trundled on to the checkpoint, which comprised two girls with a trestle table on a grass verge. It looked like a garage sale of food and drink, as they stood behind it and we pulled up.

We had a good chat and a laugh with them, as we'd done all the major climbing and could almost visualise the finish now. As we departed, one of them said, 'You're amazing. What you're doing is incredible.' This really cheered us up and we left on a high.

As well as general soreness from head to toe, my feet were

very sore. I could feel a bad blister on my right foot. We stopped after another few miles so I could inspect it and treat it. It was massive, a marble-sized ball of blood beneath my big toe. There wasn't much I could do apart from drain and tape it, then press on. We then had a difficult field of cows to negotiate, forcing us to climb a barbed wire fence, which was a slow and awkward manoeuvre with legs that wouldn't work properly.

I was having another big low, was bothered by my feet and really wasn't enjoying life. Then Dave's mate emerged on the trail ahead of us with his mobile phone in hand.

'Have you seen Dave? He's lost. He can see pylons.'

I had a big sense of humour failure and muttered some profanities under my breath. I'd got my own problems to worry about and had no spare capacity to worry about Dave.

Like a superhero, Brandon put his arm out to slow me down, stuck his chest out, took a few big paces forward and uttered the words, 'I'll sort this. You keep going.'

It was hilarious and my most vivid memory of the entire race. It often works like this, that when one of you is having a low point, the other isn't and you can take advantage of it when needed. He helped Dave's mate and caught up with me soon afterwards.

We crossed the road at Cheesefoot Head to rack up 100 miles. There were still three miles to go but I now knew that I'd run 100 miles and it could never be taken away from me. It felt good. We descended around Telegraph Hill, through the tiny village of Chilcomb and onto the final track to Winchester. We were shuffling slowly and, apart from Dave, hadn't seen another competitor since Amberley, sixteen hours and fifty miles before. Incredible.

We were slowly making our way down the track when we could hear someone coming behind us. It was another runner, travelling at the speed of a freight train, absolutely flying down the hill. He overtook us and vanished into the distance. We were shot and moving at a snail's pace and he'd flown past like he was running a 5k race. It really begs the question what on earth he'd been doing for the previous 101 miles as this was very odd behaviour.

Into the streets of Winchester, suddenly becoming conscious of how mucky we were as we hit civilisation after more than a day's running. I was desperate to finish but also very conscious not to make a navigational error in the town's streets and add even a single metre to the distance. We had no such problems and rounded a final corner to arrive on the steps of the finishing hotel, with a group of five people cheering and clapping us home. We'd done it in a time of 29 hours and 1 minute.

I didn't feel elated or like celebrating. I just had a sense of relief that I'd overcome the challenge and had run 103 miles. This was something big, a real achievement and something to be very proud of. It all seemed surreal as it hadn't sunk in properly. It wouldn't for a while as it was such a big challenge. It took time for me to accept that I'd actually done it. To run over 100 miles is mind boggling, something that your brain just cannot compute. This was something that would define who I was, something that would forever be a part of what I'd achieved in life. I was very happy.

The next morning, at breakfast in the hotel, I could hardly walk. Brandon and I chatted to a fellow competitor and his wife as we hobbled out. I'd seen other guests looking at me strangely, as I could hardly move back and forth to the buffet. As I left the room, I heard some discussion, obviously about our condition. The last words I heard were, 'They ran 100 miles yesterday.'

I welled up as I couldn't believe it was me they were referring to.

In ultra running, they say that, 'To finish is to win.' This weekend I'd won.

34 started, 22 finished, I came 14th. The race had a 35% drop-out rate.

7   There and Back

Running ultras presents a significant physical and mental challenge to overcome, putting a large strain on your body during the course of the run. This is difficult enough to deal with in isolation, without having any additional factors added, either before or after the event itself, which might impact on a successful outcome.

I always approach an event by having a very clear plan of my logistics in getting to and from it, which will eliminate all stress factors while I am actually running. This ensures that I start fresh and do not have the worry of what I will do after the finish weighing me down on the way. This reduces the pressure during the event itself, allowing me to focus all my energy and mental strength on what lies between the start and finish.

In reality, this all boils down to just two things to consider. First, a plan to arrive at the start well-rested and in plenty of time. Second, a plan to recover after the finish and get home again.

Start times can be a challenge in themselves as ultras can start at any time of the day or night. I've started races as early as 4 am, as late as 10 pm and at all times in between. I will generally drive to an event, aiming to be there a good few hours before the start. I don't relax until I'm there and have eliminated variables such as traffic that could disrupt my plan. I also like to register and use the toilets before queues build up, then simply unwind and dial-in to the event, chatting to other competitors and soaking up the atmosphere. This relaxes me and ensures that I've distanced myself from any baggage of day-to-day life well before I head to the start line. For an ultra with an early start time, I'll either get up very early when traffic is not an issue or stay somewhere overnight beforehand. This depends on how far the event is from home, how early the start is and how big the race is. For an overnight stay, I'll either camp or book a hotel somewhere close to the start. For a big 100-miler, where I'll be awake for two nights straight, I'll always arrive very early and have somewhere to have a lie down and good rest for a few hours in the afternoon.

One way to think of the best way to arrive at an event, is to consider the opposite. Imagine a race starting on a Friday evening; the worst thing you could do would be to work all day, stress through traffic for a few hours to get there, leaving barely enough time to change, register and make it to the start line. This would not be conducive to setting off on a long journey with everything pitched in your favour for a successful out-come.

Similarly for the finish, you can complete a race at any time of the day or night. I will always have a plan to cover this, based upon a predicted finishing time from the race schedule that I'll have prepared in advance. If it's a marathon or short ultra, then I'll simply change, eat and drive home. If it's a long ultra with overnight running, then I'll either have somewhere to stay at the finish, a plan to get to a train station or simply a plan to sleep in a tent or car for a few hours before driving home.

By having a plan for the finish, then I have nothing to worry about while actually running the race. If there were complex travel arrangements or a tight schedule after the finish, then this could start to affect my thinking during the race. This would introduce baggage and additional emotional drain that I just don't need on top of managing the race itself.

The biggest logistical challenge is ensuring that you are safe to drive a car afterwards, if that's your means of getting home. For long ultras and any event that goes overnight, then no one is in any fit state to drive after finishing. The level of physical exertion, coupled with sleep deprivation, means that it's simply unsafe to drive until you've had some rest and sleep. This needs planning into the schedule if you are driving yourself. I will have some food and drink at the finish, a shower if available, clean clothes and aim to get at least an hour's sleep. Events differ in the facilities available. Sometimes there may be a hall you can crash-out in, at others you may have a tent pitched at the finish. The other option is just to sleep in the car with the seat wound right back. I keep an airline eye-mask in my car and find I can sleep well for an hour or so like this. A sleep of just thirty minutes is incredible at reviving you sufficiently to be able to drive, without the danger of dozing off at the wheel. However, any journey afterwards must be taken with extreme care and at the first sign of fatigue I'll stop, get out, eat, drink and walk around in the fresh air to revive myself. If public transport is a viable option, then that's a better alternative to driving after an event.

Some races are run on a linear course, finishing at a different place from the start. Events will always put on a bus to close the loop back to the original point. While this is straightforward for the competitors, it adds travel time and waiting time to the events, many hours to an already long day. This needs factoring into the plan for the logistics.

One factor that changes this is the use of a crew. I've never had a crew on an ultra as I much prefer to be self-sufficient. This comes from my hill walking and fell running background, where I've spent many thousands of hours on my own in the mountains, where self-sufficiency and self-reliance are essential. I've also had one experience of a crew which went badly and I said that I'd never repeat it again.

I was cycling the Coast-to-Coast route with a friend, Dan, on road bikes from St Bees on the Cumbria coast to Seaham on the North Sea coast, a distance of 125 miles in a day, from sea level to the highest road pass in England and back to sea level again. We'd stayed the night before in a hotel in St Bees and the plan was for our wives to meet us at the top of the main climb over the Pennines to re-supply us for the second half of the ride. They would then meet us again at the finish to drive us home. This was in the early days of mobile phones, so we had contact with them but knew that this would be patchy given the hills that we had to ride through.

We'd ridden all morning through the Lake District and were just past Penrith, heading onto the major climb up onto the Pennines, when we got a phone call to say that the car had broken down and they were waiting for assistance. We had no option other than to keep riding as we still had a long distance to cover and no contingency plan. As we climbed up the long road towards Hartside Pass, where we were supposed to be meeting at the cafe for lunch and the re-supply, all we knew was that we weren't going to meet. We were adding up between us what we'd got with us in terms of food, drink and money. We could get water at the cafe and could buy something to eat as we had cash with us but no credit card. We both had a waterproof jacket stuffed in our jerseys but no other layers if it got cold later on. If we could keep riding and get all the way to the finish in our planned time we should be ok. The bigger issue was that we knew we'd lose phone reception in the Pennines. This meant we had no means of knowing if we could get home from the finish and we certainly had nowhere to stay or method of paying for it. The climb was hot, hard work and we were both incredibly demoralised with all these options going through our heads. I even took my helmet off and hung it on the handlebars, which I never do, as I was so bothered thinking of all the options. It just made a hard job even harder, through something that was completely out of our control. It all worked out in the end as these things always do; the car was fixed and we met up at the finish. However, we had a few stressful hours while we had no phone reception and no knowledge of what was going on with our support crew. This just added to the difficulty of doing a hard physical challenge. That was my one and only experience of relying on a crew or anything external to myself on an event. I will never do so again as I'm a naturally self-sufficient person and find that if I have everything under control myself then I'm a lot happier

However, if you do have a crew that you trust and can rely on, then a lot of the pre- and post-race arrangements can be forgotten as you can rely on them to sort all of that for you. Just make sure that you're happy with the plans and have no baggage from relying on them that you will take into the event.

My thinking is that you should do everything possible at either end of an event to reduce the weight on you within the event itself. This is just simple planning, being organised and knowing exactly what you are doing and when. Others don't worry too much about this but I feel that every percentage point you can pitch in your favour that reduces baggage, is another percentage point towards a successful finish. Not many people are this focused when it comes to looking at the details surrounding an event but I find it a simple approach and one that's been very successful for me. It's an approach that I'll always adopt.

8   Perfect Day: 10 Peaks *(July 2011)*

'The 2010 event saw 52 people, including armed forces,
adventure racers, fell runners, triathletes, ultra-distance and
elite marathon runners take on the challenge. No one
completed the course.' (Race Organiser)

The 10 Peaks is an event that was first run for charity in 2010. It covers a 45-mile route, with a significant 18,000 feet of climbing, to visit the ten highest peaks in the Lake District. It was originally intended as a one-off event that year but, as no one finished, the event was being run again in 2011. The big draw was the fact that the tough course and poor weather had defeated all starters before, so naturally it appealed to me to have a crack at it. It was also a great route over some fantastic mountains with incredible scenery, so promised to be a first class day out.

Brandon and I travelled up to the Lakes on Friday evening and camped on the edge of Derwentwater in Keswick. We registered that evening and were given race numbers two and three. The event organiser was running himself and he had number one. Numbers for all other competitors were allocated in order of entries being received. Brandon's had been the first entry, mine was the second. It felt good having the lowest numbers possible.

The start was on Saturday at 4 am from Swirls car park on Thirlmere, so the event was running a bus transfer from Keswick, leaving at 3 am. Working backwards we needed to get up at 2 am to get sorted out and walk across Keswick to the departure point. It was never going to be a good night's sleep and neither of us fell asleep before midnight. It's always hard to relax ahead of a big event, especially when the alarm is set so early.

After getting up at this early hour, silently moving around the campsite getting dressed into kit and eating a hasty bowl of muesli, we made our one and only mistake of the day before departing. Neither of us put any sunscreen on and neither of us packed it into our rucksacks. It didn't seem important in the dark but unfortunately would be a decision we'd both regret later.

After the bus to the start and some milling around to kill time, we were off at 4 am just as it was starting to get light. The route was all uphill, straight to Helvellyn summit (peak one) and a climb that took us just under an hour. The view from the top with the sun rising over the distant Pennines was breathtaking but we had to turn around and head on, as there was a long day ahead. To drop the required 2,000 feet into the valley quickly, we used a direct route which was off-path and straight down the steep hillside over steep, vertiginous ground. All other competitors around us headed down the longer route via a good path, but we were familiar with the direct route used on the Old County Tops fell race. What we hadn't appreciated was that, while the direct descent was fast in May for the fell race, in July the steepest section towards the bottom was covered in thick bracken. This slowed us considerably and, with hindsight, we would have been better heading around the path as the footing would have been much better. No time was lost versus the path but it was heavy going through the waist-deep undergrowth on a very steep slope. A lot of care was needed to avoid falling.

We then ran round to the first checkpoint at Steel End, grabbed a banana each and headed into Wythburn. There was a line of portable toilets in the field here for the overnight camp of the Saunders Lakeland Mountain Marathon that was also being run this weekend. This was an event we'd completed for the last four years but we were on a bigger mission today.

It was a long journey through the Wythburn valley and The Bog, the notorious section that needs skirting carefully as it's always very wet and boggy. As we headed through the upper section of the valley, we were being followed by a few young lads from the army. They were clearly following us and using us so they didn't have to navigate. To make it worse, they were full of themselves and their endless talk of their greatness was bugging me as we headed up the final steep climb to the intervening ridge of Green Edge. This might seem uncharitable but when you know what you're doing on an event, others that are clearly following you start to frustrate you. They're known as 'limpets' for obvious reasons, adding nothing of value but slowing you down by draining you mentally. They didn't know it but we had an ace to play.

This part of the route was still part of the Old County Tops route and the best line here is to head straight over the col, skirt the top of Long Crag and then slide off the hillside gradually to the top of Stake Pass. However, the event route suggested turning left and climbing over the adjacent summit of High Raise, before dropping to the pass. This is easier to navigate but adds climbing and is unnecessary as High Raise is not one of the ten peaks and has no checkpoint on it. We went straight over the col as planned and instantly noticed that all the chatter behind us had stopped. After a few hundred metres, I turned to look behind and could see the four lads looking confused, all confidence gone, with a map out and wondering where we were going. It was priceless and a very memorable image.

We headed down to Sticks Pass and then climbed to skirt Angle Tarn and up onto the rocky Bowfell summit (peak two). It was still early but we'd already covered a significant distance and been running for over four hours, so took a moment on the summit to appreciate the views which were fantastic. This summit was an out-and-back, so we headed back the way we'd come. As we approached the col, there were a number of rucksacks dumped on the ground. This is something that really annoys me; people leaving their rucksacks to save weight on an out-and-back section. If you're an experienced mountain walker or runner, then you're used to carrying a rucksack with you at all times so it is not something that bothers you. What would you do if you had an accident, your plan changed, the weather closed in quickly or you got lost without your gear, on that out-and-back? There's a reason for carrying your kit with you at all times. Dumping rucksacks to come back and retrieve them later, for a minimal weight saving, is something that I would not entertain.

We headed off to the highest ridge of Lakeland where the peaks came thick and fast: Great End (peak three), Ill Crag (peak four), Broad Crag (peak five) and then on to England's highest point, Scafell Pike (peak six). So far, so good, great visibility and we were moving efficiently, although it was now getting very warm.

The next section to Scafell (peak seven) was only one mile but involved losing and re-gaining 1,000 feet of height by dropping to the fearsome ridge of Mickledore, before scrambling up a very steep and rocky gully to Foxes Tarn, then climbing the scree-covered path up to the summit. There are a couple of other options for this route but they all involve scrambling and significant re-gain of height. This is a really tough section and took just under an hour, a speed of barely one mile per hour. The heat was building now as it was a perfect day without a cloud in the sky. I was low on water as there wasn't any accessible across such rocky ground, so was rationing myself until the next stream which would be in the valley below.

From here there was a major route-choice decision to be made. The event's suggested route was to retrace our steps back to Mickledore, then drop down to the Corridor Route, a well-trodden path to Styhead Tarn, followed by a climb up onto Great Gable. This would be peak eight and would then require a very long out-and-back to Pillar, which would be peak nine. A long out-and-back like this would be mentally difficult and a long slog but it was the obvious route. However, while studying the map a month prior to the event, Brandon had found an alternative. This was to drop straight off the back of Scafell, a massive descent into the depths of Wasdale. We would head through Wasdale and then have a long climb up to Black Sail Pass, before a short out-and-back to Pillar, which would instead be peak eight. We would then retrace our steps back to Black

Sail Pass, skirt Kirkfell and climb onto Great Gable which would become peak nine. The advantage of this option would be that it looped around and minimised the out-and-back section, a huge mental advantage. The disadvantage was that we'd be descending to the valley floor and adding a significant amount of climbing to an already big day. We'd discussed it at length in the build-up and both decided that the mental advantages outweighed the physical disadvantages, so we opted for this route. Very few competitors came this way but I think we made a fantastic route choice and it worked out perfectly for us.

We dropped the 2,900 feet into Wasdale where a major rescue operation was underway with two helicopters and twenty members of Mountain Rescue dealing with a casualty on Scafell where we'd just come from. What we didn't know at the time was that this was a fellow competitor from our event, who had opted for the perilous Broad Stand route between Scafell Pike and Scafell. He'd slipped and fallen a significant distance, sustaining serious injuries, requiring rescue and hospital treatment.

Both of us were feeling the heat and this huge descent turned our legs to jelly. It was a real struggle to descend quickly so we just trundled along, concentrating on losing the height and getting down to the valley. Once we hit the valley floor, another fell runner joined us who was waiting to support his friend on a Bob Graham Round attempt. This is a 66-mile run, climbing 27,000 feet over 42 peaks, with the target being to complete it in under 24 hours. Those attempting it always use support runners to carry their gear, navigate and basically help to speed them up.

We chatted to him as we trotted up towards Wasdale Head and soon realised that he was an exceptional runner, having won the Old County Tops race a few months before. He was clearly very experienced and confirmed that we'd made a great route choice over the recommended route. He left us after ten minutes to return to his Bob Graham duties. As we ran, we ate and drank plenty and kept moving. It was hot now with no breeze, so we ensured that we'd got plenty of water before heading onto the monster 2,700 feet climb up to Pillar (peak eight). This had us both struggling, so we just kept our heads down, grinding out the miles to slowly cover the distance and gain the height. At the top we were seven minutes ahead of schedule after ten hours of running, a planning accuracy of 1% but this wasn't to last.

It was now very hot, even at height, and this was sapping our energy. Sweat was pouring off us and it became apparent that the lack of sunscreen was a big mistake. There was nothing we could do but press on. We'd completed eight peaks and had turned a corner on the route now, so it felt like we were heading for home. Motivationally, this was a huge factor as we headed for Great Gable, passing other runners on our event who were heading out to Pillar while we were returning. Everyone looked wasted and in a far worse condition than we felt, which gave us some consolation, especially as everyone we now passed was behind us on the course. We were still moving strongly, albeit more slowly than planned. We lost thirty minutes on this section but summited the rocky monster of Great Gable (peak nine) by mid-afternoon.

Now for the sting in the tail. The final peak (Skiddaw) was fourteen miles from Great Gable across mountainous terrain. This was going to take a long time. Looking towards the north, Skiddaw looked an awfully long way away which was pretty demoralising. We'd always known that the last peak would be the most challenging but it was the same for everyone. We cracked on but the heat was sapping us, although the views were glorious with the whole of Lakeland spread beneath us. At least the navigation had been simple all day with such good weather.

At Honister pass we had drop-bags to replenish our food from. Due to the heat, I didn't actually fancy anything that was in my bag and had sufficient food to get me to the finish. There was the opportunity to retire here, with a minibus to shuttle you back up the valley to the finish. A few competitors were doing just that and a lot more behind us would too, but we pressed on fairly quickly. It was another big climb up to Dalehead Tarn to get over the next ridge and then a long, rocky descent into the valley below. I was flagging badly along here and just couldn't get going. The heat and distance were catching up on me. After a few miles we hit the road at Little Town and decided to take a break and have a good sort out. We slumped by the roadside. I registered that this was the first time I'd sat down in fifteen hours, which is something that very few people will ever do in their lives. This ten-minute break allowed us to get straight. I cleared the debris from my shoes, sorted food and headtorch into more convenient pockets on my rucksack, ate and drank. The powers of recuperation, both physically and mentally, that such a short break gives are incredible. We were both refreshed when we headed on again but this was only relative, as we were far from the spritely athletes who had departed the start many hours previously.

It was all valley running through to Keswick which was straightforward and ate some miles up easily. It had taken four hours to get here from the last peak and would take us another two to climb Skiddaw. These six hours were murder. We were cooked from the sun, it was hot throughout, everything hurt and as we started the immense climb of Skiddaw, Brandon was feeling sick and dragging but soldiering on as always. This climb was tough, really tough. I've climbed many mountains in my time but this was a steep route after a long day, with 2,800 feet to gain. Worse than that, we were now heading away from the finish which we'd passed within a mile of, as we skirted the edge of Keswick. This was mentally draining to add to the physical challenge of the climb. No wonder the drop-out rate was 100% the year before.

A slow plod to the top had us on Skiddaw summit (peak ten) just after 10 pm. It was dark as we left, heading down the tourist track to Keswick, with Brandon commenting that two others were right behind us, heading onto the summit. Skiddaw is a big, open mountain and you can see a long way across it on the descent. We kept looking back to see where these two runners were, as they had to be faster than us because we were crawling down slowly. However, they never came and we didn't ever see their headtorches. Brandon must have imagined them from rocks or shadows on the mountain as they certainly didn't exist.

It took us an hour and forty minutes to descend to Keswick. This is a full hour slower than I can do it on a normal day which shows how exhausted and bashed-in we were. We finished just before midnight.

Our final time of 19 hours and 51 minutes was slightly behind our nineteen-hour schedule, partially due to the heat, but ahead of our self-imposed target of twenty hours. I drank about ten litres of water en route which shows what an epic day out it had been.

After a chat with the organisers and fellow finishers, we shuffled slowly through the deserted streets of Keswick to our campsite. We had the campsite showers to ourselves at 1 am which was probably a good thing, as we had clothing and gear strewn everywhere. Showering was not a pleasant experience as I'd blistered both my feet and had pretty bad sunburn on the exposed areas of my face, arms and legs.

Less than half the starters finished which shows how tough the event was. I rate this as the greatest day I've ever had in the UK hills. The views and scenery had been awesome all day. Conditions were tough in the heat but it was an epic journey through incredible terrain and a day that will be very difficult to beat. It had been a perfect day out.

102 started, 49 finished, I came 18th. The race had a 52% drop-out rate.

9   Cycling to a Number

'Only those who will risk going too far will possibly find out how far one can go.' (TS Eliot)

After cycling from Lands End to John O'Groats in the spring of 2000, I'd proven my ability to cycle long distances and was keen to do another challenge. The trouble is, when you've cycled the full length of the country, most other ideas lack ambition by comparison. There were organised challenge rides and single day challenges, such as cycling the Coast-to-Coast route, which I completed in the summer of 2001 with my friend Dan. However, I hadn't found anything to really get my teeth into.

   Dan was also keen to do another challenge and we discussed a few options but nothing really grabbed us enough to do it. However, something that Dan said had stuck with me. Dan was a strong and powerful cyclist, much stronger than me. He could power along on the flat but I'd leave him for dead on any climbs because I was a lot shorter and lighter than him. Dan tended to focus on shorter but faster rides. Prior to the Coast-to-Coast, his longest ride was sixty miles. He doubled that maximum when we rode across the country that day. We'd joked that he couldn't keep doubling his maximum. Could he?

   The Coast-to-Coast was 125 miles and had taken us eleven hours. It was a hilly course so our average moving speed of 14 mph had been compromised. It wasn't a preposterous suggestion to double the distance and expect to maintain a similar pace. That would give us 250 miles in under 24 hours. Now this grabbed me and wouldn't let me go. I started planning.

   The first thing I knew was that we had to be unsupported. Whatever I came up with had to be achievable without relying on any outside help. I considered cycling from the River Mersey to the River Thames, which would effectively be from my house in Warrington to my parents' house in Essex. I thought Clair could drive down to Essex and bring us back but this would commit us to a long, straight line and involve committing Clair to a lot of driving.

Rethinking the logic, I realised that what we were actually trying to achieve was the longest ride that we possibly could, rather than a journey. A ride that we'd bank as our longest and never need to attempt again. A distance of 250 miles was the ultimate target but what would I accept as the minimum? I decided 200 would be an awesome fall-back if 250 was not achievable. The closer we could get to 250 the better. So why not have a route that had some flexibility in it, planning for 250 but with bail-out options available to get us to 200. In my mind 200 miles was the absolute minimum that I'd accept as success, that '2' at the front of the number being the all-important factor. To drive 200 miles takes some effort; to cycle it in a day would be incredible.

Dan was living in Derby at the time. Derby is located centrally in the country so gave a lot of route options. I realised that a big loop from his house would enable us to achieve the two desired outcomes. Firstly, we could be totally self-sufficient as it would be a closed loop circuit and we'd end up back where we started. Secondly, by being a loop we could devise a route that would enable us to cut it short in the latter phases, to knock some distance out if necessary.

I spent time poring over maps with a measuring wheel and devised a circular route that would serve our purpose. We'd ride south from Derby, heading to the east of Coventry, looping round to Stratford-upon-Avon and then to Worcester. We'd then head north, via Bridgnorth, Telford and Whitchurch. We could loop around the top of Stoke-on-Trent for the full 250 miles or loop underneath to shorten it down to 200, with options between the two distances. This seemed perfect.

We'd do it in 2002, on a convenient weekend in the middle of summer to maximise daylight. We'd set off at midnight so we'd get the night riding done first, while we were fresh and alert, not physically exhausted. We'd aim to be finished by 10 pm the next night when it would still be light, 22 hours later. If we went into darkness again it would only be for a short time as we'd set a 24-hour time limit. I prepared a time schedule for the day and photocopied sections of map to carry with us. Apart from adding lights to my bike, we were pretty much set to go.

This ride was to prove a great example of how mental preparation is key to an endurance challenge. In the week leading up to the event, I'd been at work all week, while Dan had been on a relaxing holiday in Scotland, arriving back on the Thursday. We were cycling overnight, starting at midnight Friday evening. In theory, he should be fresher than me as he wouldn't have just completed a week at work but this actually worked against him.

I'd got my bike sorted out the weekend before, as well as the kit I needed and food to eat. I needed to be prepared as I wouldn't have time during the week. Dan had been in a rush to go on holiday and left his preparations until he returned. Unfortunately, he then discovered a problem with one of his brakes and had to spend time obtaining a replacement part and repairing it. He ended up limited for time and doing this on the Friday afternoon. I arrived at his house in the late afternoon, to find him disorganised and sorting his gear out. He still had plenty of time but I was relaxed and focused on the task ahead, while he was busy getting ready. We were in very different frames of mind for the ride.

We ate some pasta, sat around chatting and attempted to get some sleep for a few hours. I slept from about 10:30 pm until my alarm went off at 11:40 pm. I awoke groggy but was actually well rested as I'd been sitting and lying down all evening. To this day, 11:40 pm is the earliest I've ever got up, a bizarre time but an hour's sleep was better than nothing before setting off.

After some strong coffee, we departed on the stroke of midnight. It was a surprisingly dark night for the time of year but the roads we'd chosen were small and there was very little traffic. We'd only have a maximum of four hours' darkness before daylight, which would soon pass. The cycling was straightforward, with either empty but dark roads in the countryside or street-lights but a small amount of traffic in the few towns we went through. We had some abuse shouted at us by late-night revellers as we cycled through Hinckley in the early hours but, other than that, the first few hours were uneventful. It was exciting to be out at night and knocking off some miles before the day started. It felt as if we were getting ahead, which was psychologically beneficial.

Shortly before daylight, we had a slight setback when Dan suffered a puncture. We were just entering a small village and wheeled his bike underneath a streetlight that was right outside someone's front door. It was 3:30 am and we silently changed his inner tube, taking care not to drop any tools or make any sounds, to avoid waking the locals. This cost us some time but we were relaxed on that front as today was about hitting the magic 200 miles and just managing our way around the route.

The sun rose soon after and we threaded our way around Coventry, gradually turning west, passing through Stratford-upon-Avon in the early morning. For me, this was the first big landmark achieved as we'd completed the southern leg of our route. Our spirits were high and we just kept rotating our turns at the front as we had been all night, heading on towards Worcester.

As we racked up ninety miles, Dan started saying that he was tiring. He wasn't in any trouble but the first signs of fatigue were setting in. It wasn't surprising really, as we'd been on the road many hours already but we still had a long way to go. I was feeling strong so started to take longer turns on the front with him in my slipstream.

We racked up the first 100 miles near Worcester which was a huge milestone. We were halfway to our lower objective. We stopped at a garage to stock up on food. On a ride like this, we only had the rear pockets in our cycling tops to carry everything we needed. I had a rain jacket stuffed in one pocket and the other two contained my maps and food but after 100 miles I'd eaten almost all my supplies. On a multi-day trip, I'll have panniers on my bike, which give extra space for carrying things but this was a lightweight daytrip and space was limited. I bought a couple of pasties, pork pie, chocolate and cereal bars. Some of this was eaten immediately as I was hungry from the exertions so far. The rest was stuffed in my rear pockets.

Shortly after Worcester we turned another corner and started heading north. The day was warming up and I removed the long-sleeved base-layer that I'd been wearing under my cycling top. I had no pocket space to stow this in so tied it round my waist. As the morning wore on it got warmer and warmer and I was very aware of the sun on the back of my legs. I had no sun cream on and was fully exposed but this was a minor worry on a route this long.

I was still going strongly all the way to Telford, although Dan was flagging a bit. Normally we're very similar in our ability on long rides so this was something we hadn't experienced before. I put it down to the difference in our preparation, the fact that I'd started relaxed and focused, while Dan had been dealing with a mechanical issue right up until the last minute. It certainly wasn't anything physical as we'd matched each other over long distances before.

I was on the front constantly now. The hills south of Telford were behind us and we emerged onto the flat plain beyond. I was pushing along as we headed up to Market Drayton at 160 miles. We'd long passed our previous furthest mileage and now the numbers were getting substantial. We were both considering our options on what we should do. For some reason, we'd covered more miles than expected up to this point on the schedule, so decided to cut south of Stoke and start heading back to Derby. We wouldn't make the top target of 250 miles but would easily exceed 200.

Soon beyond Market Drayton I started flagging badly too. I'd done over 160 miles feeling strong and it was inevitable this wouldn't last all the way home. I'd also managed to get a lot further than Dan before struggling but now we were both in it together. We were estimating another seventy to eighty miles to go, which is a huge ride in itself and not something you'd set out to ride being this exhausted normally.

My whole body was hurting by now. Not just my legs, which were inevitable, but all the contact points with the bike. My bottom was as to be expected, that always feels it after a long ride, but my hands and feet were sore from bearing my weight on the pedals and handlebars. My back, neck, shoulders and upper arms were aching from constantly looking forwards with my head lifted, which is the position you ride a road bike in. This last third of the ride was going to test us.

The afternoon was hot and thunderclouds were building. As we approached Stone, the heavens opened and we had a monsoon rainstorm, accompanied by thunder and lightning. We donned our rain jackets and kept moving, with water sloshing around the road under our wheels. As with all summer storms, it soon passed and the sun emerged strongly again to dry us out. It was 4 pm and our calculations had us finishing well before darkness. We just had to keep our bikes rolling.

There were some small hills to climb around Uttoxeter and it was here that our bike computers recorded the landmark 200 miles being achieved. It was such a lift to see this and to know that we'd succeeded in our goal, although we still had a few hours of riding in front of us. We cycled through some small villages south-west of Derby, crossed the busy A50 and then were aiming directly for the end. I could hardly move my neck as it was so sore and was getting pins-and-needles in my right hand. Dan was in a similar position and had pins-and-needles in his feet. The sheer length of time spent in one position was taking its toll but the end was in sight now, with less than ten miles to go.

Negotiating the busy roads of Derby demanded our attention, but then we had just one last, small climb before rolling down Dan's road to pull up on his drive, just before 8 pm. My bike computer recorded 230.0 miles, a very satisfying, round number. I was happy with that. We were both utterly drained, sore and glowing from a long day in the sun. We'd been on the road for 19 hours and 54 minutes.

We showered, then limped down to Dan's local fish and chip shop. We both had a doner kebab and chips which we ate silently and slowly while sprawled on his sofa, then headed for a well-earned sleep.

Departed at midnight, cycled 230 miles, home for kebab and chips. It has a nice simplicity and honesty to it. I'm very proud of what we achieved that day.

It took me a few days to recover. The timing of our finish was useful, as we were in bed by 10 pm and I slept for ten hours, straight through the night. I was stiff and sore for a few days which was to be expected. The pins-and-needles lingered in the little finger of my right hand for three days which was a worry but it was only temporary.

On the face of it, it was a completely pointless exercise to cycle that distance and return to where we started. It had been an incredible day which was all about one thing, achieving a big number. We did that. Am I disappointed that we didn't manage 250 miles? No, not at all. We smashed the 200-mile mark and 250 was simply a big number to pull us well past that. It worked. The number that we achieved shocks people when I tell them. Even seasoned cyclists, much keener than myself, are amazed when I roll that number out. It's just ridiculous to think about covering that distance in one day on a bike but that's what drew us to it. I'm extremely pleased to have this achievement in my box of accomplishments.

We cycled 230 miles, at an average speed of 14 mph. I've never met anyone who's done anywhere near this distance or would want to try.

10   Hard Graft: OMM Elite *(October 2011)*

'The Original Mountain Marathon is a test of endurance,
navigation and mountain survival. Held in some of the most
remote locations and at a time of year when conditions can be
extremely challenging, an OMM is meant to be hard.'
(Race Organiser)

The Original Mountain Marathon (OMM) started life in 1968 as the Karrimor International Mountain Marathon (KIMM). Despite the name, it is not a marathon. The full-length course was conceived as a double marathon, run over two days on an unpublished course in the hills, for teams of two, who must carry all their gear for the duration. It also has a number of shorter courses, all run over two days with an overnight camp. The Elite course is the longest and toughest, staying true to the double marathon concept. This race has a rich history and is seen as the fore-runner to modern adventure racing.

In 1993, I ran the C course of the KIMM which was held in the Queensberry Hills of Southern Scotland. This was one of the shorter courses on the event, being three levels down from the top Elite course. The Elite was for super-humans. I was only 21 at the time and relatively inexperienced in the hills, although my navigation and running were good through time spent orienteering, running and hiking while at university. It was a big challenge and I was pleased to finish it. At this time, there was also a mountain bike event called the Polaris Challenge, which followed exactly the same format but on bikes. I completed this five times while at university, every time with a different partner. After leaving university, I didn't think I'd ever compete in such an event again. I certainly didn't ever consider that I'd run the OMM Elite course.

The mountain marathon format that the OMM introduced has been adopted by a number of events and is considered a standard format. The event will consist of a number of courses to suit different abilities. These will be specified by approximate distance and expected finishing time for the winners. The event location will be given up-front in terms of the general area in the country where it will be held but the exact location of the event and its starting point will not be revealed until a fortnight beforehand. Competitors run in teams of two and must carry all their gear to be self-sufficient in the hills for two days. This includes each individual's personal gear, comprising clothing to cope with all mountain weather conditions, sleeping bag and survival kit, as well as shared items, including a tent, stove and food. The focus of the event is on navigation so all electronic navigational aids are banned. Each team starts at staggered intervals to prevent following other competitors. The course for each day will be unknown until the start of that day, when it will be provided as either a pre-marked map or a list of grid references to plot yourself. The race will involve navigating to about ten controls, each comprising an orange and white flag with an electronic box attached, in which each team dibs their dibber, to show that they've visited. A dibber is a small two-inch plastic stick which is attached to one competitor's wrist. When it's inserted into the box at the control, it bleeps and flashes to register being there.

Day one will be the longer of the two days and will take competitors out to a remote camp in the hills where they will spend the night. The next morning, they will pack their kit away and repeat the format, with the finish back at the event centre. The cumulative time for the two days is added together to give a total time.

One of the mountain marathons in the UK that has adopted this format is the Saunders Lakeland Mountain Marathon, held each July in the Lake District. I ran this with Brandon in 2007, completing the third hardest course out of six, finishing comfortably in the middle of the field. The year after, we ran the second hardest course and again finished in the middle. In 2009 and 2010, we ran the hardest course; we were now amongst the elite runners, with less than twenty teams competing. Both years we finished three-quarters of the way down the field, which we felt was respectable. We are not the strongest runners but are both excellent navigators and make up for our lack of pure speed by making good route choices and minimising our mistakes when micro-navigating into a control. The ultimate mountain marathon challenge was the OMM Elite and we discussed whether we should do it or not. We knew that it would be a very tough challenge, but the time was ready to test ourselves as we now had the required experience to be accepted.

In October 2011 we headed up to Scotland to test ourselves on this blue-riband event. What a test it was.

The event was based in Comrie, central Scotland, about fifty miles north of Glasgow. I drove the 250 miles up from Warrington on the Friday afternoon, picking Brandon up along the way. We camped at the event centre, using a four-man family tent, rather than the tiny tent we would be carrying with us. This gave us the space to use luxurious airbeds to try and get a decent night's sleep before starting, as well as saving the hassle of re-packing our rucksacks again the next morning to add in a tent. We were starting at 8:27 am the next morning, so had to be up, ready, tent packed away and on an event bus by 7:30 am.

All preparations went to plan and we were on the bus with nothing but two rucksacks containing all our gear for two days in the hills. We were dropped off at the next village where we had a mile's walk up a hillside track to the start. It was raining heavily and we wore full waterproofs. The forecast was grim and it wouldn't stop raining all day. This was going to be a very unpleasant day out.

On the dot of 8:27 am, we picked up our laminated maps with the control positions marked on them and we were off. A quick scan of the route showed very few paths and a few long legs where we'd have to consider our route choice carefully. The first leg was a short one of only one mile, straight across a heather-covered hill and into a boggy area beyond. This was a good, simple start to get us tuned-in to the day ahead. Legs two and three were uneventful, although the rain was driving and we were having to navigate very carefully the whole time due to the lack of paths. The third control was on top of a 2,000-feet high peak and visibility was very low as we were in the cloud. As we left the peak and descended through the cloud on a compass bearing, we were heading to a stream crossing below. We heard the stream long before we saw it. Arriving on its bank, we were presented with a scene of horror. The stream was massive, in spate and was a raging torrent of white water.

'How are we going to get across that?' we asked each other.

There was no option to track up-stream or down-stream to find a bridge or other suitable crossing point, as this would have taken us miles out of position. We gripped each other by the shoulders and carefully waded in. The current was strong and threatened to sweep us away. We coordinated our feet movements by telling each other to move, so that we always had three feet firmly on the river bed. The water was freezing cold and thigh deep but, with hearts pumping due to fear, we gradually inched across to the far side. The crossing was a heart-stopping epic but was only the first of many that we'd have to complete that day.

Controls four and five were difficult to find as they were in indistinct ground in the mist. On fell races and ultras, checkpoints are normally large, manned and easy to locate. They are positioned on a prominent feature such as a peak or a path junction. Not so on a mountain marathon. This is a navigational event and the controls are made challenging to find. They are small flags, tucked in a feature of the land away from obvious view. Typically, they will be positioned so you can't see them from the direction you approach. This means that your navigation has to be spot-on or you'll shoot right past. Both controls four and five required us to head over the brow of a hill and drop onto them from above, both being tucked into a small stream in a re-entrant on the hillside. A re-entrant is basically a wrinkle in the contours, like a small gulley running up the side of the hill.

We'd been out for quite a few hours now and the rain was incessant. Despite having full waterproofs on, we were both wet and miserable. Every now and then we'd see another team but they were few and far between, so we were mostly on our own. We'd covered barely a third of the distance and had seen nothing but featureless, mist-covered moor. This wasn't fun for anyone.

We slogged on and picked off control six, which put us onto the crux leg of the day. This presented us with a seven-mile straight-line leg across pathless moor, skirting a number of hills and looking like it could be hours of marching through heather and rock-strewn roughness. The key was to find a route which picked up easy ground and use any of the very few paths. There was a path about a mile and a half north of us, which was off-course but would take us on a meandering route to nearly the halfway point of the leg. We took compass bearings and headed for it. It was a good move because when we hit it, we could switch off and just trundle along, making easy ground for two miles or so, before taking a small indistinct path around the next hillside for another couple of miles. We then had a high ridge to cross or traverse around to the north. We elected to head north and around, dropping into the head of the valley that we wanted, but this was not before we'd had a few more heart-stopping moments crossing streams. Each one could be heard like a freight train in the distance, well before we could see it. Every time, we'd look up and down the banks for a more convenient crossing point, before grabbing each other and wading in. The power of water is frightening and every one of these crossings had our eyes wide with fear. We were careful and got through each one without either of us being swept away.

We headed on into the valley which contained our overnight camp but this was still a few hours further down. We had to remain high on the hillside, contouring around to locate our controls. We'd now been out so long that it got dark. We put on our headtorches but knew we were in trouble because we still had three controls to find and they're hard enough to locate in daylight, let alone in darkness. The next one was a stream junction in the midst of a number of stream junctions, halfway up a remote, pathless, Scottish mountain. There was water pouring off the hillside; everything looked like a stream. We needed to locate the third stream along and counted our way across them until we hit our one. Then we proceeded up it. We met another pair also looking for the control. They were confused as to why it wasn't where they were. We told them we thought it was higher up. I led the way up the side of the stream but the hillside became almost vertical. We had a raging torrent beneath us and in the darkness I was trying to find a way up, only able to see as far as my headtorch would shine. All I could do was grab the heather in my gloves and scramble up the slope.

This is my most lasting memory of this dreadful event. It was pitch black and I could see only a short distance in my torchlight. I was clinging to a near vertical slope, relying on my gloved hands and the strength of the heather. I couldn't hear myself think due to the noise of the raging torrent just below us. Brandon and two others were following me upwards. I didn't know for sure if I was heading for the control or not.

I just thought, 'What am I doing here? This is ridiculous. One slip and we've all had it.'

It was one of those moments that makes you realise what being alive is all about. We were in a ludicrous position and had only ourselves to rely on to get out of it. We could have turned back down, given up the hunt for the control and retired from the event by simply following the stream to the valley floor, turning right and picking up a path down to the camp, a few miles away. However, we were focused 100% on the job in hand so pressed on. All my senses were in over-drive and life was focused on simply getting out of that predicament and finding the control. Nothing else existed. All the hassles and woes of modern life were forgotten, material possessions had no use and any other future arrangements or thoughts did not exist.

We were on a Scottish mountain looking for an orange flag in the dark, in the torrential rain and with terrain that was doing its utmost to stop us.

We headed up and five minutes later found the control. It was a massive relief.

Turning around, we headed back down in the darkness to the valley floor but we weren't finished. There were two more controls to find halfway up the other side of the valley. The first was straightforward, so we headed quickly up and across the hillside towards the last, again counting streams as we crossed them. We found a control in the stream that we thought we wanted but it had the wrong number on it, so it was for another course. We headed further along the hillside, thinking there would not be two controls in the same stream a few hundred metres apart. Time to the 8 pm cut-off at the finish was now very tight but we still couldn't find our stream. Even though it was pitch black, I could sense the hillside turning a corner which meant that we'd gone too far. There was a fence above us on the map so we headed up to that, then back-tracked along it to hit the last stream that we'd crossed. We then dropped straight down the stream and found our control. What an ordeal but we could head to the finish now. We ran down the hillside and onto the path at the bottom, running to the finish as fast as we could on very tired legs, arriving within a few minutes of the course closing.

The whole day had been a grind from start to finish. The rain, the stream crossings, getting caught out in the dark, finding those last two controls and the desperate worry about being timed out at the finish. We'd been running for over eleven hours and I was drained, both physically and mentally. Now we had to pitch a tent, feed ourselves and get ready to do it all again tomorrow. There was no respite.

The overnight campsite was a field adjacent to a large stream. The whole area was very boggy and muddy, having been churned up by the feet of hundreds of competitors who'd arrived many hours before us. We pitched the tent in the far corner and filled all our bottles with water from the stream to give us sufficient to cook with and make cups of tea. Finally, we could retire into the tent to get warm and dry.

A mountain marathon tent is tiny. A single bed is bigger. There's enough room for two adults to lie down, shoulder-to-shoulder and that's it. You can't even sit up as they're very low too. All movement has to be coordinated between you. If the weather's good, you can sit around outside, cooking, drinking and sorting your kit out. When it isn't, then you're crammed together in the smallest space in which it's possible to sleep two people.

There's absolutely nothing to do at one of these overnight camps, apart from chat, eat and drink. You'll get to know the other teams camped next to you as you exchange war stories of previous events you've done. You might meet others that you already know as you walk around the camp, fetching water or heading for the portable toilets. Phones don't get reception and you're completely isolated from the outside world. This is one of the great appeals for me because all you have with you are the bare essentials to survive for two days in the hills. Less is definitely more, as you minimise the weight that you'll be carrying. We'd arrived late tonight but most competitors would have been relaxing and living a very basic existence for a few hours, which is completely at odds with the hectic pace of life today.

The only entertainment that exists at an overnight camp, apart from talking, is to review the map and check the results. We'll look at that first day's course and the route we've taken. We'll discuss it, to see if there were any better choices or if we can understand any places where we went wrong. We'll relive the highs and lows and walk our way back through the day. This is a task that I always enjoy but I like to leave it until after we've been in camp for a few hours as something to look forward to. The results are normally pinned up somewhere and updated regularly as teams come in. Again, we'll stroll over to take a look to see where we lie and how many teams have retired.

Tonight I didn't care about either of these. I was exhausted. I took off all my wet layers and lay down in my sleeping bag in just my shorts and base layer. Brandon did the same and started cooking through the tent door. I was so tired that I just fell asleep while he was talking to me. I was knackered and just conked out. I didn't sleep for long because Brandon started moving about as he poured boiling water into our food sachets.

We both needed to eat and drink to replenish our reserves for the next day. This would normally be something that we enjoyed at an overnight camp but today it had become purely functional. It was getting late and we needed to cook sufficient food for both of us which takes time on a tiny stove.

We didn't finish eating until late and then both had a restless night in the cramped tent. The ground was uncomfortable and I only had a very thin layer of foam under me, which was the padding from the back of my rucksack. We were woken at 6 am by a bugler playing to wake all runners. This gave us a little over two hours to eat breakfast and get everything packed away into our bags. I was stiff as a board but gradually got some life into my body as we moved about and got warm.

The fastest team from day one set off at 7 am. They were followed by other teams who'd finished within an hour of their time, setting off on what's called a 'Chasing Start.' This means that if you finished two minutes down on the leaders, then you would set off two minutes after them. The result is that it becomes a pure race to the finish at the end of day two. All teams that finished day one outside an hour of the leaders had a set start time from 8 am onwards. At 8:21 am we were on our way again.

The weather was vastly improved today. There was no rain and it was bright but chilly. Higher up there was a strong, cold wind with cloud on the higher ground. The first half of the day contained a couple of very big climbs, up steep, rough hillsides. These were broken up by fairly quick running on paths along ridges where we made good progress. The wind was very strong and we kept our hoods up and heads down to keep the worst of the cold out. Our spirits were high as this was far better than the incessant rain of the day before. The streams were noticeably lower today and our route kept us mostly on high ground so we didn't have too many to cross.

After six hours of running, the rigours of the two days were catching up on us both. We were climbing up through the cloud on the pathless slopes of Ben Chonzie, a 3,000-feet high Munro mountain. Visibility was only a few metres and we were aiming to drop over the shoulder of the mountain a quarter of a mile north-east of its summit. However, our navigation was off and we headed almost over the summit before dropping very steeply down the far side. We were a quarter of a mile out-of-position without knowing it and with very low visibility. We dropped and dropped but could not match our location to the map. With hindsight, it's obvious what we did but when you're in thick cloud, on a windy mountainside and are exhausted, you make mistakes and can't correct them. We eventually dropped down out of the cloud and managed to re-locate ourselves, forcing us to re-climb and contour around the steep slopes until we found our control half a mile away. This was demoralising and wasted time and energy, neither of which we had. This was the closest that either of us have ever come to bailing out of an event, as the fatigue and build-up of the last two days got to us. What options did we have to give up? We were on a remote Scottish mountain and the only choice was to get ourselves to the finish, so we might as well keep going.

The next control was equally hard to find. We climbed an intervening ridge, then had a long descent through broken ground to find a re-entrant. Unfortunately, we ended up in the wrong re-entrant. We headed up and down, checked maps, looked for any features to re-locate off and wasted yet more time. We were now seriously worried about being timed out again. Eventually we found the right re-entrant, found the control and got out of there as fast as we could.

The running sped up now as we left the open moorland and

could use paths to take us towards the last few controls. As we pushed our pace along, in our fatigue we made another navigational blunder. We're both very good navigators but we made exactly the same error, showing that our mental agility was suffering badly from fatigue, exacerbated by the need to move as quickly as we could to avoid the time cut-off at the finish. There were a series of path junctions which would normally be easy to navigate. Unfortunately, one was on a bend and this was enough to throw us and for us both to take the wrong option. As we ran further, we realised that we were dropping rather than climbing and after a quarter of a mile confirmed the mistake. To correct the error, we could either run back round the paths or climb straight up the hill, both options wasting yet more time that we didn't have. We headed straight up the hill, pushing ourselves as fast as we could.

With only a few miles left to the finish, we took much more care after this. It was getting dark now and was very gloomy as we headed into the forest but there was no time to stop for headtorches so we just kept going. We picked off the last control in the dark and dashed along the final run-in to the finish, barely able to see what we were doing. We'd been out for over nine hours and were spent when we finally crossed the line. The last few hours had felt as if we were the only competitors still out on the hills but the marshals said there were still 100 pairs out on the shorter courses.

Over the two days, we'd run for 20 hours and 38 minutes, covering 53 miles and climbing 14,000 feet. Approximately 80% of it was off-path, across rough and often steep ground. It had been a hard slog all the way and touch-and-go against the cut-off times both days but we'd finished. On the Elite course, we were the last of the finishers but we had finished. A third of the field hadn't. What an achievement.

It wasn't over just yet though.

We headed back to the event centre, changed quickly and set off for home. This was a five-hour drive in the dark, requiring concentration while shattered, and I had to drop

Brandon off in Glasgow on the way. It was nearly midnight when I got home and I had to be in work the next morning, so there was no down-time or enjoyment after the event, just a quick shower and then bed.

I was shattered the next day and very sore. My feet were swollen from the rough ground and I ached everywhere from the distance run over hard terrain while carrying a heavy rucksack. I thought I'd just need the usual few days of recovery. That evening I started to feel unwell. I went to bed early but was up most of the night, with diarrhoea and vomiting. For the next two days I ate practically nothing and drank only water. By Thursday, I was eating plain food but then got too adventurous, resulting in another night spent back and forth to the bathroom. It wasn't until nine days after finishing the race that I felt fully well again. Brandon was exactly the same, coming down sick on the Monday evening too, with exactly the same symptoms. We'd spent the whole race drinking water from streams and must have drunk some that gave us a sickness bug. It was the event that just kept taking and wouldn't let up, even though we'd finished days before.

The whole experience was a grind from start to finish. The travelling, two dawn-to-dusk days on the hills, bad weather, rough ground, dangerous stream crossings, no down-time at the end and then a sickness bug too. I had no sense of satisfaction or fond memories of it until months afterwards. On reflection, it's one of my biggest achievements but it didn't feel like it at the time because it took so much out of me. Hard challenges are strange like this; the satisfaction and fond memories take a while to develop, as the memories of the hardship and difficulties slowly fade to leave just the good memories.

I won't ever do the Elite course of the OMM again. It was too full-on to be enjoyable at our pace. We were basically hanging-on at the back, just avoiding the cut-offs, which shows we were only just at the minimum standard required to compete at that level. We had no room for error and that shows in how much it took out of us both. It was an incredibly tough event but to be able to say that, 'I have completed the OMM Elite,' is something I'm very proud of.

56 pairs started, 38 finished, we came 38th. The race had a 32% drop-out rate.

11   Gearing Up

'By failing to prepare you are preparing to fail.'
(Benjamin Franklin)

One of the large differences between running ultras compared to shorter races is the amount of gear that you need. You're out for longer, exposed to changeable weather, generally on tracks or in the hills and so need to be self-sufficient without relying on much support from others. This means carrying an appropriate amount of kit so you can remain comfortable, keep fuelled and hydrated, navigate and generally look after yourself for any issues that arise.

In my experience, runners tend to fall into two camps over kit, as follows. These are gross generalisations but they will get the point across.

The first are those that have come into ultras from an athletic background. By this, I mean that they would class themselves a runner or an athlete and have probably progressed into ultras through road or trail running, building up the distance through marathons. The focus from this background tends to be on speed, hard data (such as split times or heart rates), competitive spirit and focusing on the running only. For relatively short runs, no kit is required, so it is alien to have to start wearing and carrying more. I would summarise this group by saying that they focus more on the result that they want to achieve, rather than on the process of the activity required along the way.

The second group are those that have come into it from a mountain background, such as hill walkers, fell runners, climbers or those with a breadth of general outdoor experience. As ultra running is slower than pure running, this is a common route into the sport, coming from a distance perspective rather than a speed one. It's a natural progression for hill walkers to move into fell running as they gain confidence and can move more quickly in the hills. There are also organisations such as the Long Distance Walkers Association who hold events that naturally bridge the gap between days out in the hills and competitive races. The focus from this background tends to be less about the hard data of time and results but more focused on the broader aspects of a day out in the hills, which includes being comfortable and carrying a reasonable amount of kit. I would summarise this group by saying that they focus more on the process of doing the activity and are less focused on the end result, in terms of finishing time.

Excusing the generalities given, what it amounts to is there are those that carry slightly more than they need and those that carry slightly less. In broad terms, I would expect the athletes to carry less than required and the mountaineers to carry more. At the start of an event will be those that are lined up in running vest, shorts and a tiny bumbag. My thoughts will be, 'They'll never finish; they don't have sufficient clothes or food with them.' At the other extreme will be those in full length clothing, with hat, gloves and a large rucksack and items clipped everywhere. My thoughts will be, 'They'll never finish; they're carrying too much weight.' In reality, these are extreme views and there's a whole spectrum in between.

In most sports, there's an accepted level of kit that works for everyone, whether that be for football, tennis, cycling, cricket, road-running or any other sport. In these cases, the kit required tends to be the best approach to achieving a good result, so everyone uses the same with just slight style and manufacturer preferences. This is not so in ultra running. It's an unorthodox sport and there are no right and wrong answers. The amount of kit that I take will suit me. What suits someone else is down to them and needs to be found through experience. If you take too little clothing and food, so you end up cold and hungry, then that's fine if you're comfortable with that minimalist approach. However, if you'd rather be warm and well-fed, then take an extra layer and a bit more food than you think you'll need.

I've come into ultra running from a mountain background. On long ultras I'm also not racing as such but running to finish in a decent time and hopefully enjoy the whole experience. I therefore tend to err on the side of taking slightly too much kit.

The great thing about ultra running is the variety. People wear and take everything and anything. If it works for you and you feel comfortable, then go with it. Bizarre hats, strange tops, shorts, long trousers, any type of footwear that suits, rucksack, bumbag, hydration pack, sandwiches, energy gels, cake, hotdogs, water, sports drinks, hi-tech gadgets, battered old maps; it doesn't matter. Just do what you're used to and what you're comfortable with. A large part of ultras is dealing with discomfort, so the last thing you want is to kit yourself out thinking that's what the right gear is, when in fact you're not comfortable. Wear flip-flops and a sombrero if that's what you're used to and you know you can keep going in them.

If I run a marathon, then I'll be running hard for a time. I'll wear shorts, t-shirt, watch and use a small bumbag to carry some energy gels and my car keys. To run on the hills, I'll take a rucksack with some warm clothes, food, drink and navigation gear. To run an ultra, I'll add more food, headtorch, safety and first aid items. To run a long ultra, you can send drop bags ahead to re-supply from. I'll usually send a bag to the major halfway point containing a set of running shoes, socks, change of clothes and re-supply food. This gives the option of changing shoes if the first pair have rubbed and saves carrying all the food from the start. All this needs planning, bagging and labelling.

What I won't do is tell anyone precisely what to take. Gear choice is highly personal and only experience of trying different things will allow you to know what is right for you. When running a long ultra, you need to be comfortable with every item that you've got with you, knowing how and when to use it so that you have no surprises en route.

My gear choice will depend on the time of year and the terrain. For mountains in the winter, I'll take far more than for a low-level run in the summer. For an ultra or long day out on the hills, I would consider the following options for my kit.

Shoes. This is the most important piece of kit that you'll

select. Choice will depend on the terrain and what you're comfortable wearing. I have a range of running shoes but for a long ultra will tend to wear trail running shoes which give a good compromise between grip and good cushioning. I have fell shoes that are great for grip on steep ground, well-cushioned trail shoes that are very good for distances up to about sixty miles on rough ground and also super-padded ultra shoes that I've worn for 100 miles. I've had some good experiences and some bad ones with all these shoes. There is no right and wrong answer and you just need to ignore all advice apart from your own experience. Unfortunately, there's only one way to find out whether a pair of shoes is comfortable or not over a long distance. So select a pair that's comfortable over shorter distances and wear them in well.

Gaiters. These are useful for rough ground. They are small over-gaiters that fit snugly around your ankles and over the top of your shoes, with an elastic fastening under the sole to hold them in place. They prevent stones, heather and other debris from falling into the opening of your shoes. I tend to wear them on events that have a lot of off-path running.

Spikes. In winter, if conditions are icy then I have microspikes that clip around my shoes with a rubber grip. These are effectively mini crampons that give you spiked grip on icy surfaces. They are quick to attach and remove from your shoes and provide essential grip on ice when running in the hills in winter conditions.

Shorts/leg-wear. Personally I like the tight, cycling-style running shorts, rather than traditional running shorts. I don't wear underwear underneath them and don't feel the need to wear normal shorts over the top as some do. I'm used to wearing cycling shorts on a bike so this works for me. I don't get any chafing issues which I have done with traditional running shorts. When the weather gets cooler I wear the three-quarter length tights which are basically just a longer version. If it's cooler still, I'll wear full-length running tights but I'll wear these over the shorts for warmth and also as I find it more comfortable this way. Previously I've tried various makes of running shorts and other leg-wear but find the tight clothing comfortable, hassle-free and easy to manage.

Tops. My usual running attire is a long-sleeved, thin, base-layer top, with a technical t-shirt on top. Depending on the weather, I'll take a second thin base-layer, second t-shirt, long-sleeved technical top and a thin fleece. I've run overnight in exposed sub-zero temperatures, wearing all six of these layers, plus full waterproofs and still been cold. For emergency use in winter, I'll also carry a lightweight down jacket.

Outer layers. My opinion is that these are the second most important items after shoes. For anyone who's spent time in bad weather on the hills, you'll know that a good set of waterproofs are essential. That's the case for a five-hour day-walk in the hills. Now think about spending up to forty hours outside in potentially bad weather, at night too. It's not worth skimping. I have a decent, breathable, fell running jacket with full hood and a decent pair of breathable, waterproof trousers. Nothing keeps the wet out completely but good waterproofs are the best you can do to keep reasonably dry and comfortable. They can be the difference between finishing and not. On many occasions I've worn my jacket for over twelve hours straight and a number of times for more than 24 hours. I estimate that I wore my last jacket for over 600 hours before replacing it. If you're serious about this game, then buy decent waterproofs.

Warm items. I'll always have a fleece hat with me, no matter how warm the weather. When you're tired you get cold and overnight runs are always cold in the early hours. I'll also carry a buff which is brilliant for keeping cold air from going down your neck, plus doubles as a balaclava or lightweight hat. In summer I'll take a thin pair of running gloves, in winter a thicker pair of wind-block fleece gloves or fleece mittens with waterproof over-mitts. In cooler weather I'll also take a balaclava.

Rucksack/bumbag. For trips to the hills or ultras, I always

use a small twenty-litre rucksack. I've tried various bumbags and rucksacks over the years but find a simple rucksack, with accessible belt pockets for food, easy-to-reach bottle holders on the sides and a lid pocket works for me. Race vests are very popular these days but I'm not convinced and have never tried one. I've always used a rucksack, it works for me and that's what I stick with. I always use a number of fully-waterproof inner bags inside it to keep everything dry inside. I also have a small front pouch that clips onto the rucksack straps that I'll use on long ultras, that's useful for stuffing items into as I move, such as gloves, camera, route notes or snacks.

Poles. The use or not of poles prompts more debate than any other item except shoe choice. In Europe they're very popular but in the UK traditionally less so. For me, this comes down to personal choice. The advantages are that they assist on climbs and descents by spreading your load and assisting stability. They're great on difficult terrain such as when off-path on heather. I also find them good on overnight runs when dozing off, as they stop me stumbling about as much. The downside is that they stop you having your hands available for other uses such as eating, drinking and navigating. They also require care around other runners, as many users are completely unaware of those around them and obstruct or even hit others with them. They are awkward when dealing with gates and stiles, so particular care is required here, as it's very easy for them to flick up and catch people behind. So for me there are both advantages and disadvantages in their use. For shorter events I don't bother as I don't feel they're necessary. On 100-milers, I'll use them but not for the whole time, maybe just half the time and especially overnight to aid stability. I have a pair of lightweight, aluminium, folding poles that are easy to carry in a rucksack when not being used.

Navigation. I take an old school approach and navigate using a map and compass. Most races have these on their essential kit list but it's not enough to just carry them; you do need to know how to use them. Compass use baffles many people but there are only essentially two skills that you need to master: setting the map to match the orientation of the ground, as well as taking a bearing and following it. GPS is popular with others and I'll occasionally use one in very indistinct terrain in mist or darkness. However, far too many people rely on GPS to know where they are, without actually knowing where they are, if that makes sense. Personally, I always run with my map stuffed down my rucksack belt where it's accessible and I will always know where I am on it. I've experienced others using GPS who were either clueless on its use or could use it but couldn't actually reference it to the ground being travelled over. Whatever method you use, only practice and experience will make you proficient and confident. So practice in training and develop confidence in your own ability to get from A to B. I will also have a laminated schedule tucked in my map, with checkpoints, mileages, estimated schedule and cut-off times on it. This is so that I always know where I am against a schedule and can manage my progress against it. Some events have detailed route notes which I'll carry with the map.

Watch. Running watches have changed beyond all recognition from when I started out. My view is that a GPS watch that gives you distance is useful but unnecessary for ultras. A simple watch that you can record splits on is all that's needed. For marathon running, I'll regularly be looking at my watch as I monitor pace and distance to judge how I'm progressing against my target time. For an ultra, however, I'll be tracking my progress over the ground with a map or from local knowledge. Distance is less important and I'll work off time rather than distance, as I find that much simpler and more motivating.

Lights. A headtorch is essential for running in the dark. This doesn't have to be expensive as the technology is a world apart from where it was a few years ago and good headtorches can now be bought cheaply. I look for a couple of features which I have on mine that I find useful. I like an adjustable beam, so that it can be kept as a wide pool of light to pick out the ground that you're moving across but can also be focused into a tight beam when you need to navigate and look for features in the distance. I also like the head to angle, so that it can be kept pointing downwards at the ground for general use but then adjusted up for navigating. Finally, I like the brightness to be adjustable so it can be kept fairly dim to save batteries most of the time but put on full brightness when navigation becomes more difficult. Battery life can be a problem on long, dark nights and changing batteries is always a nuisance in the dark, so it's good to be able to adjust the power to manage this. I will always put fresh batteries in before an overnight run and carry a spare set. I will also carry a tiny emergency headtorch just in case my primary headtorch fails. This might seem unnecessary but my view is that a headtorch failure will end your run more than any other piece of kit and this extra weight is negligible. Finally, if it's going to be misty or navigation will be very technical, then I will also carry a small but very bright hand-held torch. This can be used to pick out features ahead without having to move your head to re-point your headtorch. It also has the advantage in mist that it doesn't reflect directly back into your eyes off the mist, which happens with a headtorch.

Maintenance. A number of small items are required to look after yourself en route or in case of emergency. Anti-chafe cream is essential to reduce chafing between your legs and on your feet and lower back. This can be as simple as the tried and tested petroleum jelly or there are lots of more expensive specialist products. I've tried a few but always now use a product that works for me, which comes in a toothpaste-style tube and doesn't ruin your clothes. Sufficient painkillers for the entire event, both paracetamol and ibuprofen. Caffeine tablets for overnight runs. First aid kit, sufficient to deal with cuts, grazes or minor injuries. Sun cream if it's summer because you'll be exposed all day and can get caught out, which happened to me at the 10 Peaks race. Finally, mobile phone, cash, credit card and camera.

Running cap. For long summer runs only, to keep the sun off your head. I often wear it backwards to shade the back of my neck too.

Ski goggles. For extreme winter conditions, to keep wind and snow out of your eyes.

Food. To be able to run for many hours, you need to be able to eat as you go. This is often a problem for runners who are not used to running beyond half marathon distance. When many runners start training for their first marathon, eating becomes a major hurdle to overcome because it's not a skill that comes naturally to most people. To run further though, it's essential you master it because your body needs some form of fuel intake to keep the engine running. I've never had an issue with eating while exercising due to many hours spent hill walking and cycling over the last 25 years. Food falls into two categories, food at checkpoints and food that you carry yourself to eat between them. At checkpoints I'll eat whatever is on offer but typically stick to non-sweet items. So I'll have sandwiches, wraps, pasta, hot food, pies, pastries, soup, crisps and biscuits. For eating on the go, I'll have muesli bars, sweets, chocolate, peanuts, raisins and energy gels. I aim to eat one item each hour, with some variety to choose from so that I can eat what I feel like eating at any given time, rather than having no options. I store the food in the belt pockets of my rucksack so it's easily accessible.

Drink. The same as with eating, it's essential that you can drink on the go. This is much easier than eating and isn't generally a problem to most people. I've tried different things over the years but keep it very simple now. I just drink water and always use bottles so that I can track how much I've drunk and how much I've got left. I'll typically carry two bottles: one on a front shoulder strap and one in a side pocket. This gives me up to one litre of fluid. If it's hot, then I'll have a third bottle in another side pocket to give me one and a half litres. I'll replenish my water bottles at checkpoints but will also refill from streams on the hills if necessary, always taking the water from as high as possible and where it's clear and flowing freely. I've drunk from streams thousands of times and only ever suffered an upset stomach once, at the OMM in Scotland, so I believe the risk is low. Apart from water, I'll drink tea or coffee at some checkpoints and occasionally coke but I try to dilute coke with water as it can cause stomach problems with its high sugar content.

Kit choice in ultra running is highly personal and different from individual to individual. It's an area of huge debate which I think is unnecessary. In my opinion, if you're asking questions on what to take, then you're not experienced enough to know what gear you'll actually need with you. There's only one way to find out what works and what doesn't, what you like and what you don't, and that's to get out and try different approaches. I have kit and methods that work for me but that doesn't mean they're necessarily right or that they'll be suitable for anyone else. It all comes down to personal choice, experience and getting it all organised before you set off. Unfortunately, poor gear choice can end a race, so it's worth experimenting to get your approach right beforehand. Although I've said that gear choice is unconventional and down to the individual, there is however one golden rule: do not try anything new on race day.

12 Gaining Confidence: South Downs Way 100
(June 2012)

'Nobody is going to finish this damn thing for me, but me.'
(Anon)

It was two years since I'd run my first 100-miler and it was time to do it again, mostly to prove that it wasn't a fluke or a one-off. Since 2010, the South Downs Way Race had changed hands and was now being run by a much larger organising group as one of a number of 100-milers in their portfolio. They had changed the event and reversed the direction, so the start was now in Winchester and the course would be run west to east, finishing in Eastbourne. The route would also follow the inland option of the trail close to Eastbourne, cutting out Beachy Head and the Seven Sisters, as well as reducing its length by three miles to exactly 100 miles. The changed route still had 13,000 feet of climbing though.

Leading up to the event, I'd had an exceptionally busy week and not slept well. I travelled down to Winchester on Friday after work but was shattered, falling asleep on the train to London, where I met Brandon before the final leg to Winchester. We stayed the night in a hotel a mile from the start.

The race starts on Saturday at 6 am. The logistics of this meant getting up at 3:45 am to get to the start for registration. This was not ideal when I was already tired with a full day and night of running ahead. I was concerned about how tired I'd be overnight.

The pre-race briefing contained the usual safety warnings: to look out for your fellow competitors, help each other and keep safe. There was a show of hands for those running their first 100, with over half the starters in this group. It was only my second 100, but it felt good to no longer be a novice as I knew what lay ahead.

At 6 am, the 163 runners set off on two laps of the sports field. This was taken very slowly as there was a long way to go.

There's always a lot of competitiveness at a start which is fine for the front-runners but a major error for everyone else. We sat at the back of the field chatting to a couple of other runners and just enjoyed it. Then it was out onto the trail. We were 161st and 162nd out of the field. If we were playing it right, we'd not be in these positions by the time we arrived in Eastbourne.

The first few miles were all about dialling into the event, keeping very slow, laughing, joking and enjoying it. These miles were fun and easily banked. We had on-off rain for a while but it was warm. The first twenty miles were uneventful but we just ignored everyone else as we gradually gained positions. Not that positions matter; you just have to do your own thing on a long ultra. Queen Elizabeth Country Park came and went at twenty miles and we passed a mountain biker who'd taken a nasty fall a mile later. We stopped to help but he seemed ok; we said we'd run on and send his mates back for him. Selfishly he wasn't our problem to sort out and his friends weren't far ahead.

From twenty to thirty miles we achieved the first big mental landmark which was marathon distance. This is always good but by now I had aches and pains which was very sobering given that we were barely at a quarter distance. You're constantly looking for problems in these early stages. My achilles tendons were hurting as I'd been suffering with them all year and they were taped up, my right knee had some twinges and I was generally feeling tired but nothing to worry about that wouldn't be expected after running for a few hours. There was nothing that could be done apart from not letting the thoughts get on top of me. We'd run an awfully long way but were only really starting out. Big ultras are a huge mental battle, always with the weight of the unimaginable distance remaining being balanced against the increasing pain from a body that's physically being abused.

At Cocking at 35 miles, we took ten minutes to put on fresh socks and re-lubricate everything. Chafing is a potentially debilitating issue so anti-chafe cream went everywhere, especially on my feet. It's messy but effective. This was also a chance to clear the trail debris from my shoes. What felt like large stones were actually only small pieces but it was good to sweep them all out. The pleasure of getting rid of wet, gritty socks for fresh ones gave me a new lease of life. There's an old army expression, 'Any idiot can rough it.' Time spent getting sorted out is always a sound investment for the miles ahead. I removed all the achilles tape here too; it had served seven hours and was starting to ruck up. Sore achilles are less bother than potential blisters.

We'd gained steadily on our schedule up to here and kept it up all the way through to the major halfway checkpoint at Washington at 54 miles. The day was warm but there was a cool breeze and we just kept drinking plenty and keeping on track. Washington was the re-supply point where we had drop bags in a village hall and some hot food. As we walked into the hall, someone was throwing up. Another competitor was flat out on the floor, being dealt with by paramedics. These are not uncommon sights on ultras. We ate pasta and drank tea, while having a good sort out. I put on fresh socks, a clean top and put a few extra bits of food into my rucksack to restock those I'd eaten. I had the option of a shoe change but didn't bother as I had no issues with the ones I was wearing. We were 65 minutes ahead of schedule and in high spirits.

The next seventeen miles to Clayton were awesome. There were a series of hills to climb as the main South Downs Way escarpment is bisected by roads running through valleys. We got ourselves into a strong rhythm of hill climb, jog along the top and then down. Then we'd repeat it for the next hill. Our schedule had slowed but we were going strongly, so gained loads of time to move two hours ahead of schedule. It was just dark when we reached this 71-mile checkpoint. Another clean set of socks and yet more anti-chafe cream and we were ready for the night.

Brandon has a view that eighty miles is halfway on a 100-miler and I agree with him. Some runners at this 71-mile point said to us, 'We're on the home stretch now.' In my opinion, the home stretch on an ultra is the last mile if not quarter mile. Forget what's behind you, it's what's ahead that matters. Taking the condition most people are in at 71 miles (dog tired, sore feet, everything hurting, feeling awful) and with 29 miles to run over hills through darkness, you wouldn't get me out the door normally. We repeated the words, 'Home stretch,' often after that as a morale booster.

We were slowing down due to the attrition but still moving strongly for the next six miles to Housedean. I was hurting everywhere, my feet were sore and I had pain on every foot-strike. I'd started feeling sick due to the endless eating and had been taking painkillers for a while. The remaining 23 miles through the night over hills were not appealing when I felt this bad, but I had to just focus on the next section. This was eight miles to Southease which should take about two and a half hours.

As we climbed the large hill on the other side of the valley, the tiredness of the day started to show. This was where it started deteriorating. It was 1 am and we still had quite a few hours of darkness to get through. We both started to fall asleep on our feet. This is difficult to understand if you've not experienced it but I was literally falling asleep while climbing up the hill. When you've run for so long and it's the early hours, then you need sleep. If your brain's not occupied with eating, talking, navigating or concentrating on technical ground, then you literally fall asleep while running. You doze off, then stumble or lurch sideways, come back awake, then repeat and repeat. It's horrible. It's absolutely horrible. You can do nothing about it and it just keeps happening. You eat caffeine tablets, chocolate and sweets but nothing stops it. When it goes further you start hallucinating (I didn't get any hallucinations this time but I have on many other runs). It's not dangerous because your eyes don't close for long and you come out of it with a bump. It's the most horrible experience I've ever come across in life because you just want to sleep and you can't. Your body is getting to its lowest ebb and many an ultra runner has curled up on the trail to sleep in these conditions. We both kept staggering about, then jerking awake, then repeating. Finally, we got onto a long descent on a decent track where we could start moving more quickly and came back awake. It had been a hard, slow section but we ticked it off as we arrived at Southease at 3 am.

All the checkpoints through the second half of the course had dead bodies at them; competitors who had dropped out ahead of us and were waiting to be swept up by the broom wagon. Some of them looked in a right state. We weren't that bad but I was physically wrecked and emotionally drained. We took a fourteen-minute break, drank some tea, joked with the marshals and had some Dunkirk-spirit banter with the other runners. Let's be honest here, by 83 miles, you will always know that you've had a very hard day out. Your body hurts everywhere, your feet burn, your legs are stiff and hurting, your back, shoulders and neck are sore from the rucksack, plus you desperately need sleep. It was only seventeen miles to go. This is further than most runners have ever run, we'd been awake for nearly 24 hours, I couldn't get out of a chair without using my arms and I was dead on my feet. On the plus side, I was in better shape than anyone else I'd seen recently and we gained six minutes on our schedule over that last section, despite the sleep issues. Relatively speaking, we were in good shape.

Now it was time to seriously break things down. The remaining route could be split into three simple hops. Eight miles over the top to Alfriston, four miles over the next hill to Jevington, then a final hill and four miles to Eastbourne. I wasn't even thinking of hops two and three; all I was focused on was the next section.

It was only eight miles to Alfriston. I can run that in under an hour at home. It would take two hours and forty minutes tonight. This section was absolute hell. The wind was bitterly cold, the rain was horizontal and it was a high, exposed section. I had all my clothes on, buff pulled up as a balaclava, hat, gloves, hood up and was still cold through to the bone. My body had no reserves left to keep warm as well as run. All I could do was keep moving as quickly as possible to generate some heat. I was focused on the knowledge that there was a valley a few hours ahead, where we'd get out of the wind at a checkpoint and where friendly marshals awaited. The course loops a bit here, so looking back over the hills we could see headtorches of runners two or three hours behind us, which was a small consolation. We felt for everyone up high, who'd be suffering as badly as us.

Daylight arrived which is always special when you've run all night and lifts the spirits. The run down into Alfriston was agony on hard, stony trails but it was another section ticked off. Despite everything, we gained another four minutes on this section.

The next four miles to Jevington was over yet another hill. Heads down and keep going. Every step was closer to the finish which still seemed a long way away. Daylight brought some sunshine so warm clothes were no longer needed but every step was agony. We gained another nine minutes against our schedule.

Then it was just four miles over the final hill to Eastbourne and the final run-in. The final two miles through Eastbourne seemed like twenty after such a distance and in so much pain. They were endless. We were moving at a very slow jog, walking at times, and neither of us could go much faster as we'd given everything to get this far. We turned the corner into the finishing stadium, picked the pace up to a slow jog and headed onto the soft track which felt like carpet. Half a lap and we were done. There were claps from the few people watching, a handshake, a t-shirt and a finisher's belt buckle. We then slumped down in a couple of chairs, utterly drained. A bacon butty and tea arrived. A few other finishers came in and we all exchanged congratulations.

We'd covered 100 miles in 26 hours and 32 minutes. We'd gained eighty positions since leaving the start field a day before.

The trouble with ultras is the logistics surrounding them too. Dog-tired and unable to walk, I had to get home from Eastbourne. I slept on the train to London, then was a slow-motion, stiff-legged, comedy-act on the tube to Euston. I slept again on the train back to Warrington, with an alarm set to ensure I didn't end up in Glasgow. While hobbling in slow motion down the steps at Bank Quay station, an old lady asked if I was ok and if I needed a hand. Another crazy memory from a trip to the hills.

On Sunday I was wrecked. I didn't eat anything for twelve hours afterwards because I couldn't. I had a two-hour sleep as soon as I got home, then was back in bed at 8 pm and slept for ten hours again. My body clearly needed a lot of rest to recover from the rigours of the race. A day later and I was still as tired as you can get, stiff all over and had grazes on my back from the rucksack rubbing. My lower legs were swollen and I was struggling to move. On the plus side, I'd avoided all blisters due to good shoe choice, regular sock changes and plenty of anti-chafe cream.

Our finishing time was better than I'd expected but what gave me the most pleasure was that our approach and execution were perfect. Our planning was rock solid and we were in control the whole way through, gaining on the schedule consistently all day, even in the last sections. We knew where we were at all times versus the schedule, what we were doing, agreed plans between us, took time where needed at checkpoints, kept our spirits up and kept up a decent pace all day. Even in the lowest of lows in the last twenty miles we beat our schedule.

One view I have is that anything up to about twenty hours is ok and enjoyable. Once you're beyond this, your body's had such a pounding that the whole experience is just downright miserable. This weekend strengthened that view.

This business of running 100 miles is highly unpleasant but it has a certain draw to it and this race confirmed that I'm good at getting through it. The next step was to run a much harder

100-miler, the Lakeland 100, an awesome 105-mile circuit of the Lake District with 23,000 feet of climbing, arguably the toughest race in Britain. We'd already entered and were now ready to test ourselves on that course.

Beyond that, there was the possibility of the Ultra Trail du Mont Blanc (UTMB), an incredible 106-mile circuit around the highest mountain in Western Europe, with a frightening 33,000 feet of climbing and billed as the toughest foot race in Europe. That was beyond mere mortals like us, surely?

163 started, 117 finished, I came 81st. The race had a 28% drop-out rate.

13 Training

'If you want to play the game, you have to train.' (Anon)

The first requirement for an ultra runner is to be physically fit enough to cover the race distance. This might sound sensible enough but can actually be quite a hurdle to overcome, especially as you build up through longer distances to new levels that you've not covered before. In running sub-marathon distances the upward steps are relatively small as you only need to get up to 26 miles. So in simple terms, you could build up from, say, four miles, by adding a mile a week over four months up to a long training run of twenty miles. Then the last six miles can simply be done on the day when you're well rested and motivated. For an ultra, building up to big distances requires some pretty large steps once you're past forty miles.

When training for a race up to marathon distance, there are many, many training schedules that are readily available. These can be followed religiously or adapted to suit the individual. They are often based on different goals or assumptions, such as a target finishing time, a pace or a number of training days per week.

I've never attempted to religiously follow a training plan. I find it too restrictive and too rigid to be realistic as it doesn't take into account factors such as how you're feeling, tiredness, any niggles or injuries and how much time you have available when fitting it around your other commitments. I've always found it far simpler to work on a structure of a long run each week and fit other training in around this. This gives the flexibility that I need to be able to fit it in around work and family plans. If a training plan is prescriptive in the distances, speeds and day on which to train and rest, then anything that disturbs this becomes a negative influence that pulls away from this structured plan. For a professional athlete then it would be fine as it would be their priority versus other life factors. For me, I might be away with work, too tired from a long day or simply looking after the kids. Sometimes I may just have plans that cannot be moved that restrict the time available. I'll simply work around this by moving rest days, doing a long run during the week rather than on a Sunday, training twice some days by cross-training or whatever else it takes. As work and family commitments are often not known more than a week or even a few days in advance, then clearly a rigorous schedule isn't going to work for me. For others it might be fine, if you've got sufficient flexibility in your life to accommodate it and the right mindset for it to work for you. For me, it doesn't, and I don't feel the need for that rigorous structure so I've never done it.

The way that I train is to keep my approach simple and focus on having an outline plan that's roughly right, rather than a fully detailed plan that will end up being unachievable. A lot of training plans focus on building up the mileage, when training for a marathon for example. For myself, I generally don't need to do this as I run races all year round and always have the ability and right mindset to be able to run far enough. What I will need to do though is specific training for a particular type of event. So for a flat road marathon where I'm focusing on a good time, I'll want to do more long road runs, for a big mountain event I'll do more climbing in the hills and for a 100-miler I'll want to have done a few other ultras as mileage build-up, ideally with one at sixty miles in the lead-up. From this I can look at my time available, particularly if I want some training days in the hills which can take up a whole day. These will have to be slotted in where they can around existing commitments, rather than adding them to a schedule being prepared in isolation. I'll then make some rough notes on what I want to do along the way but keep this very simple, so as not to add too many restrictions. Then I'll simply plan each week as it comes, once I know what other commitments I have that week.

Setting short-term goals is key but I keep this as simple as I can. I like to set targets based on a certain amount of exercise of any type per week. For example, I'll target five hours per week during the winter made up of any sport. This could be achieved by, say, two one-hour turbo sessions in the garage before work, a midweek one-hour evening run and a long solo run at the weekend. That's just four different days of exercise, with variety, that would be easy to motivate myself for, with three rest days. If I miss one of the turbo sessions, then I wouldn't beat myself up over it but would simply add something else in later in the week to target still hitting five hours. It's very simple but it works for me.

I prefer to work in time rather than mileage for a few reasons. The first is that by focusing on time I can combine different types of training such as running, cycling or gym and add them all up together to give a total. This is impossible if you use distance. Secondly, I can fit it into my life more easily because it's simple to visualise how long a session will take. This sounds strange but I've had times where I've only had a set amount of time until I need to do something else. I've then gone out for a run of a set distance, found myself running a bit slow and then doing lots of mental maths as to what time I'd get home, showered and onto the next thing. This adds pressure and negative energy. If I know I've only got, say, a one-hour window, then it's very easy to run for forty minutes, leaving time to shower and get ready afterwards. I would simply run for twenty minutes in one direction and then retrace my steps to give forty minutes. This happens frequently when I'm away with work. Often there is a short window between the day's work and a meal, which gives me just enough time to approach a run in this manner. I find that little tricks like this ensure a positive mindset to my training and give me the ability to cram the training in around other commitments.

I often like to get up early and exercise first thing so that it's out of the way. Early morning is the best time to run from home as there is very little traffic on the roads to worry about. I'll also often do an hour on my turbo trainer in the garage in winter before work which fits in well. One of the benefits is that it's easy to plan for morning exercise because other things can't crop up during the day to disrupt my plan. Also, once completed, I feel very satisfied that it's done and I'm ahead on my day rather than having to play catch-up later. I can train quite happily without having eaten anything beforehand, so doing a long run first thing on a weekend morning doesn't cause me any issues. This doesn't suit everyone, as I know some people prefer evening training, need to eat breakfast first or any number of other preferences. For me, given a choice, I would always opt for training first thing in the morning before breakfast, although I have no issue training at other times to fit in with the rest of my day.

Fitting your training in around eating can be a challenge and can catch you out sometimes. This works both ways, having eaten too much beforehand or not having eaten enough. By training first thing in the morning, this variable is eliminated because the day hasn't started. I've had times where a window has opened at short notice and I've chosen to do something that's compromised by my eating patterns. This can happen when plans change at a weekend and there's an opportunity to do some exercise but I've maybe just eaten my lunch. Typically, I wouldn't run for at least two hours after lunch or three hours after a bigger meal. This is despite the fact that I'm very good at eating and exercising from years in the hills. However, no one is good at running after eating a solid lunch. The opposite issue occurs when I go out on my bike for a few hours in late morning. It will have been a few hours since breakfast and I've had occasions where I get the 'hunger knock' on the bike. In marathon-speak, this is the equivalent of hitting-the-wall, a complete lack of energy that results when you've depleted your reserves, that can only be recovered by eating. I recognise this now and make sure I've got energy food with me when I go out at this time. I don't often get caught out with this at other times of day, so I can only conclude that generally my eating and drinking patterns compliment my training.

I'm a big fan of cross-training, especially cycling to compliment the running. I find that by mixing two sports, I'm motivated and have the ability to do more sessions of greater duration without getting bored. I also benefit from mixed terrain running, in that I'll run on the roads from home or when travelling, but my primary focus is running on the hills which is a completely different undertaking altogether. I also mix the cycling up between road biking and turbo training. I tend to do more road cycling during the summer when there's increased daylight, as well as weather and road conditions being more favourable. Turbo training is good in winter or when I can't leave the house because I need to be there to keep half an eye on the kids. I'm not a member of a gym but I will always use a gym when I'm staying at a hotel because it's something different and adds variety and interest to my training. By mixing things up, I find that I can train daily when I'm having a focused effort, without overdoing any one thing, stressing my body too much or becoming bored and struggling for motivation.

Training on the specific terrain that you're going to be doing an ultra over is good practice. So for a mountain event, it's more beneficial to be running in the mountains than on the roads. The variety of terrain is quite broad, such as good trails, roads, rocky paths, grassy hills, open moorland, peat hags, heather, boulders, steep slopes, gentle climbs, on-path, off-path and a myriad of other surfaces. I like to spend time on terrain similar to that of the event so that I'm getting used to it. Running over heather and peat is probably the slowest as it's such tough ground to get over. If you've not experienced it before, then it can come as quite a shock from travelling over paths and other well-trodden routes. I've spent a lot of time on varying terrain and would always advise anyone to train on what you'll be covering in an event. This has the dual effect of being very good specific training for the event itself and also ensuring that you're preparing mentally and will not have any surprises on the day with what's underfoot.

There are standard rules about training and building up to a higher level. The standard road running guide is to increase mileage by no more than 10% per week and to have an easier week every third week. This is good advice for relatively new runners and those building up to an event longer than they've done before. However, once you've been an established runner for a few years, you learn to listen to your body more than just following a standard rule. I'll only follow a build-up rule after an injury that's stopped me running. Typically, I will have maintained my fitness through cycling and then start to reintroduce the running. The key consideration is where to pick up again. I always use time for this, so I'll start with a test run of maybe twenty minutes, then leave it for a few days. I'll then do a thirty-minute run and rest again. Very quickly, I'll be up to an hour of gentle running. What I'll do is keep the frequency between the runs fairly wide, so do just two runs per week, but increase the distance reasonably quickly. Once I've done a few runs at one hour or longer, I'll stop increasing the distance but increase the frequency of the runs instead. This way I'm not building up both the distance and the frequency of runs at the same time. I'll do this as much by feel as any structured or planned percentage build-up. I've used this approach many times when returning from injury and it works for me.

For ultra training, I find the two best ways of running long distances and duration are to run in the hills or to run other events. If I run on the road, then I struggle to motivate myself to run for more than about two hours or so. If I go to the hills, then I can happily run alone all day so long as I've got some food with me, the weather's not awful and I've planned an interesting route or one that meets some objectives that I've set myself. The pace will be slower but I'll get significant time-on-feet training that I just cannot do otherwise. Even running on trails in less hilly areas doesn't motivate me for long runs but long training runs in the Lake District, Snowdonia or Yorkshire Dales do.

Running other events as build-up training runs is a good approach and one that's widely used in many sports. It's common practice to use half marathons in the training for a full marathon, not that I ever have. Similarly, I'll use marathons as training events for ultras. It's a good way to motivate myself for a very long run which achieves something in itself. I'll also run shorter ultras in training for the long ultras. However, due to the length of all the races that I do, I would never underestimate one. All marathons and ultras demand respect as they're never easy.

A final and very important consideration in training is to factor in adequate rest so you don't literally run yourself into the ground. It's so easy when highly motivated to train every day, pushing the intensity and drain yourself. It's also very important to rest after very long training runs in the hills or after races. I've come unstuck myself by getting out again quickly after a race because I'm looking towards the next one. Now I've learnt that it's just as important to let your body recover and your mind refocus, rather than treating life as an exercise treadmill that you have to keep on pounding. After a big ultra, I'll assume that I'm taking complete rest for at least a week, maybe a fortnight if it's a hard 100-miler. Then if I feel ok after the race, I might cut this a bit short but I would always favour some gentle cycling which is less stressful on the body, as opposed to getting out running again.

Another time to take a break is when you're unwell. If I'm under-the-weather, then I might do some slow running or cycling but I certainly won't put any pressure on myself to push or do a lot of it. Taking a complete break for a few days or a week will do you no harm and will allow your body to recuperate. In fact, I find that after a period of illness I'll restart my training with little or no loss of form, but will return mentally refreshed and motivated so there can actually be a net gain. I've found that I do best by treating illness and these breaks positively rather than worrying about the loss of a few hours of training.

My approach isn't an orthodox one or one that you'll find in any training guide but it works for me and I've had a lot of success using this method. I've run some reasonably fast marathon times and many long ultras as a result. If I were to adopt a more structured and focused approach, then I'm sure that I could improve my speed and improve my marathon personal best. However, I wouldn't mentally engage in this approach, it wouldn't fit in with my busy life, it wouldn't fit my goals of running long rather than fast and I wouldn't enjoy it. What I do have is a method that works for me. It's also an approach that I can maintain long-term, all year round and is only interrupted by periods of injury, which are generally minimised because of the variety that I do. I wouldn't care to advise anyone else what will work for them, except to try different things and find an approach that keeps you fit, motivated, positive and allows you to achieve your goals.

*'The forty hours available to complete the course may seem
manageable upon your first calculations but don't be fooled.
The climb, descent, rugged terrain, darkness and tricky
navigation generally ensure a 50-60% failure rate over the
100-mile course. Seasoned ultra runners have tried and many
have failed, a finisher's medal in the Lakeland 100 is one of the
most treasured possessions you will ever receive. There are few
things in life for which you will have to work so hard, show
such commitment, desire and the simple stubbornness to keep
going.' (Race Organiser)*

Having finished the South Downs Way 100 a couple of times,
the next step-up was to attempt a harder 100-miler. As the
terrain gets harder, the pace slows and the time required to get
to the finish increases. This then adds additional complications
such as having to run through two nights without sleep, rather
than just the one. In order to step up another level, Brandon
and I entered the Lakeland 100 in 2012.

This one's a monster. It's known to be the toughest single-
stage race in Britain. It's a 105-mile circuit of the Lake District
with 23,000 feet of climbing. It's a valleys-and-passes route
rather than taking in any summits. The start time is 5:30 pm on
Friday evening, with time cut-offs en route and a forty-hour
time limit. We would expect to take 39 hours, with a finishing
time of 8:30 am on Sunday, requiring us to run right through
both nights and deal with the associated sleep deprivation. This
would be a big test.

In preparation for the event we decided to run an overnight
recce of a large section of the first half of the course which has
the harder climbs. We drove up to Keswick on a Friday
afternoon in May, dumped the car in a side street and caught a
bus back through the centre of the Lakes to Ambleside.
Ambleside is the 89-mile point of the race and our plan was to
run the last section of the route to the finish in Coniston, so we

could recce the part that we'd be covering at our most tired. Then we'd do the first third of the course over the hard climbs back to the car at Keswick. This would be fifty miles and we estimated it would take sixteen hours.

We ate chips in Ambleside before departing, which will seem strange pre-run preparation to runners used to shorter distances. However, we were heading off for a long time and needed something decent to eat beforehand. After setting off, the first few hours in daylight passed quickly. It brought back memories of having run the Lakeland 50 race the year before, which is run on the same weekend as the 100 but covers just the second half of the course. We had run the fifty-mile race as a first recce for the 100, tonight was our second recce. We'd be well prepared come race day.

It got dark as we headed over the fells to Coniston and we were then a lone pair in the mountains, miles from anywhere at times, on a crazy adventure to run back to the car. There were no particular problems on this run although the night seemed endless and the only thing we had to look forward to was a flask of tomato soup, drunk with buttered rolls in Eskdale at 2 am. We were both tired after a week at work and struggled later in the night. So much so, that we had a big discussion heading through Wasdale as to how we were going to cope on the actual event, as the terrain was tough and had sapped our energy. We both questioned whether we had the ability to finish the full race as we were struggling badly on just one portion of it. We were running for eighteen hours that night, a massive unsupported run that served as a reality check for the actual race. Much as the overnight recce for our first 100-miler on the South Downs Way had done before, this one temporarily knocked our confidence. We were both experienced with long days out in the Lakes but hadn't expected it to be as tough as it was. Once again, the exercise was valuable because we emerged much stronger and more focused on what was required because of it. We were under no illusions as to how hard the event would be, which ensured we both focused 100% on arriving at the start line as prepared mentally, as well as physically, as we could possibly be.

Two months later the event was upon us. We headed up to Coniston on Friday lunchtime, registered and spent the afternoon chilling out by our tent, chatting to a couple in the neighbouring tent who were running the event together as husband and wife. They asked me about the UTMB race in the Alps and whether I'd ever considered entering it. I told them that I'd looked at it but would only consider it after I'd completed the Lakeland 100 first. They said they'd ask me again after the race.

The start was the usual, 'Everyone looks fitter than us,' so we just hung around at the back and off we all set. The first section is seven miles over the Walna Scar road (a rocky track) to Seathwaite in the Duddon valley. We trotted along at the back chatting to our friend John, who told us this was his 'Coming of Age' race, as it was his 21st 100-miler. It was a nice warm evening and very pleasant.

We then headed over to Eskdale. This section is a bit tricky to navigate but we knew the route from our recce and there were many runners about so it was uneventful. As it's through woods and boggy ground, our feet were constantly wet which was unavoidable. Then it was over another boggy section past Burnmoor Tarn where we put on headtorches and headed into Wasdale Head. We'd covered nineteen miles in just over five hours, seventeen minutes ahead of schedule. A great start.

Now we were into the first night and the big climbs: first over Black Sail Pass into Ennerdale, then over Scarth Gap into Buttermere and finally over Sail Pass to Braithwaite. These were steep, rocky climbs in trail shoes with wet feet. This was problematic because our feet rolled about on the rocks and started to get sore from being wet. There wasn't much we could do about this, apart from look forward to clean socks later. We had quite a few competitors around us and these big passes were impressive at night with headtorches stretched out ahead and behind us.

We met lots of characters as we ran all these sections with John. We met a guy who was on his 45th 100-miler, another who had done 125 mountain marathons and a guy who looked familiar until we realised we'd met at the penultimate checkpoint on the South Downs Way 100 the month before. All this made the time pass quickly as we headed over the mountain passes.

Our pace was good through the night. By Braithwaite, dawn was breaking and we were 54 minutes ahead of schedule with 33 miles covered. We took time here to change into fresh socks and sort ourselves out. My feet were sore and shoes were wet but nothing could be done about that.

We headed around Keswick and onto an easy navigation section around Skiddaw. It was light now but I was very tired and started to doze off on my feet. Then another competitor came up from behind and we chatted for five minutes which broke the spell. I was wide awake again.

At 41 miles at the Blencathra checkpoint, we were in good shape but there were a lot of competitors dropping out here. They all looked a shadow of their former selves as they waited to be picked up by the broom wagon. Ultra checkpoints are funny like this; seemingly fit individuals, covered in mud and looking like corpses laid out everywhere. It was rumoured that thirty runners hadn't survived the night. It was also said that the front-runners were, 'Through Howtown and on a sub-twenty hour pace.'

We shook our heads in disbelief and headed off.

Shortly after this, John dropped behind on one of the climbs and told us to head on. We swapped him a few miles later for Brian, who was running his fourteenth 100-miler. He was struggling but he decided to pick up his pace, to stick with us as he needed dragging along. We would end up running with Brian to the finish. We all had sore feet but had now moved 71 minutes ahead of our schedule by Dalemain at 59 miles.

Dalemain was hilarious. The Lakeland 50 starts here at midday and does a four-mile loop around the Dalemain Estate before picking up the last 46 miles of our course. We arrived at 12:17 pm so they were out on the loop, due to return shortly. There was a marquee set up for the 100 runners where we all had hot stew and a drop bag to re-supply from. Imagine a mess tent in a war zone and you've got the image; half-dead bodies in various stages of undress, some moving, some coherent, some completely out-of-it. We sat on the grass outside amongst the bodies, changing socks and sorting ourselves out. The 600 runners on the fifty-mile race came roaring past, all bright-eyed and bushy-tailed, spotlessly clean, all compression clothing, fancy gear and electronic gadgets, fit and young and full of the joys of spring, heading off on an adventure with boundless enthusiasm. We were all spark out on the floor, decrepit old men covered in stew and mud, with no shoes on and stinking to high heaven after a night on the fells, with red eyes, matted hair, sore feet and old battered kit everywhere. The contrast is just hilarious and I bet they wonder how anyone finishes the 100. They were great though; the respectful shouts of encouragement as they passed were very touching and much appreciated.

Inspection of our feet gave a common problem: trench foot. Having wet feet for so long causes them to swell up and go soft, white and wrinkly, like after a long bath but ten times worse. Pound them on unpredictable trails and rocks for hour after hour and they get very sore. Then they blister. I had no blisters at Dalemain but very sore feet. There wasn't much I could do but air them and put on fresh socks, knowing there was trouble coming.

As we followed the tail-end fifty-mile runners out of Dalemain, a female marshal joked, 'You're clearly doing the hundred.'

'How do you know?' Brian asked.

She laughed and started running next to us doing a silly shuffle to show us. We exchanged some banter, she showed us sideways and backwards running because she knew we could only shuffle forwards.

'Well if you think it's so easy you should join us,' Brian told her.

'I did it last year,' she replied.

'Really? What time?' he asked.

She sheepishly answered, '28 hours. I won.'

Incredible. We were all stunned, congratulated her and she ran with us for about half a mile more. Little experiences like this are what it's all about.

We ran all afternoon and evening to Kentmere, gaining time on the schedule with feet getting more and more sore and getting ever more tired. The descents were now very painful and I'd started taking painkillers to try and take the edge off. Everything was on track and we were 83 minutes ahead of schedule at 82 miles. We had a good feed and sort-out at the checkpoint before heading off up the rocky Garburn Pass into our second night. I was apprehensive about this as a single overnight is hard enough, let alone two back-to-back. I'd previously asked John what the second night was like and he'd downplayed it, 'Much like the first really.'

There was only one way to find out for myself.

At this point things changed quite drastically. I'd sum it up by saying that I enjoyed the first 28 hours and 82 miles. The next 23 miles took eleven hours. They were the hardest and most painful eleven hours of my life. Over the years, I've been through a lot of tough and painful times in the outdoors, but I hope never to repeat what happened this night.

The pain in my feet was getting bad. They were blistering all over due to the trench foot and to run on blistered feet is challenging. If the terrain is flat and predictable, like a road, then your brain tunes in to the pain and dulls it, so it's manageable. Somehow the brain predicts the pain coming with each foot strike in a rhythm, 'Ow-Ow-Ow,' so you can deal with it. When the terrain is rocky trails and gradients, you get this constant pain as a backdrop, plus shooting pain as your feet roll at different and unpredictable angles. Then more blisters form and more pain comes. If you've blistered one part of your foot, you tend to favour another part. When you get multiple blisters on both feet then things get bad.

I was dealing with this pain through to mile 89 at Ambleside. Dreadful thoughts were creeping into my mind: 'Can I take this pain for sixteen miles further? Am I going to make it? Only two hours and I can have more drugs. I have to finish because I'm not coming back. Just hang on in there. Just get to the next checkpoint. Just get up this climb. Just keep moving.'

We were now losing time against the schedule, which was a concern for the final cut-off if things deteriorated but we still had plenty in hand. We had bigger things to worry about.

After Ambleside my feet became less of an immediate concern because I was getting a sharp, shooting pain up my left shin. This was pure agony. Mixed with my feet it was the worst pain I've ever experienced and, believe me, I've gone through a lot in my outdoor exploits. It was gone 1 am, I was on my second night without sleep, I was still a long way from the finish and this had been thrown into the mix. All I could do was shorten my running stride, which slightly took the edge off the pain. I made it to the Chapel Stile checkpoint at 3 am and all but collapsed into a chair. I must have looked bad because a fellow competitor asked if I was ok, as I was shaking.

'I'm fine. It's just been a long day.'

Gallows humour always works but I was worried. If I look bad, I must be bad. Coffee and soup. Ibuprofen, paracetamol and caffeine tablets. Sorted.

Brandon was having his own troubles. He was shattered. He kept dozing off. Near Elterwater he stopped on the track and fell completely asleep while just standing there. Luckily Brian came up behind him and woke him up or else he'd have just toppled flat onto his face. I had no problems with sleep deprivation all night through, as luckily the pain I was experiencing was so great that it kept my mind focused on dealing with it and there was no chance of sleep issues. This was the horrible reality of what we were going through.

As well as our own personal problems, we were also dealing

with the weather. The previous night had been warm with on-off showers all night. I'd worn shorts, t-shirt and a waterproof top. The day had been warm and no rain, which was perfect. For this second night, a cold wind had cropped up and the rain was much more persistent. I was in full waterproofs, thermal, t-shirt, light fleece, hat, buff, the lot. It was downright miserable. When you're at a low ebb this is all you need. We were all cursing the rain and the cold as it made an unpleasant experience all the worse. I kept reminding myself that it's supposed to be hard and wouldn't be a challenge otherwise.

Heading through Langdale in the dead of night was a blur of pain. My head just kept saying, 'Keep moving. Only two more valleys. Only six hours to go.'

This was hell. Absolute hell. Ultras aren't ever easy but this was horrific, another level entirely. It still brings tears to my eyes thinking about it, even years later. Every footstep was blinding agony. I'd been feeling sick for hours due to the pain but had to keep eating. Brian was suffering the same with feet and nausea. Brandon was not quite so bad, relatively, but he was still dozing off. We were the walking dead. I just wanted a fast forward button to get me to Coniston. I wanted it to end or to fall unconscious or someone to strike me dead. It was the worst experience of my life.

Daylight came. Fifty-mile runners that we'd overtaken earlier kept coming past but we were grinding it out. On through Little Langdale and into the final checkpoint at Tilberthwaite at 102 miles. I was a few hundred metres ahead of Brandon and Brian here and waved that I was going to continue straight up the climb. If I had stopped here, I would not have finished. Incredible as that might seem after 102 miles, I knew I had to go straight through. Runners have retired here before and I know why. When you're in agony, you just don't care and to stop here would have been terminal for me.

The final climb. I caught Peter up (your race number is on the rear of your pack and had your first name in huge letters and either 50 or 100 on it). I knew he was a 100 runner long before I could read his pack. He was barely upright. We chatted. His feet were like mine. He was in slow motion and wincing with every step. He offered me a sweet. Shared pain, shared goals, shared sweets. Memories.

Brandon and Brian caught us up a mile into this section, then we hobbled to the final descent into Coniston. This descent is rough and rocky at the best of times, with unpredictable footing. The shin pain was not a worry as we were moving too slowly but the foot pain was off the scale. Brian said every step was like walking on razor blades. Peter and I think he was understating things somewhat. We were all on the verge of tears as the pain was that bad. It makes me go cold just thinking about it. We only had a mile or so to go but every footstep shot up through my whole body. I knew I'd finish now but it was small consolation as I just didn't care. Pay me a million pounds and I wouldn't do that descent again. Seriously, I wouldn't. I'm a fell runner, I'm used to pain, but I do not have enough profanities in my vocabulary to get this across to you. It was just awful.

We hobbled to the finish at the school in slow motion as broken men and checked in. Then we were taken into the hall to huge applause from earlier finishers. Very emotional. We'd run 105 miles across rough ground in 38 hours and 47 minutes.

Unknown to us, John had retired after 66 miles at Howtown. His legs hadn't fully recovered from a recent 100-miler in the Pyrenees. He was waiting for us at the finish, somehow standing behind the organisers' tables where the medals were being given out. He was full of congratulations for us, shaking our hands and so happy that we'd completed it. It was a very special moment.

This was the worst experience of my life but my greatest ever achievement. The time didn't matter. All that mattered to me was that I'd finished. I had still finished every race that I'd started.

This race nearly broke me. Those last eleven hours of pain were the worst eleven hours of my life and always will be.

Normally I don't care much for the medal I get at a race; I just dump it with the others. After finishing, I wore mine all day under my top where I knew it was but no one else could see it. A few weeks after the event, I had it framed along with my Lakeland 50 one from the year before. These are the only medals that I have on display at home. I earnt this one and it means a lot to me. I explored new depths on the second night. I wouldn't wish that level of pain, suffering and misery on anyone for five minutes, let alone eleven hours, but it didn't crack me. The old ultra saying is, 'To finish is to win.' Once again I'd won.

The fall-out from this race was big. My feet were shredded, with too many blisters to count and some massive ones too. I was still losing large amounts of skin off my feet six weeks later. My lower legs had swollen fit-to-burst and I had bruises on both shins, the left one a foot long. Nothing had hit me; it was internal damage causing bruises. I couldn't wear shoes for two days, only soft trainers and they were bothersome so I had to take my slippers to work. I was still limping three weeks after finishing and didn't run again for six weeks due to continued shooting pains in my left shin. My legs and feet were wrecked.

After finishing, the couple in the tent next to us had been true to their promise. 'So, do you now want to run the UTMB?' they asked.

'No, I have no need to. I've finished this one and I don't need to do it,' I responded.

How wrong I was but what do you expect if you're asked a question like that after running 105 miles in agony and haven't slept for two nights?

263 started, 136 finished, I came 127th. The race had a 48% drop-out rate.

15 Motivation

'Doubt kills more dreams than failure ever will.'
(Suzy Kassem)

Running an ultra is a big commitment for anyone, both in the time required to prepare adequately and also in terms of the physical and mental demands that it will put upon you. It's not something that you enter and then simply turn up on the day, hoping to get around. Once you've entered an ultra, then you're on a timeline towards the day of the event and an ever-decreasing number of days to get yourself to that start line adequately prepared.

The three considerations going into an ultra are to be ready physically, logistically and mentally. Getting your level of fitness up to an adequate level is the primary consideration. This normally comes easily as it's the focus of most people who exercise. Then organising the logistics around the race isn't too onerous in terms of time so can be fitted in around other aspects of life fairly easily. The key final aspect is to get yourself mentally prepared for the event.

This is the process of becoming confident that you have the physical ability, the technical skills and the right equipment to get yourself successfully to the finish line. It's a process of getting your head into the right frame of mind so you know that you've left no stone unturned in your preparation before the start. Essentially, you must be highly motivated to put the effort in to commit yourself to the event. This is not easy, as it requires a lot of time and effort in amongst the other pressures and distractions of life. In my opinion, it's not necessary to be extreme by cutting out all other pleasures and leading a monastic lifestyle, but you do need to be committed and be able to motivate yourself to put the effort in.

The starting point for ensuring your motivation is high is to question how committed you are to the event. The weeks or months approaching it can stretch endlessly in front of you, which can feel like a treadmill that you've jumped onto and can't get off until it's over. So the first thing is to have a reality check and ask yourself why you're doing it and how badly you want to complete it.

In terms of why I want to do an event, my motivation varies but it normally fits into part of a plan. For the big ultras like the 100-milers, they will be my focus for the year and I will know more than a year in advance which of these I'm going to do. Other events will then be part of my build-up plan towards these, to get some large mileages under my belt, which I find easier on another event rather than doing very long training runs myself. Some events I will do every year because I enjoy them and they fit nicely into the calendar, while others I'll select because I haven't done them before and want to experience them. Whatever my motivation, I will have pre-selected the event, entered very early to ensure a place and will know that I'm running it because I want to. I build a plan for each year around these events, which will also take into account other commitments, such as holidays, to ensure that it will all work in a balanced way with the rest of my life rather than disrupting it. I'm therefore mentally committed to every race from the start, which ensures that my ability to motivate myself for each one starts at a high level.

Looking at how badly you want to complete an event becomes more important as the severity increases. If you go into something half-heartedly, then that's fine if it's relatively straightforward. The nature of ultras is that they're all very demanding, so you will get found out if you're not fully committed. When I enter a 100-miler, I'm absolutely 100% committed and have tunnel vision in the build-up. I want to finish it so badly that nothing will stop me. I know I'll be devastated if I don't finish and that motivates me to ensure that everything possible is in my favour to make this happen. I'll think about it every day for months ahead, I'll count down the days and will find myself visualising a successful outcome as I go through day-to-day life. When the event gets closer, I'll be thinking about it constantly, imagining that I'm an aeroplane on final approach to landing. Everything will be focused on my approach into the event and lining everything up with the runway for a smooth landing at the start line.

For shorter events, my motivation will be where they fit into the overall plan of what I want to achieve. I have no interest in short races that are less than a marathon so I wouldn't be able to motivate myself to do them. My motivation is completing some long-term goals, such as building towards a focus race, getting in the 100 Marathon Club or bagging as many mountain peaks and ascents as I can. These things define me. A 10k road race doesn't work towards any of these so I'm not doing it. Running up Snowdon or running a road marathon does, so I will.

I'll remind myself that I'm physically fit, mentally strong, organised, focused, determined, a doer and an achiever. I have as much experience in the mountains as anyone else, most of it alone and being self-reliant. I've run long ultras multiple times before, I'm comfortable being self-sufficient in the hills, both day and night, I'm a strong navigator and all my kit is tried and tested from many hours running in the great outdoors. These are all factors in my favour to be a success at this. So on that front, I'll be as well prepared as anyone else on that start line and far better prepared than most competitors. This isn't arrogance, it's just a simple statement of fact. While my fitness may only be average amongst the field, my preparation, knowledge and experience will be greater than that of many others, which increases the odds of a successful outcome versus the average competitor. This confidence in my ability is what allows me to motivate myself for the event because it helps me to visualise a successful outcome and know that if I prepare adequately then the chances of me finishing are high.

Assuming that you've got the initial motivation to commit to the event, how do you maintain it throughout the build-up? There are lots of ways of achieving this but you need to find what works for you and not follow something prescribed by others. Ultra running is unconventional, everyone is an individual and the methods used by different runners will be completely unique. This will be far more so than for athletes training for other events, where more standardised methods of training and motivation will tend to work for everyone.

I have a few simple methods that I use to keep myself motivated and ensure that I complete the necessary training and preparation. It's all quite simple but it works for me. The key one is that I keep a log of all of my training. I've been doing this for over twenty years and it's as simple as a spreadsheet into which I enter details of what I've done. I've recorded all my exercise, whether it be running, cycling, hill walking, gym or other things. I've also recorded all the mountains that I've climbed as part of the log. I record slightly different information depending on what type of exercise it is, but I'm always consistent in what I do record. There are far more sophisticated ways of doing this now with the modern technology of running watches and cycling computers, but I've got a method that works for me and that I trust. The advantage of the spreadsheet is that it allows me to enter everything that I choose and then use the data for analysis purposes afterwards. This is great for motivation because I can always find something positive in my current situation, backed up by the data. For example, if I'm resting because of an injury, I can always look back at other similar periods and see how quickly I recovered back to a good level of fitness afterwards. This dispels negative thoughts from my mind because the anxiety of being injured is very quickly put back into perspective from what I've been through before.

I have some simple summaries that I always focus on, such as how many hours a week I've exercised or how many hours I've run in a month. This keeps me focused on adding another session in or extending a planned one if I've set myself some specific goals along the way. Typical goals will be a long run of a certain duration or a certain number of hours' exercise in a week. I always keep the goals simple and focus on being roughly in line with them, rather than worrying over the absolute detail of them. For example, if I've targeted a long run of eighteen miles but only do seventeen, then that's in the right area and the slight shortfall will have no detrimental effect in the long run. It's all about keeping positive and focusing on what you have done, rather than what you haven't. In this example, a seventeen-mile run is a long distance in anyone's book and the one mile short of the target is nothing in the grand scheme of things. Too many people beat themselves up over what they didn't achieve, rather than focusing on the positives of what they did. By focusing on the positives, the motivation will be there to continue. By focusing on the negatives, it will be much harder to feel motivated to repeat it again.

Sometimes it can be difficult to motivate yourself for a specific training session. This is especially so in winter, when it's cold, wet, dark and life is generally more tiring. At other times when life's really busy it can be easy to skip doing things that are hard, like training. If you're really struggling for the motivation, then my approach is not to set any specific objectives but just get started. If I'm running, then I'll just head out and think that I'll be satisfied with ten minutes running around the block. Once I'm out then inevitably the ten minutes will turn into something longer but it enabled me to get started in the first place.

I use a similar trick to motivate myself for long road runs. I'm not a fan of these as they're very much a means-to-an-end but they are key to endurance training. Rather than heading out to run, say, eighteen miles, I'll go out with the mindset that eighteen miles would be great but I'll be happy to run for an hour and I'll just see how I go. I find this takes the pressure off myself and nine times out of ten I'll end up doing the long run that I'd originally planned. Long runs can be quite daunting as anyone using a standard marathon training schedule will know. I find that by treating it as a shorter run that might continue into something longer, I can motivate myself more easily to be in the right mindset to finish it.

As I like to cross-train using cycling, then this can be used to vary my training and do something that I'll enjoy more. Some days running seems a chore but a ride on my bike or a spin on the turbo trainer in the garage might appeal instead. A lot of runners are just that, runners, and they will do all their training running on roads. I like the variety of road running, fell running, trail running, turbo-training, gym and cycling, which gives me sufficient options that I don't get bored and demotivated. While my training is therefore not highly specific and I won't achieve my true athletic potential in terms of pure time, it is very effective in banking large amounts of exercise which is great for an ultra runner. It's also great for avoiding injury. Essentially, I'm ensuring that I enjoy what I'm doing so I rarely find myself without the motivation to train.

I'm not a person who needs company to train, such as a running or cycling partner. I've always enjoyed my own company and this applies to exercise too, so the vast majority of the training that I've ever done has been alone. This isn't for everyone and one of the best ways to keep motivated is to train with a partner or a club. I've never had a problem with it, although I do enjoy running with others and with the running club. Again, for me this creates variety, which I think is essential to keeping well motivated.

In terms of keeping focused on an event and doing all the preparation necessary, I'll take a long-term view towards it and count down the days to the start. I always have countdowns running to all my races in my spreadsheet and like to chalk off key milestones like 100 days to go. I'm not sure why I started doing this but it's something that I've always done. The effect it has is to ensure that events I'm working towards are constantly on my mind. It keeps me mentally focused on them, so that I'm visualising them and also prompts me to do the necessary logistical preparations for them sufficiently early in the build-up.

Visualising events is important. More specifically, visualising your success at them is important. This is easiest if you've been successful at that event before but can actually be achieved if you've done one that's similar. Nothing builds confidence and positive energy more than reliving the finish of a hard challenge and the memories of how it felt at the time. I find this incredibly rewarding and one of the best techniques there is. I love the feeling of a hard job well done and just knowing that I'm heading towards that again helps to motivate me to put the effort in towards it.

I find that looking back at where I've come from is useful too. This can be small things that will help to boost me, such as: this is the most exercise I've done in a week for a while, I've done more mileage than this time last year or that's the longest or fastest run that I've done for a few months. This is highly motivating because there will always be something going well which boosts my confidence, rather than it being easy to lose sight of this.

It's important to keep yourself positive, despite all the potential negatives that can occur. I always try to turn negatives into positives, with the thinking that great things can be achieved no matter what your starting point. When I first ran sixty miles on the way to my first 100-miler and was naturally shattered afterwards, I was informed that, 'You'll never be able to do 100 miles if you're like this after sixty.' While this was a negative comment, my immediate reaction was that they were wrong and I would use this comment as my motivation to be successful.

I like to be inspired by the achievements of others, which makes me keen to be successful myself. I've read a lot of books on sporting and physical achievement. Sports biographies of professional sportsmen are always a good insight into the mind and motivation of someone who has excelled in their arena. This is very different to my own situation where I don't have the natural talent and exceptional dedication that they possess to reach the pinnacle of their sport. However, aspects of their thinking and approach can always be learned. I've always enjoyed books on outdoor pursuits, such as ultra running, cycling, mountaineering, polar exploration, round-the-world sailing and other adventures. These all have a touch of the madness and focus that all outdoor pursuits require. I can identify more with these individuals than with professional sportsmen. I have some books that I've read multiple times because they inspire me to think about the hardships, efforts and ultimately success that is being written about. I find this a great way of motivating myself to keep moving towards my own goals, even if the sport that I'm reading about is very different to my own.

Finally, I have lots of little motivational sayings or quotations that I use in my head to keep myself going at various times. These can be anything at all, lines from songs, quotes from books, cliched sayings, but no matter what others think of them, if they work for you then I think they're worth using. My own personal favourite is, 'Remember Roy Castle,' referring to the late, great trumpet player who presented the TV program *Record Breakers* when I was growing up. This always ended with Roy singing the theme song *Dedication*, with some very distinctive lyrics. I'll often think, 'Remember Roy Castle,' and sing the lyrics in my head, as my motivation if I'm struggling on my bike or not tempted to get up for an early morning training session.

Keeping motivated to achieve a hard challenge is not easy but I've found little tricks that help me, none of which are complex but all of which work. This is the key to how I get myself to the start line of an ultra, knowing that I'm as physically, mentally and logistically prepared as I possibly can be.

Above: Climbing
Craigysgafn,
Snowdonia. *(2004)*

Right: Descending with
Brandon to finish the
Saunders Lakeland
Mountain Marathon.
(2008)

DIWEDD

3.28.05.

(Photo by David Baldock)

(Photo by Alastair Tye www.fellrunningpictures.co.uk)

Above: Finishing for the third time at the Snowdonia marathon. *(2008)*

Left: Running through a storm at the Welsh 1,000-metre Peaks Fell Race. *(2009)*

Above: Descending on the International Snowdon Race. *(2009)*

Right: Completing my first 100-miler with Brandon at the South Downs Way Race. *(2010)*

Above: Cloud inversion from Cadair Idris, Snowdonia. *(2010)*

Left: Becoming the first person to complete a double round of both Wainwrights and Nuttalls. *(2011)*

Above: From left: me, Brandon, John and Jon at the High Peak Marathon. *(2013)*

Right: Relaxing in Chamonix after finishing the CCC. *(2013)*

Above: Climbing Snowdon. *(2013)*

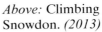

Left: Running with Greg at the Old County Tops Fell Race. *(2014)*

Above: Getting sorted out at the halfway checkpoint of the Lakeland 100 with Brandon. *(2014)*

Right: Finishing the Lakeland 100 with Brandon. *(2014)*

Above: On Snowdon summit after my 101st ascent with Clair, Harry and Kieran. *(2016)*

Left: At the start of the UTMB with Brandon. *(2016)*

16   Frozen: High Peak Marathon *(March 2013)*

'The High Peak Marathon can test a competitor's fitness, endurance and navigational skills to their limit. The route is at least 42 miles long and for much of it the terrain is pathless peat bog. The dark, lack of sleep and winter weather add to the challenge. All entrants should therefore be certain that they have the fitness, navigation and general mountaineering skills required to make a safe passage.'
(Race Organiser)

Despite the name, the High Peak Marathon is not a marathon at all. It's a 42-mile race with 7,000 feet of climbing, for teams of four, around the Derwent watershed in the Peak District. The terrain is a mixture of path and open moorland, with a significant amount of the route covering what can only be described as a nightmare mix of peat, heather and bog. The route is largely indistinct and featureless, so teams need to be strong navigators to find their way across this ground. All electronic navigational aids are banned, so the reliance is on using map and compass skills to navigate. As if that's not hard enough, it's held at the back end of winter, when the weather is almost guaranteed to be poor. Teams start at staggered intervals, with the slowest first, to spread them out and discourage following. Finally, to add to the already considerable challenge, it's run overnight, with the first team departing at 10 pm, so a large amount of the race is run in total darkness. It's held on a Friday night when most people will have done a full week at work beforehand and are not starting fresh. It's a real grind from start to finish and only attracts the hardiest entrants.

It's difficult to get into this event. There are only fifty teams each year and it's oversubscribed. There's an application process, with a complex ballot to select the successful ones. John had entered a team for a number of years with mixed success. In November 2012 he emailed Brandon, myself and another ultra runner, Jon, who I didn't know at the time, to say

139

that he'd got us into the 2013 race. I didn't know whether to cheer or cry.

On the day of the event, I'd worked until about 3 pm, then had a few hours at home to relax. After eating some pasta and drinking a full pot of coffee, I headed off to the start in Edale to meet the others.

After a rigorous kit check, followed by cake washed down with a couple of cups of tea, we were ready to roll. The first team left at 10 pm to applause from the other runners, then we were second out into the darkness two minutes later. We were all well wrapped up against the cold, as the temperature was below zero and would only get colder. It had been around freezing all week and we were hoping this might work to our advantage. Boggy moorland is easiest to cross, either after a long, dry spell when it has dried out, or in winter if a prolonged cold spell freezes it solid.

The first section is straightforward with a short run along the road and a climb up to Hollins Cross on the Mam Tor ridge. Then it's along the ridge for a mile or so to the peak at the end, Lose Hill. We overtook the first team along here so we were now the front-runners on the course. We exchanged some cheery chatter with the marshals at the checkpoint, then headed swiftly down into the valley. It was a reasonable descent to Hope and then straight into a stiff climb up out of the valley to the rocky top of Win Hill. Navigation on this section was easy, as we all knew the route without having to use maps so far. Another steep descent down to the next valley, then a couple of miles trotting along the road out onto the open moor. It was a very clear night and as we headed around Stanage Edge, we could see headtorches descending from Win Hill, a few miles behind us. This was the case all the way to Moscar, a fantastic view back at 1 am with 200 headtorches strung out across the hills behind us. All of them were gaining on us, apart from that first team.

As we ran into the checkpoint at Moscar, the first team to overtake us caught us up. From here until daylight, there would now be a slow but steady stream of teams coming past. Moscar was one of the two checkpoints on the A57 Snake Pass road, both of which had food. We stopped for a few minutes to refill our water bottles and eat sandwiches and cake. All our water was ice cold and it was an effort to drink it on such a cold night.

We had now completed the first major section and headed out onto the toughest section in terms of navigation and terrain. We climbed up onto Derwent Moor, where there was a stone path across the moor to start with, so it was good underfoot and easy to navigate. These stones didn't last and the terrain was to keep deteriorating. We made good, steady progress through to Sheepfold Clough, chatting amongst ourselves but relying heavily on John for navigation as he knew the area well and had recced it as he lives locally in Sheffield. The other three of us were keeping in contact with our maps, so I always knew where we were and that John was doing a great job of guiding us.

Beyond Sheepfold Clough, the ground gets less distinct and it becomes harder to follow the line of the watershed. Other teams were grouped around us as we climbed up higher onto the moor. I'm not sure how it happened but I lost the other three here as we climbed slowly up. In the dark, everyone looks the same as you can only see what's in your headtorch beam and the lights of others. I realised that the guys I was with were not Brandon, John and Jon. It was 3 am, bitterly cold and it started to dawn on me that I could be in trouble here. I didn't know whether the rest of my team were ahead or behind me. I trundled along but could feel the panic starting to rise up in me. How had I lost them? Where could I have gone wrong? When had I last seen them? How could I figure out if they were ahead or behind me? Indecision wracked me until I realised there was only one option open to me: I needed to speed up and start overtaking people until I found them. If I didn't catch them in, say, ten minutes, then they must be behind me. There were many other teams around me here so I didn't have to worry about navigation as I could just follow them. I just needed to start overtaking them all, so I sped up and ran as fast as I could across the rough moorland.

I went past twenty or thirty people but couldn't find them. I was starting to panic again because it then struck me, what if they were looking for me and taking some alternative action? Out of the darkness ahead of me emerged a fence with a stile. This was a rare feature on the moor and a natural point where they'd have noticed me missing as they climbed over it. I realised that if they were ahead of me, then they'd be standing there but they weren't. So they had to be behind me. I decided to stand and wait in the darkness for them and hope that they'd turn up. I didn't like the idea of retracing my steps and was seriously worried because we could be hunting for each other for hours on this moor if we weren't careful. I wasn't worried for my safety as I knew that I could navigate myself off to safety if I had to bail out. However, I was seriously worried about how long we could be hunting for each other in weather that was well below freezing. Also I wasn't happy that I'd messed up and jeopardised our team finishing the event.

I waited, watching all the people that I'd just overtaken coming up. In the dark, all I could see was headtorch lights until they were right on top of me and I could see their clothing to know it wasn't my team. Eventually, after what seemed like an hour but was probably only five minutes, they arrived. I could have hugged them. They hadn't even noticed I was missing and were just chatting away as they trotted up. I'd been having a serious panic and they hadn't got a care in the world. There was no harm done but this just shows how easy it is for something to go wrong on an overnight run. The only thing I can compare this twenty-minute period to, is the panic you feel when you lose a child, then the sheer elation when they turn up as if nothing has happened. We climbed the stile and trundled on.

We were on the high moor and the night was crystal clear. We could see lights of towns and cities for miles around. Sheffield was a glow across to our right and other towns were glowing further north. It was an incredible night.

142

As we headed across the moor, we were getting towards the notoriously boggy sections. We'd been dropping in and out of the peat hags for a while, noticing that the ground was solid under our feet. Rocky sections had been icy so we'd been very careful across these. Frost had been on the ground for a while but now we were all forming frost on our rucksacks and backs. I've been out in extreme cold many times but generally during the day and don't recall getting covered in frost before. I've been out in conditions where my clothing has frozen or walking poles have jammed solid but frost was a new experience to me. In our headtorches we were all becoming reflective with the white frost on us. I had six layers of clothing on, with gloves and over-mitts, balaclava, buff, hat and my hood up with the drawstrings pulled to minimise my exposure to the cold. It was absolutely freezing and we had to keep moving to generate heat. After finishing, we were told that it was minus seven degrees and it certainly felt like it. Luckily there was only a light wind so wind-chill wasn't too bad a factor.

The benefit of this extreme cold was that the ground had frozen solid. We hit the worst section where we expected to be picking our way around wet sections and sinking. We just sailed straight across it. It was such a boost to be able to move quickly through it. We had to be careful of ice so I was taking short strides and paying close attention to every footstep but we were flying, relative to our previous expectations.

At this late stage in the night, I'd noticed that it was becoming increasingly difficult to drink water from my bottle. I thought it might be faulty. I mentioned it to Brandon but he confirmed the same with his. Closer inspection showed why: our bottles were freezing. Eventually the top of my bottle froze solid and the only way to drink was to unscrew the lid. The contents were a semi-frozen slush. It wasn't pleasant drinking it due to the severe cold but was necessary to keep hydrated. The conditions were harsh but we were in good spirits and moving well towards the daylight.

On our team, John, Brandon and I are all lightly built.

However, Jon is an ex-paratrooper and built like a tank. As we cruised across the frozen bog, every now and then there'd be an exclamation from Jon as he went straight through into the icy bog below. Each time he'd sink in, wallow around and occasionally his momentum would cause him to go right over and be lying flat out. Sometimes it would need one or two of us to help drag him back out again. It was amusing for us but not for Jon.

We cleared this section and agreed to stop at the checkpoint at Swains Head to sort our gear out. This was the first time I'd taken my gloves off for hours and this confirmed how cold it was. After grabbing some extra food from my bag and putting it into more convenient pockets, I was struggling to close the rucksack up as my hands froze. I was also shivering and my teeth were chattering now that we'd stopped. I was getting very cold, very quickly. We only stopped for a few minutes but it was a relief to get my hands back into my gloves and start moving again to generate heat.

There were no other teams near us now, as all the faster teams had gone past us. We headed up onto Bleaklow where the ground was firmer and more solid but there were patches of ice around. The first signs of daylight were appearing in the sky as we headed on a slight downhill slope. We were in two pairs spread out, as we moved around peat hags to find good lines through the broken ground. Suddenly there was a shout from my right and I saw Brandon vanish as he tripped over on a very icy section. He was with Jon and disappeared behind a raised piece of ground, while Jon went after him. The shouting continued but I couldn't see what was happening. John and I continued around the front of the raised ground and backtracked to him. He was on his hands and knees below a six-feet drop, checking for injuries and gradually getting back to his feet. Jon was with him. He'd tripped on the rough ground, fallen onto an icy slope, before vanishing over the drop. He was ok, with just cuts and grazes to his knees but it could have been a lot worse.

It was getting light now but there had been a mist descending for the last hour or so. We no longer needed our headtorches but still couldn't see far because of the low cloud. We got to where we thought the next checkpoint was on Bleaklow Head but couldn't find it. We all had our maps and compasses out but couldn't see far enough in the mist to locate it. We headed on and then back-tracked to where it should be. It wasn't there. We all stood there poring over John's map together and checking compass bearings, confused. We decided to move on and start circling around to look for it. After 200 metres we stumbled over it. The marshals apologised that they were slightly out of position. This cost us about ten minutes. While this didn't matter in the overall scheme of a long day out, it was frustrating as we were all so cold. Now this was resolved, we'd completed the most difficult section and could head towards the top of the Snake Pass.

As we dropped off the moor towards the Snake checkpoint, it was fully light but the mist was thick and it had started snowing. The snow was reasonably heavy so visibility was poor. There's a good path off here so navigation wasn't an issue but it just felt like the weather wasn't going to give us a break tonight. We'd all fallen over a number of times due to the icy conditions. I had my worst fall along here when I stepped on a sloped, icy block and my foot went completely from under me. I went down hard onto the rocks on my right side but luckily fell backwards slightly onto my rucksack which cushioned the fall. It knocked the wind out of me though and I made sure I was stepping very gingerly from there all the way to the top of the Snake Pass.

At the checkpoint we had sandwiches and cake and messed around with the marshals. At all the checkpoints, the marshals were wrapped up warmly against the cold but were in fancy dress. At this one, they were dressed in women's underwear over their bulky clothing. We had photos taken with them all, as they kindly refilled our water bottles with boiling water to defrost them and get rid of the ice.

It was 8 am and we'd now covered 29 miles. We were heading for home. The snow continued for about half an hour but then the whole picture changed. The snow stopped and the mist lifted as we headed along the Pennine Way onto Kinder Scout. It was a crystal-clear morning and the views across to Manchester were fantastic. It was a perfect winter's morning to be out on the hills, especially after having run all night. As we skirted the edge of Kinder Scout on rocky paths, we had to keep stopping to take layers off as the temperature rose. By the time we crossed Brown Knoll and headed towards the final section of Mam Tor, I'd removed all but two layers and my rucksack was crammed full of all my excess clothing.

We crossed the road at Mam Nick, ran around the side of Mam Tor and back to Hollins Cross where we'd first hit this ridge nearly fourteen hours ago. We descended back into the Edale valley, with John and Jon rocketing off ahead, while Brandon and I trundled steadily down behind them. We arrived back at the village hall with a finishing time of 13 hours and 54 minutes.

After changing at the car and heading back into the hall, we all sat there exhausted, enjoying the fantastic stew and eating huge quantities of the chunky bread on offer. It had been a massive night out in the extreme cold with our bodies using a lot of energy just to keep warm, let alone cover the distance. The advantage was that with the ground frozen solid, our progress had been rapid through the worst sections. In fact, the conditions this year resulted in very fast times and the course records for all categories were broken, which showed how cold and frozen it was.

The High Peak Marathon is a unique event and survives as one of the traditional, old-school events on the annual calendar, having been run for forty years. Don't be fooled by its length of only 42 miles. It's a very testing race and one that I'm proud to have finished.

We returned in 2014 with the same team and finished in 15 hours and 3 minutes. The frozen ground was the difference, saving us over an hour in 2013, which is a huge amount of time and shows just how difficult the terrain is when it's not frozen solid.

44 teams started, 38 finished, we came 36th. The race had a 14% drop-out rate.

17   Peak Bagging

'Great things are done when men and mountains meet.'
(William Blake)

If there's one thing in life that I like, it's a good list. I have lists for everything, whether it's things I've done, things I'm working on or things I plan to do in the future. I've got lists of all the books I've read, football and rugby matches I've attended, sports grounds I've been to, holidays taken, countries visited and others.

In terms of exercise, I have lists of all my race results, 100 Marathon Club qualifiers, training sessions and race split times. I record data for all of these in a large spreadsheet so I have a lot of information that can be analysed for future planning purposes.

I have one list that surpasses all others: mountains.

This is my favourite list. It catalogues every peak I've climbed, my route, distance, height ascended and other information. I've covered 8,513 miles in the mountains, climbed 570 different peaks, made 2,133 ascents, climbed 2.2 million vertical feet in 661 days and made 74% of these trips alone. I know all this because I keep lists.

I'm often told that I have an obsessive personality and I think this is all the evidence that's needed to prove it. When I start something, I become obsessed with it and have to do it to the extreme. It's just how my brain works and how I'm used to existing. That's why I was drawn into ultra running. I can't just run a few 10k's; I have to start at marathon distance and go from there. It's not just exercise that I do this with, it's everything. If there's a list of something, I'll want to do the lot. I've been to 27 of the 92 football league grounds; I want to visit all 92 but will wait until I retire and visit them all with my brother, when we have the time to do it. If I find an author I like, I have to read all their books, preferably in order. I've taught myself to solve the Rubik's cube and have a personal best of 1 minute and 18 seconds. This is slow compared to the world record of sub-five seconds but, in a parallel with my running, speed doesn't interest me. Going longer does, so I have large cubes up to a big 10x10x10, which takes me just over an hour to solve. I'm now looking at buying the largest available which is 13x13x13 simply because it is the largest.

Please don't ask me to explain this mindset because I can't. I'm just an extreme obsessive in everything I become interested in. I'll never be fast but if you want someone to keep going at something when everyone else has given up, then I'm your man.

When I started climbing hills, I was always destined to need to know how many there were and attempt to climb them all. It was inevitable. The result is I've now spent a significant part of my life bagging peaks and have catalogued every single trip but how did it start?

I was brought up in Essex which is a flat county with no hills, so it didn't start there. However, my Nan lived in the West Country in a small village called Bleadon, on the edge of the Somerset Levels. Close by were the Mendip Hills, with the prominent Crook Peak above the M5 motorway, as well as the isolated Brent Knoll rising up from the Levels themselves. My favourite activity when staying was to climb one of these hills. Neither is very high, both only being about 600 feet above sea level, but for some reason they fascinated me. This was where the seed was sown.

When I moved north to go to university in Leeds, I spent a lot of time orienteering and mountain biking. This took me into the hills of northern England, areas that appealed to me and I wanted to explore more. After university, I moved to the North West and started walking in the hills, using my map-reading skills from orienteering, coupled with my general fitness from running and cycling. After a few years, I'd done a moderate amount of hill walking, having climbed the major peaks of the Lake District, Snowdonia and Peak District. Then I hit a tipping point where it accelerated rapidly.

In 1998, Clair went to work in New Zealand for seven months. I needed something to occupy my time so I started heading to the hills to walk every weekend. I was living on the outskirts of Liverpool so driving to any of the major upland areas of the Lakes, Snowdonia, Yorkshire Dales or Peak District took only an hour or so. I quickly climbed all the 3,000-feet mountains in Snowdonia and the Lakes, as there are less than twenty of them. I particularly liked Snowdonia and wondered how many mountains it contained. I did some research and bought a book of Mountain Tables, which listed all the mountains of England and Wales above 2,000 feet. Immediately I had a list and a mission: I wanted to climb all the 2,000-feet mountains in Snowdonia, of which there were 145.

I was off and I've never looked back.

One of the things I enjoy about peak bagging is the planning. You don't undertake to climb all the peaks on a list by adopting a random approach as you'll miss some. Mountains naturally fall into groups and these are always fairly logical. Their location between roads is the most common grouping. In Snowdonia, the northern mountains of the Carneddau, Glyderau and Snowdon are all bounded by roads and split nicely by them. Using the book of Mountain Tables, I listed the initial groups and identified which peaks I'd already climbed. I then reviewed maps and distances and started devising walking routes that would pass between the peaks. This would then generate a number of walks to be undertaken to bag them all. There would be multiple trips required into each area to pick up the different peaks, sometimes over-lapping and sometimes requiring strange route choices. Part of the planning exercise was to link up the peaks sensibly into an interesting route that had to be circular from a convenient parking place.

I bought guide books so I could read descriptions of different ascents, conditions of paths and make my own decisions on routes and on how difficult their sections would be. My approach was to focus on planning a single group of mountains at a time, starting in the north and working south. I

150

didn't always walk them in that order. Sometimes I'd work through a group methodically before moving on, but at other times I'd skip from one area to another for interest.

While peak bagging might sound a very strange way to approach spending time in the hills, it has an advantage that a non-structured approach doesn't. As you attempt to tick off peaks, you visit all the corners of the region that you wouldn't otherwise consider. It's natural to head towards the most popular, well known and generally the highest peaks. This is very apparent in Snowdonia, with crowds of walkers on Snowdon and a reasonable amount on the Glyderau, southern Carneddau and Cadair Idris. Beyond these popular areas, the remaining hills are far less frequented. Peak bagging takes you to every peak, including all the little known ones and some very remote ones too. Without the tick list approach, I wouldn't have discovered many parts of Snowdonia, as I simply wouldn't have had a reason to go there. I'd have missed out on the variety of the landscape, the remoteness of the wilder areas and the sense of really getting to know the area well by spending time walking across all of it.

Peak bagging's an adventure and much like exploring as you head into a new area for the first time, off the beaten track and with the hills to yourself. It's fantastic for improving your map-reading skills as every trip out requires navigating over new terrain that you haven't been to before. Hence, it never gets boring and offers a different challenge on every trip. It suits my logical approach to life, love of lists and desire to get out into the hills at every opportunity.

I started ticking Snowdonia's hills off my list, initially at a fast rate. I'd focus on routes where ridges quickly linked multiple summits and enabled a good number of peaks to be bagged in one day. Then progress soon slowed, as all the low-hanging fruit were picked. The peaks became more remote, more widely spaced and with longer distances to trek into them and between them. These were the connoisseur's hills, the little frequented ones that I was all alone on and would walk across all day without seeing another soul. These hills may not be as exhilarating as their loftier and more popular brothers, but in many ways they were more rewarding as I explored the unknown corners of our country.

Over the next two years, I kept plugging away and eventually, in January 2000, I completed my objective with all of Snowdonia's mountains climbed.

I'd gained considerable experience in the mountains through this period, not only in Snowdonia but in other areas too. Naturally I was drawn to bigger things and I'd already decided that I wouldn't stop there. I intended to climb all the 2,000-feet high mountains in England and Wales. These are referred to as Nuttalls, after the couple who catalogued them, in the same way as the Scottish Munros are named after the man who listed them. There are 443 Nuttalls, from the Cheviots north of Newcastle, through the Lake District, North Pennines, Yorkshire Dales, Peak District, all the way through Wales and finally two lone ones down on Dartmoor in Devon. It was going to take a lot of effort to visit all these different places and stand on top of all of these peaks.

One thing that falls perfectly for me is the location of the mountains of England and Wales. If you could pick a location that was central to them all, it would be Warrington, where we've lived for the last eighteen years. It's at a crossroads of the motorway network and 90% of the 2,000-feet mountains are within a two-hour drive. I don't mind driving, so I can day-trip these easily and on occasion will do some much longer day-trips. The longest was a 600-mile round trip to climb the two peaks on Dartmoor, picking up two odd ones in the Brecon Beacons on the way back. Another epic day was a 430-mile round trip to the Cheviots, to walk a long and tough 24-mile route on a very hot day to bag six peaks. Ridiculous trips but such happy memories.

For me, this is all part of the fun, getting out and seeing the country, with a reason for doing so. I've driven many tens of thousands of miles to bag peaks, mostly on my own and enjoyed every trip. Peak bagging has taken me across the North of England and Wales many times over and at all times of year. I feel that I've seen more of our country than most people, simply because I've spent so much time driving around the countryside, parking up and then climbing up hills.

I like being in the hills with others but have spent the vast majority of my time there alone. I've always enjoyed my own company and have never struggled for motivation, so I don't need that buddy that many people require to get out and do something. There's something very rewarding about climbing mountains on your own, relying on no one but yourself and being totally self-sufficient with just your rucksack on your back. I usually tell Clair roughly where I'm going and the time I expect to be back but I'm never very specific, which I know is not good practice. 'I'm off to the Lakes, back at five,' is a typical example.

I'm self-sufficient, very competent and take responsibility for myself in the great outdoors. So I'll always return. What I always do without fail though is send a text when I get off the hills to say I'm down safely and will be home at a certain time. Often I'll have to wait until I've driven out of the hills to somewhere with phone reception but I always do it. The only time I failed at this was after the Tour de Helvellyn race in December 2013 in the Lakes. This was a gruelling day in bad weather and I'd been running alone for nearly eleven hours, longer than expected. Somehow I'd got water in my mobile phone so it wasn't working and I couldn't report in to Clair before setting off for home. Driving over Shap summit on the M6, I suffered a tyre blow-out and found myself stranded on the hard shoulder, waiting for more than an hour for roadside assistance. I was well overdue off the hills but had no means of letting Clair know where I was. The Highways Agency eventually rang her to let her know that I was safe, just delayed. This might sound trivial but my view is that I always like to let her know that I'm safe, as I'm often out alone in testing conditions, in remote and inhospitable places, as was the case this day.

After completing the Snowdonia peaks, it took me another two years to finish the rest of the peaks in England and Wales. It was an incredible experience, visiting many different areas in every kind of weather imaginable. The final peak was Fan Hir in the Brecon Beacons, which I climbed in January 2002 with Dan, who I was planning the 230-mile cycle ride with at the time. It was a miserable day and we climbed my final five peaks in a circular route with very low visibility for the whole day. As we stood on the peak that completed four years of planning and effort, I felt no elation and no cause for celebration. It was simply a relief to have finally achieved what had taken me so long. It was raining and we could only see about ten metres in the mist as we stood there in the cloud. I just wanted to get off the hill and get dry. I simply said to Dan, 'That's done, let's go home now,' before we headed off on the three-mile walk back to the road where the car was parked. The satisfaction came later at knowing that I'd achieved something special.

As part of this round of peaks, I'd spent a lot of time in the Lake District to bag the 170 peaks there. I'd bought the whole set of Wainwright's famous guide books to assist in the planning. Alfred Wainwright is a Lakeland legend and his set of seven hand-written guide books catalogue 214 Lakeland peaks, based on his own arbitrary definition of a peak. Of these, 117 overlapped the list of 2,000-feet mountains that I'd climbed, leaving 97 that didn't. My second mission was to climb these remaining 97 peaks to complete a round of all the Wainwrights.

The definition of a mountain is a topic that can affect these lists. Wainwright's list is straightforward as it's his personal selection with no specific rules, so it can never be argued. However, the original list of 2,000-feet mountains that I climbed has changed slightly over the years. The basic definition is that a peak must be 2,000 feet above sea level, with fifty feet of re-ascent from the highest intervening col. These then subdivide into separate mountains and subsidiary peaks, with rules as to which camp they fall into, based on how far apart and how

154

much re-ascent there is between them. The change to metric maps from imperial ones has complicated some classifications at the borderlines, due to height measurements being rounded up or down. Those peaks affected have sometimes been re-surveyed and there have been a few height changes made over the years. The most notable being the elevation of Glyder Fawr up to 1,001 metres in height from its previous 999, which took it above the 1,000-metre mark and changed the course of the Welsh 1,000-metre Peaks fell race. The list is settled now but has gained a few peaks since I started and lost one or two as well. If a peak was added, I'd make sure that I went out and climbed it to keep my list complete.

The classification of peaks can get very pedantic but that side of it doesn't interest me. Although I found that I needed to set some rules for what constituted climbing a peak or not when it came to recording multiple ascents. The initial climb of a peak is never in doubt as I will always walk in from a road, which will result in an ascent from a valley or a pass. The difficulty comes when you're doing multiple peaks in one day. It's accepted that you can climb a subsidiary peak from a separate mountain and count it. Then what happens if you return back over the top of the main summit again afterwards? Does that count as a second ascent? My rule is that it doesn't. Once I'm on a particular mountain with its subsidiaries, I only count one ascent of each, until I've either returned to a recognised starting point (typically a road) or have climbed another completely separate mountain before returning.

The other small area of detail is whether you have to go right up and touch the very highest rock. This isn't an issue on the vast majority of peaks, as you can stand right on the highest point. Some peaks have prominent rock formations on their summit, however, which are a few feet above the main bulk of the hill. For example, Glyder Fach in Snowdonia has a big pile of rocks on an otherwise fairly flat summit and Helm Crag in the Lakes has the Lion and Lamb rock formation on its summit. No one can dispute that you've climbed the peak if you stand next to the base of these rock formations as you're clearly on the summit but the highest point is technically at the tip of these rocks, a few feet higher. My personal rule is that I will scramble up to the tip once so that I've touched the highest point on the first visit. On repeat visits I think this is unnecessary and pointless unless I particularly want to do it. The exception is where the jumble of rocks is what gives the peak the required fifty feet of re-ascent from the surrounding area, such as Castell y Gwynt in the Glyderau mountains of North Wales.

Completing the Wainwrights took me into many of the outlying areas of the Lake District which I hadn't explored before. This changed my perspective on the hills, as I'd always been drawn to the highest peaks first and then those over 2,000 feet. I found that some of these were fantastic little hills at much lower altitude, such as the lowest of them all, Castle Crag, in the jaws of the Borrowdale valley. Exploring the hills between the higher peaks, at the end of ridges and in the outer areas of the Lakes was well worth the effort and all part of the enjoyment of completing this list. After another year of effort, I ticked the last one off in January 2003. I'd purposely kept one specific hill back for this: Mungrisedale Common, tucked away behind the bulk of Blencathra in the Northern Fells. Many people believe Wainwright included this one as a joke because it's not really a peak but more a lump in the hillside with a couple of stones on it. For this reason, it seemed appropriate for it to be climbed after all the others.

I enjoyed completing the Wainrights far more than I did the Nuttalls because it added more breadth to my walking. I was no longer just climbing the highest but had experienced a lot more of what Lakeland had to offer. I thought now that I'd completed these two peak bagging challenges, I had no further need to tick peaks off a list and could just enjoy random days out in the hills. However, I discovered that once you've started peak bagging, you don't ever stop. I didn't focus on it actively for the next few years but slowly I was completing a second round of both sets of mountains and would make sure that I picked up odd peaks when I was out. On family holidays to South Wales, Devon and the North East, I'd head out to the hills to climb peaks that were a long drive from home, all in the aim of doing round number two. I wasn't as focused as I had been on round one but was slowly reducing the number remaining in both sets of hills.

In February 2011, I ran over Great Mell Fell in the eastern Lakes to complete my second round of Wainwrights. It was a typical day for peak bagging; cold, wet and dreary with no views, even on the relatively low hills that I'd run over that day. I became the 59th person to complete a second round, which seemed a greater achievement than the first time due to the low number of people who had done it before me.

All completions of rounds of the popular peaks in the UK are logged by the Long Distance Walkers Association (LDWA) and listed on their website. This is done on an honesty basis, which surprises some people, but how else can you do it? Why would anyone cheat it anyway, as it's such an obscure achievement? I hadn't registered my first completions of either challenge until I'd nearly completed my second round of Wainwrights. It had been a personal challenge both times and I didn't feel the need to have them logged but once I was within a few trips of completing the second round of Wainwrights, I registered my claims with the LDWA. I felt I wanted multiple rounds officially logged, as much for the LDWA's records as for any need of my own.

Once I'd completed two rounds of Wainwrights, I looked at how many people had done two rounds of the Nuttalls. It was only six. I was already 85% of my way through them for a second time, so naturally I focused on finishing them off as this was a very select group of peak baggers.

As I worked through the spring of 2011 to increase my total, I checked how many of these six had also climbed all the Wainwrights. It was only three but none of these had ever completed a second round of Wainwrights. It dawned on me that if I could complete my second round of Nuttalls, I'd be the only person to have ever done a double round of both sets. What I didn't know was if anyone else was nearing completion of a second round of either that would beat me to this.

So it became my mission to do it as fast as I could. I took every opportunity to add to my total, heading out midweek if I could to pick up odd ones, as well as at weekends for the bigger trips. I made some long trips to South Wales, on a few occasions running in darkness and not getting home until the early hours. It was my most intense period of peak bagging because I had the opportunity to do something that no one had ever done before. Granted, it's a slightly obscure challenge, but it was there nonetheless and I was determined to be the first to achieve it. I finished in a mad flourish, with four trips to the hills in twelve days to clear the final peaks in the North Pennines.

The final peak was Cross Fell, the highest point in the Pennines and one that I'd kept back as a good one to finish on. I ran it with Greg on a wild Wednesday night in October 2011. The vast majority of my walking and running in the hills has been done alone but I'd been with Dan for my first Nuttall completion and it seemed fitting to have Greg with me for the second. Both my Wainright completions were made alone but the Nuttalls are an altogether bigger challenge, with greater height, more peaks and being spread across the country. It was nice to be with a good friend for it.

We parked at Knock and ran straight up the access road that runs to the radar station on Great Dun Fell. It got dark as we headed up and started raining too. On a cold October evening like this, you wouldn't normally want to be running on the hills but this was a special night. I actually needed to climb three peaks to finish, Great Dun Fell being the first. It was then an easy run along to Little Dun Fell and then only one remained. It was half a mile of gentle downhill, then half a mile up onto the large flat summit of Cross Fell. It was dark, windy, raining and visibility was low but eventually the summit cairn appeared out of the gloom. It was done. We lingered long enough for Greg to take a few photos and then headed back.

158

I've never been so satisfied in my life as on that return run. This was special. I'd achieved something that no one else had. Slightly obscure, yes, but it was a unique achievement. It had taken me thirteen years from start to finish but it was done. I don't ever feel that I have to do things to prove myself or my ability to anyone else. The only person I feel the need to impress is myself and I have to keep doing these things to gain satisfaction of a challenge well done. This was my finest hour, not in terms of difficulty, but in terms of sheer dogged determination to keep heading out to different places and ticking items off a list. I was very proud of what I'd done.

We drove to Appleby-in-Westmorland to get fish-and-chips but missed the chip shop's closing time by a few minutes. Greg bought me a pint of Jennings in the Grapes Inn, then we bought pasties from the shop in the square and ate them in the car. It was a fantastically understated way to celebrate but one that I loved.

I have so many happy memories of days out in the hills, either running or walking, and in so many different places. I could write an entire book on my experiences but the most vivid memories tend to be the ones in extremes of weather. The most difficult weather to contend with is strong wind. It's usually windy up high so I'm used to that, but I've been out many times when it's strong enough to be dangerous, especially given the nature of being on difficult mountain terrain. The highest winds I've ever been out in were when bagging some peaks in the southern Carneddau mountains of Snowdonia. I'd specifically picked these hills because they offered big, grassy run-offs to the south with no crags, so I'd have plenty of escape options and no technical ground to negotiate if the wind became too much for me. This was essential if I was heading out in such extreme conditions, so that I could extricate myself safely if need be. I can only describe the conditions as comparable to walking through treacle. It was almost impossible to stand up, I was constantly thrown about and when walking into the wind, I was working at my limit to make any

159

progress at all. Breathing was difficult and as I climbed onto the shoulder of Creigiau Gleision, the wind was so severe that I felt like I was suffocating. There was literally no air to breath, as the wind screamed over the hillside. The weather station across the valley recorded wind speeds of a constant ninety miles per hour that morning, gusting to 103 miles per hour. As conditions were so extreme, this was a rare occasion when I'd been using GPS to navigate for safety when in the cloud; this GPS was a fully waterproof unit, guaranteed for full immersion in water for up to thirty minutes. Conditions were so severe that the wind drove rain into its casing and destroyed it through water damage. This demonstrates how incredibly ferocious the conditions were, as this should have been impossible. It was a real test of my ability to keep safe, a very intense experience, but also very rewarding to challenge myself in such weather.

Winter conditions with snow and ice are also some of the most challenging conditions but are worth it, as the mountains look fantastic in winter. I've run in these conditions many times, with mini crampons on my running shoes. However, when conditions are more severe, or I'm climbing on steep, technical ground, then I'll walk with crampons and an ice axe which offer greater protection. One of the hardest climbs that I've done under such conditions was Scafell Pike in the Lake District. I've climbed this peak many times but on this particular day there was snow right down to the valley floor. I walked in from the Langdale valley, which is a reasonable trek, with the final climb being up from Broad Crag col to the summit. This is an easy path in summer, although steep and rocky. However, on this day it was a steep slope of snow and ice. I climbed up fairly easily by digging my crampons and ice axe in carefully. There are large drops to both sides here and a slip on such ground in such conditions would be fatal. As is so often the case though, the problem wasn't on the ascent but on the return. As I descended, it became too steep for me to be comfortable. I was the only person on the mountain that day and there were no foot holes or steps from other climbers to use, only my marks from the ascent. I had to turn around to face the mountain and back-climb down. I'm not a climber so only have one ice axe and this was a very perilous operation, carefully planting my crampons before releasing the safety of my axe from the slope. The problem with back-climbing is that you can't see where you're going and have to keep looking down between your legs. The drops sucked dizzyingly below me the whole time. It took twenty minutes to reach the safety of the col, a time when the adrenaline was flowing and my whole being was concentrated on being firmly attached to that slope. At times like these, you're genuinely frightened as one small slip would be the end. Experiences like this in the hills are the only time in my life that I've experienced genuine fear, something that heightens all your senses to an incredible level that you will never experience in normal daily life.

Rain, hail and snow all cause difficulties as they restrict the visibility. Rain isn't too bad, although when it's driven horizontally by the wind it gets into everything. Hail is always painful; all you can do is pull your hood down tightly and turn your face away from it. Snow is most challenging when up in the cloud, as the whole world turns white. Your eyes have nothing to focus on, the sky is the same colour as the ground and there is no distinction between the two. It's a surreal experience, is very confusing and feels as if you're going mad. On one day while crossing the summit of Bowfell, I used the trick of throwing a stone in front of me, to give me something to aim for and for my eyes to focus on as I crossed an indistinct world of white.

Snow on the ground can make for very heavy going. If it's deep, then you have to literally wade through it, waist deep at times. Ground that you'd cover in minutes in summer, can take hours in deep snow. At other times, the snow develops a crust that you can walk on above the deep snow below. Sometimes this is not quite strong enough to take your weight, so you'll take a few steps then break through and fall. Without snowshoes, the only option sometimes is to literally crawl across it. Walking on Post Gwyn in the Berwyn mountains of North Wales one winter, I had to crawl for thirty minutes to cross a really awkward section. I'd have looked ridiculous if anyone could have seen me, but it was a better option than to keep falling through the crust.

Thunderstorms in the hills are a serious hazard. In normal life, they're something that's happening above you, while you're generally indoors. In the hills, you are exposed at high level and feel as if the storm is around you, rather than above you. I've only been caught out a few times. Once was while on the summit of Stoney Cove Pike in the Lake District. It was late afternoon on a hot, summer's day and thunder had been rumbling around over the distant Pennines for a while. Just as I left the summit cairn, lightning flashed and there was an enormous bang of thunder right on top of me. All I could do was get away from the summit as fast as I could, to find a hollow a bit lower down the hill to shelter in. I crouched down here, well away from the summit until the storm moved away. Another memorable time was climbing Moel Cynghorion in Snowdonia with Greg in the dark. We watched a thunderstorm flashing away, a few miles ahead of us over Moel Eilio. As it was dark, we could actually see the storm moving across our path from the lightning flashes, heading east towards the Glyderau mountains, so we were safe to continue behind it.

It's not just bad weather that remains memorable. I've had some fantastic days on the hills, all year round, with clear visibility and the ability to see for miles. Not just in this country either; I've spent time walking abroad, in the Rockies in both Canada and the USA, the Appalachian mountains of the USA, the Alps, Pyrenees, New Zealand and some of the Canary Islands. As the foreign trips were always holidays, the weather tended to be good, with fantastic days out and mountain scenery that you just don't get in the UK.

One of the most spectacular weather effects that I've experienced is cloud inversion. This is being on a mountain above the cloud. I've experienced this many times and it's typically a similar experience; you head up into the cloud, expecting another dreary day with no views. As you climb higher, it will start to get a bit brighter and you'll sense light above you. Then the cloud will clear and you're above the top of it, with mountains laid out above a sea of white. It's always incredible to see and something that heightens the mountain experience.

Good weather or bad, I've never let the weather forecast distract me too much from getting out into the hills and bagging peaks. If you head out enough times, then you'll get some great conditions. If you always watch the forecast and delay for a better day, then you could miss out on some of the rich experiences that the hills have to offer. In my experience, the forecast is often right but not always so. My approach is just to head out, be prepared, know my limits and take the right clothing to survive it. Weather is such an important part of being out in the hills, making the same routes completely different in different conditions. It's part of why climbing the same hills over and over again never gets boring.

Peak bagging is part of my life and something that I'll always continue to do. Currently I'm 78% of the way through the Wainwrights for a third time and 53% of the way through the Nuttalls. I'm not actively pursuing these third rounds but once these percentages hit higher numbers, you know exactly what I'm going to do.

Peak bagging is a bizarre past-time but one that's given me great pleasure over the years. I plan to continue doing it for many, many years to come. I'd recommend it to anyone, so long as you like driving, climbing mountains, bad weather and, above all, lists.

18   Running Flat: Thames Path 100 *(March 2013)*

'Keep Moving Forward.' (Walt Disney)

The Thames Path 100 is a 100-mile running race from London to Oxford along the national trail that runs along the River Thames. This makes it a flat course and one suited to runners, as opposed to mountain athletes, with fast times possible. This doesn't make it easy. There is no such thing as an easy 100-mile run due to the distance involved. I'm definitely in the mountain man category and wouldn't class myself a runner as my training mileage is relatively low. So this event gave me some particular concerns. Firstly, hills naturally break a route into sections which suits my approach. There would be no hills this time, just a 100-mile stretch of trail. Secondly, everyone has to walk uphill on a long ultra, even the winner, so this creates natural breaks and rhythm changes. No hills gives no variety to break things up. Finally, walking or running uphill, flat and downhill all use slightly different muscles in your legs. Running continuously on the flat doesn't.

The build-up to the event was problematic to say the least. It was off the back of a very hectic few weeks in general, so I was tired and hadn't had time for my usual focus in the lead up. Then the weather started to play its hand. The Thames was on flood alert in numerous places along its length so the organisers made the only decision they could to allow the event to take place, which was to change the course. Rather than run from London to Oxford, we would have to turn back after 38 miles as the river was flooded above here. The danger was that if you couldn't tell where the river ended and the path started, it would be too dangerous to proceed. So at Cookham we would turn around and head back 27 miles the way we'd come to Walton. We would then be turned around again and head 27 miles all the way back up to Cookham. A final turn-around to head back ten miles to the new finish in Windsor. The course would be somewhere between 102 and 104 miles, so-called 'bonus miles' being necessary as checkpoint positions could not be changed at short notice. We would pass through the finish at Windsor three times during the race at miles 28, 48 and 82. Mental toughness would be needed to keep going when an easy option would be to bail out here.

The weather then continued to cause stress. Snow was forecast for Friday and duly arrived on schedule. It was uncertain what disruption this would cause to the train schedules and if I'd be delayed getting to London. I had a worrying morning at work keeping half an eye on the weather and the travel news, then a taxi to the station and onto the train on Friday afternoon. Finally, I could relax as I was on my way.

The race start was at 10 am on Saturday. Brandon and I stayed at a cheap hotel a couple of miles away so there was time for a decent breakfast beforehand. Other athletes would be horrified as we ate porridge and cooked breakfast but this would set us up well for the day ahead. The weather was miserable, with sleet, rain and a cold wind. It was enough to make you moan generally but was really depressing when we knew we'd be outside for nearly thirty hours straight. Ultras are all about mental preparation and mental strength; everything had made this one very hard to get set up for mentally. I always say that you can only play the hand you're dealt, so all we could do was start and see how it all panned out.

Registration and the kit check were busy, with lots of competitors making the most of the last time we'd be indoors for quite a while. Of the 250 entrants, only 164 actually started. Bear in mind that the entry fee was about £110, so it's a lot of money to pay and then not turn up. The weather and late course change undoubtedly added to the usual injuries and other reasons for not starting. We were briefed, then all trouped outside, an air-horn was blown on the riverside and we were away. It was raining, cold and miserable but we were in high spirits as we departed.

We had an arbitrary schedule to run on, as we didn't know the course. Normally I'd recce a race beforehand to gauge conditions and time, but due to the location of this one it wasn't practical. So I prepared a schedule based on breaking the whole route down into sections between checkpoints, then times for each section based on a minutes per mile pace from experience. This was twelve minutes per mile in the early stages, sliding out to nineteen minutes per mile beyond mile eighty. Finally, some stopped time at each checkpoint was factored in. This was then all hastily changed at the last minute for the revised route. Our targeted finishing time was 27 hours and 24 minutes, which was slower than we'd run on the South Downs Way the year before but seemed reasonable for a flat course that didn't suit us and cold weather.

Due to the weather, most competitors were well equipped and well wrapped up. However fast you are, 100 miles means you're going to be out an awfully long time and with the temperature just above freezing we couldn't skimp. I was wearing full-length leggings, two thermal tops, two t-shirts, hat, gloves, buff and waterproof jacket. I had an extra, long-sleeve top, a thin fleece and a balaclava for night-time. Even then I was cold waiting before the start but the best way to keep warm is to generate your own heat through moving. I would regulate my temperature during the day by taking my hat, gloves and buff on and off.

The first twelve miles to checkpoint one at Walton were uneventful. It was an easy trot along good paths, admiring views of the river, Hampton Court and other places of interest. We were near the back of the field, chatting to other runners and just trotted along, banking early miles. We were conscious that the pace was faster than the schedule due to the easy underfoot conditions, about 9.5 minutes per mile. To put this into perspective, that would get you close to a four-hour marathon finish, an easy trot but a bit fast for a 100-miler. We were thirty minutes ahead of schedule at Walton which was nice but caused concerns that we'd started too fast. We hadn't as we weren't exerting ourselves unduly. It was just easy going.

We grabbed a quick handful of food and moved on.

Immediately we hit a wet section of trail and slippery mud. It was only a short stretch but we had to pick our way around puddles and slowed down drastically. After my experience on the previous year's Lakeland 100, I was being very careful to keep my feet dry to avoid trench foot. The mud soon passed and we were away on a good track again.

The miles then passed fairly easily up until mile 25 at Old Windsor. There were a few muddy sections but generally it was easy running and we were about forty minutes ahead of schedule. The concern we both had was that our legs were feeling tired from the constant flat running. This was to be expected; if you run a marathon your legs get very heavy after about twenty miles but then you only need to do a few miles more. Both of us had heavy legs with the best part of eighty miles left. It was mentally testing and worrying. On a 100-miler you're always looking for issues because the sooner you spot one, the sooner you can deal with it. On shorter runs you just keep going but on long ultras you need to keep monitoring yourself and correcting problems early.

After Old Windsor the trail deteriorated rapidly in places. We hit prolonged sections of wet, slippery mud. This was a nightmare. We couldn't get a grip on it so were slithering about. It was slow and energy-sapping and we had to be careful not to fall over. As we slowed down, we weren't generating as much heat and got cold too. However, we got to Windsor in good spirits and I suggested to Brandon that we should change socks here. A marshal kindly pointed out that 100 metres beyond the checkpoint was a large section of knee-deep water. That made it an easy decision to delay the sock change until the next checkpoint. The standing water was under a railway bridge and could be avoided by either clinging to a fence and bank on one side, or slithering above the river clinging to bushes on the other. We went for the bushes this time but on all subsequent passes (three more) went for the fence. It became known as the 'assault course' section.

The next 10 miles up to Cookham started well, out of

167

Windsor and round to Dorney Lake, the 2012 Olympics rowing venue. We then hit long sections of muddy trail; a good few miles of slithering around, twinges in leg muscles from slipping, other competitors caked in mud from falls and general swearing and losing patience with the underfoot conditions. We'd also started looking out for the front-runners now as we knew they'd be on their way back after the turn-around. The leader came past us when we were at mile 34. He was at mile 42 with a six-minute gap to second place. All the way up to the turn-around at Cookham was a mix of path and horrible, slippery mud, acknowledging faster runners heading back.

We had a cup of tea at Cookham while sorting ourselves out, with anti-chafe cream on feet and fresh socks. I'd got a few blisters on the side of one big toe but nothing to worry about too much. I put a fleece on for the night as the temperature was dropping.

We then turned back and headed for the mud again. What gave us a massive mental boost was that everyone we now passed was behind us in the race. This was a strange experience but made us feel good. Before we got to the worst section of mud near Dorney Lake it got dark. This made it all far worse as our headtorches didn't pick out the definition of the mud. Add to this the fatigue of many hours on our feet and the pace slowed dramatically. It was very frustrating and mentally hard to be slipping about and picking our way around the wettest sections rather than just heading onwards.

The weather had been sleet and snow flurries all day, some rain but nothing too bad. It was bitterly cold though and whenever we got slowed by the mud we felt our temperature dropping. I didn't ever get teeth-chatteringly cold as I have done at times, but I was constantly chilly. This was just a miserable and unpleasant experience which we had to endure for the whole duration of the race.

We arrived back at Windsor at mile 48 and were served some warm food: a bowl of pasta which was gratefully received. I had the option of a change of shoes here but hadn't got any issue with the ones I was wearing so stuck with them. It was 8:30 pm and we were setting off into the night.

At this point I was bearing up well. My feet were sore, my legs and back were aching, I'd got some pain in my shins, knees and ankles and a few chafing issues but nothing to worry about unduly after nearly fifty miles. I'd started taking ibuprofen and paracetamol to dull the pain and was in good shape. However, things went downhill within a couple of miles of leaving Windsor, as my right ankle started hurting. Properly hurting. You get a lot of pain on long ultras and different parts hurt more at different times. What you have to do is distinguish the problems from the general level of pain noise. This ankle pain developed quickly and was serious. Within a couple of miles, it became an intense burning sensation right across the top of my foot and ankle. I tend to rate the pain on a one to ten scale as I go. The worst I've experienced was full-blown level ten on the Lakeland 100 so I have a good feel for the levels. This was a level seven or eight. Not an issue if we were at eighty to ninety miles but at fifty miles it was a serious problem. I had a look and my ankle looked swollen but it was hard to tell in torchlight. I loosened my laces right off and we continued to the next checkpoint at mile 54 where I'd have a proper look at it. I'd finished every race I'd ever done but this was hurting badly enough to make me limp; it was sufficient for me to be thinking that I might not make this. I was seriously worried and thinking of my options.

To add to the stress, another problem cropped up too. My trusty headtorch was going very dim. It had fresh batteries in it but was fading fast. The batteries were going after only three hours or so when they should last twenty hours. This was not a problem yet as I had a spare set but had it got a fault? I had a backup torch in my rucksack but that wasn't ideal because it burns a battery an hour as it's extremely bright and used for detailed navigation. New batteries revived the headtorch but I had no more. Brandon said I could have his spares later in the night if necessary. It would be a long night with about twelve hours of darkness and burning batteries at this rate wasn't going to see me through to morning. This was just another niggle to worry about and use the mental reserves up.

At the checkpoint, I had a good look at my ankle and thought that it might just be the tongue of my shoe rubbing, which over fifty miles had flared up. The top of my foot looked bruised. So I strapped up my foot and ankle with the bandage from my first aid kit, released my laces back an eyelet and kept my shoe very loose. It was an instant, miracle cure. The bandage padded it and sorted the problem. I went from a huge low to a huge high. Tiredness and darkness exaggerate all emotions on ultras.

We headed on down to Walton, where at mile 65 we would turn around again. It was 1 am and we had porridge and tea in the freezing cold. We were alone with the marshals and this was an absolutely magic experience and one of my most intense memories of this overnight run.

I have lots of blurred memories from running through the rest of the night. We were both shattered and at 4 am or so I was struggling to stay awake and kept dozing off on my feet. I was fighting sleep as the trail was easy to follow and I wasn't mentally stimulated. As we headed into Staines I saw a bench ahead. I told Brandon that I just needed to take a break for a second. So I lay down on the bench with my feet up on its arm, which was not comfortable, and I had a two-minute nap. I wasn't asleep, just eyes closed and resting. Two other runners came up at that time and I heard one saying, 'Get him up, he can't sleep there, he'll freeze.'

Brandon dismissed him with, 'He's ok.'

Two minutes was all it took and I was wide awake after that. The body is incredible and I just needed a pretend sleep to revitalise my brain.

We headed back off towards Windsor, with more mud, another change of headtorch batteries, legs getting more and more tired, more walking breaks, running getting slower but eventually it got light and we arrived at Windsor again for a third time. Somewhere we changed socks but I can't remember where. It's crazy on these long runs, you get so many intense memories of detailed things happening but can't necessarily piece it all together into a big picture afterwards. That's absolute dog-tiredness for you as you exist in a blur of pain and exhaustion.

We'd now covered 82 miles, with just ten miles to Cookham and then ten miles back again to be finished. It was 6:30 am, we'd been up all night and were at the actual race finish with a couple of guys already there who had just finished. This was very hard to get ourselves up from and get going again but the job wasn't done yet so off we went.

The last twenty miles were just a death-trudge through the mud. The wind was bitterly cold and we were wrapped up against it. It kept trying to snow, the mud was getting worse as we got more and more tired and the pain everywhere was getting bad. We made it to Cookham ok, got the huge mental boost of turning around for the last time and then just ground out the last section back to Windsor. The final few miles were agony. Every mile seemed like ten, every footstep hurt, I thought it would never end. We had one final trip through the assault course and we were finished in 27 hours, 23 minutes and 22 seconds. After 102 miles, we finished 38 seconds ahead of our plan, which was a quite amazing forecast with a planning accuracy of 99.96%. Awesome.

The feeling at the finish? Relief.

I had no highs, no excitement and no sense of achievement. Just absolute relief that the ordeal was over and that I could finally get warm and go home. The out-and-back course, lack of hills, headtorch problems, foot problem and weather made this event a pure grind from start to finish. It was very testing, very cold, very slippery and very, very hard. A lot of pain and a huge mental battle to get through.

For the fourth time in my life, I'd run 100 miles. It wouldn't be the last. However, it was now time to take on a different but equally difficult challenge, not in straight distance but in terms of the amount of climbing on the course. In August, Brandon and I had an entry for the Courmayeur Champex Chamonix (CCC), the UTMB's sister race in the Alps. We would be testing ourselves over the last 100 kilometres of the UTMB course in one of the hardest races in Europe.

We were done with flat 100-milers and were heading back to the mountains where we belong.

164 started, 87 finished, I came 64th. The race had a 47% drop-out rate.

19   It's not about the Bling

'I just felt like running.' (Forrest Gump)

For most of my life, I've not been a member of a running club. I've never had a problem motivating myself to exercise and to train for things I've wanted to achieve. I've always been happy running, cycling or hill walking alone. I've not really focused on road running which is the staple of most running clubs, far preferring to be off in the hills doing my own thing. I came into running from a mountain background, so my focus is different to that of the stereotypical runner. I'll always say that I'm not a runner, which causes amusement to others but it's just not how I see myself.

As I ran more road marathons and spoke to lots of club runners at these events, I realised that I'd like to be part of a club, as much for the social aspect as for the running. It would have to be local to my home so that I could make it work with my generally busy life. There were two established running clubs in Warrington but neither was actually very convenient to me in terms of location. There was another club in St Helens but again that wasn't particularly convenient. During 2014, I learnt of a new club that had started up and that met at my local pub, one mile from my house. I finally joined Warrington Running Club in March 2015.

The club is a local success story, having grown from nothing to over 450 members in the space of just three years. It comprises a great bunch of people, some big characters and is an incredibly friendly group. What I find great above all else, is the encouragement and support that everyone gives to each other. While running is a very natural thing to do, it's not necessarily easy, so the support of a club is very good for anyone less confident in their abilities or wanting to improve significantly. There is such a range of experience, backgrounds, abilities and focus on different distances or disciplines, that there is always advice and support available for everyone.

All members support each other to achieve their personal goals and improve, which is just fantastic. I love the encouragement that everyone is given, for anyone achieving anything at any distance and any speed. We're all different, our goals are all at varying levels and we should applaud anyone that sets out to improve themselves through running. This shines through at our running club like nothing else I've seen in any other walk of life. The sense of everyone willing every other individual on to improve themselves and achieve their goals is incredible.

Personally, I've had some very positive things said to me about my running and how it motivates or inspires others in the club. This shows the positive energy that the club radiates which can be so rare in the modern world. It's quite simply amazing to be a member of a group that is so warm, so supportive and so enthusiastic.

Being a long-term solo runner, I've developed my own methods, thoughts and perspective on running, which I thought was normal. However, since joining the club, I've realised that I'm not in the mainstream and that I have a different take on running to most other runners. It's been quite an eye-opener, so I've compiled my top ten areas in which I see things differently.

1: Running in a group. I've run with friends many times but to run in a club group is different. There's a camaraderie and competitiveness between individuals with a love for the same sport. There are Run Leaders, Run Assistants, sign-in forms and certain rules to abide by. There is also a certain etiquette such as pointing out hazards to others. Even to an experienced runner such as myself, this takes a little bit of adapting to.

2: Stretching. When I run alone, I don't stretch beforehand or warm-up as such. I just set off at a gentle pace and then speed up a bit after a while. When you're with a club you have these little rituals to go through, a bit of a jog round the car park with some high knees, sideways and other variants thrown in. It must look crazy to any passers-by. Then after the run, there's stretching to do, all standing around in a big circle, which is good practice but not something that I bother with when alone. It all adds to the running club experience so I don't have a problem with it, especially as it teaches good practice to newcomers to the sport.

3: Distance accuracy. When I run alone, I start my watch when I set off and stop it again when I get back. I'm not obsessed with numbers but I do log everything in a spreadsheet afterwards. I only record my distance to the nearest half mile. This is because in the old days of measuring maps, you couldn't really measure much more accurately than this with the traditional pencil-and-paper method or with a measuring wheel. So I'll record my mileage rounded up or down to the nearest half mile which is good enough for my purposes. The advent of GPS has brought a new level of accuracy that's great for tracking distance and speed while running but I think causes some strange side-effects. The first is the obsession with pin-point accuracy on the distance. I'll round up from 9.75 miles and down from 10.24 miles to give ten miles. So for me a 9.75-mile run is ten miles, even though it's a bit short. At other times I'll have run an extra half a mile at 10.24 miles to record the same distance. It all balances out over time. I've found that most runners record their distances far more accurately because their watches give them this ability. In extreme cases, 9.99 miles does not count as ten. It needs to be 10.00 miles to count. I've even know people running up the road for a few hundred meters to get the data up to the correct number. Not everyone is like this but my focus has always been on recording it roughly rather than precisely.

4: Time accuracy. Lots of runners stop their watches when we get caught at a road junction. I wondered what was happening when I first observed this, everyone bleeping their watches off and then back on again a few seconds later to eliminate the stopped time from the run time. I've never worried about this, as a few seconds here and there isn't going to make that much difference. In fact, in ultra running or running in the hills, minutes are lost at checkpoints, eating, navigating, toilet stops, or simply admiring the views. I understand why the Run Leader will do this to record the pace for the front of the group but it always amuses me.

5: FOMO. *Fear Of Missing Out.* This relates to having to enter an event because everyone else is, otherwise you have the fear of missing out and not being a part of what's happening. My take on this is that I don't enter an event just because other people are. I enter because I've chosen that race for myself, whatever that reason might be. I'll usually know my focus races a year ahead and then each autumn I'll plan the next year's races around other commitments such as holidays. I've never entered an event because someone's said to me that, 'Everyone's doing it.' I think that's part of the ultra mindset, maybe being selfish about what you want to do because you need that focus, you need commitment and a plan to keep you on track for the events that you want to be successful at. Conversely, I don't find much FOMO for the races that I enter, especially the 100-milers.

6: Support. I see running races as something that I do alone or with a partner for the pairs races and longer ultras. Even if I'm with a partner, then we'll be self-sufficient and just off doing our own thing in the hills. I rarely have support at a race and I don't need it. Clair and the boys have seen me finish a few marathons, as have my parents and Clair's parents. Beyond these few races though, the rest I've just headed off and completed. The running club, however, does things differently, they do it in style and it's just amazing to observe. If someone's running a race locally, members will turn out to support. The support crew will be decked out in the club's primrose and blue colours and make a lot of noise. There's an incredible camaraderie between club members and everyone supports each other wholeheartedly in each other's events. With my long background of solitary running in the hills, I'm not used to this. When I've run marathons with the club, it's always an incredible boost to pass the support crew at the roadside as they cheer me on. The club is about so much more than just the running.

7: Phones. When I go for a run, I leave my phone at home or in the car. When I run in the hills or run an ultra, it's safely in a waterproof bag at the bottom of my rucksack. On many trips to the hills, there's no reception anyway so the phone is completely useless. However, I've discovered that most people run with their phones which they use for music, photos and communication. How they do this without dropping or destroying them is beyond me. If I'm running, then I like to isolate myself from the world and focus on it. I think that one of the great advantages of ultra running is getting away from technology and living a simple existence in travelling from A to B under your own steam. I think I'm very old fashioned in this regard but I like the quiet time away from the distractions of modern life.

8: Training. In the traditional marathon training season during the spring, club runners across the country focus on their schedules. These are typically five or six days of running each week, focusing on increasing the long run each week, doing tempo runs, intervals, speed sessions, recovery runs, hill reps, something called Fartlek (I have no idea what it is) and all manner of other things. I don't like to use a specific schedule or even do the variety of training. I just go running. I'll focus on knocking out a few decent long runs along the way but I won't use a schedule. Brandon once said to me, 'As soon as a running schedule comes out, it gets too much like work and you've lost me.' I won't criticise anyone for taking this approach because it's a very successful methodology but it's not for me.

9: Injuries. This is a constant theme at all running clubs due to the nature of the sport. I've had my share of injuries along the way and when I'm injured I'll be out-of-action for weeks or even months. It amuses me when I hear someone say, 'I'm injured, I'll rest for two days, then I'll be back at full strength next week.' I think this is a terminology issue, as I'd class relatively minor injuries as niggles and I have these all the time. All my injuries stop me dead in my tracks and each time I think they're career-ending.

10: Medals. These get referred to as Bling. I run races for the challenge, the experience, the memories and the sense of satisfaction and achievement. I also run races to rack up the number of races I've done, for example in my quest to become a member of the 100 Marathon Club. I have quite a few medals and other mementos from races, such as slate coasters from marathons and fell races in North Wales, belt buckles from 100-milers, race numbers from some of my biggest races, magazine mentions, wristbands and punch cards. I keep all the memorabilia in a shoebox, with the exception of my first Lakeland 100 medal which I had framed because it took so much out of me and took me to a level I didn't expect to attain or ever expect to repeat. Most running club members love medals. Some will even only enter events that award them. Some race series award a medal for each race and then extra medals for doing multiple races or having done the event before, which are popular. I always enjoy receiving a medal. However, I would never enter or not enter an event based on whether it has a medal or not. For me, it's a nice by-product of the event, a nice trinket to take home and add to my shoebox. What I treasure more than any of this though, are the many fantastic memories that I've banked over the years, as well as the sense of satisfaction at having put myself through some big challenges and having achieved what I set out to do. I always say that I've got the stories to take with me to the old folks' home and that's what's important to me above all else. No one will believe my tales when I get there but I'll know what I did.

Clair is also a member of the running club. She thinks it's great for support, loves the club runs for mid-week motivation and takes part in races as part of a large group. She understands where I'm coming from with my observations because she knows me and my mindset so well. Clair runs with the club a lot more than me, while I go to the pub for a few pints and a chat more often.

Warrington Running Club is a quite amazing group of positive people. I love the club but know that I see things slightly differently to most members. I think that's ultra running for you, a bit different and slightly removed from the mainstream. I wouldn't have it any other way.

20   Big Mountains: Courmayeur Champex Chamonix
(August 2013)

*'A mountain race, deep into wilderness, with numerous
passages of high altitude (above 2,500 metres), in difficult
weather conditions (night, wind, cold, rain or snow), that needs
very good training, adapted equipment and a real capacity of
personal autonomy.' (Race Organiser)*

The Courmayeur Champex Chamonix (CCC) is part of the
Ultra Trail du Mont Blanc (UTMB) series of races run from
Chamonix in the French Alps. The main race itself is the
UTMB which is a 170-kilometre trail circuit around the Mont
Blanc massif, with 10,000 metres of climbing. This is known as
the toughest foot race in Europe, with debate as to which is
harder, the UTMB or the Lakeland 100.

The CCC is run over the last 100 kilometres of the UTMB
course by busing all runners through the Mont Blanc tunnel to
Courmayeur in Italy, then running back to Chamonix with 6,000
metres of climb. As a stand-alone race the CCC is one of the
toughest in Europe, equivalent to a less hilly 100-mile race. Set
against the full UTMB, you can be lulled into thinking you've
taken the easy option. You haven't; the drop-out rate of 30%
proves that.

Having completed the Lakeland 100, Brandon and I had the
calibre to take on the full UTMB but we'd opted for the CCC
to familiarise ourselves with the event, get a very hard Alpine
race under our belts and enjoy it more than we had the
Lakeland 100. It was a massive challenge in itself but would be
a useful recce if we wanted to come back for the UTMB in
future. This was exactly what we did when we ran the Lakeland
50 the year ahead of the Lakeland 100.

Sometimes with ultras, the logistics are more stressful than
the event itself. Registration for the race was on Thursday,
closing at 7 pm. I flew to Geneva and met Brandon there on
Thursday afternoon. Another friend, Mark, was doing the same

race and on the same flight as me. We then all had bus transfers booked to Chamonix. The luck of which bus company we'd booked with meant that Mark made it to registration (but only just) while we missed it. Now for the worrying part; nowhere did it say that we could register on Friday morning. We had to be on a bus to Courmayeur by 7 am so time was tight. None of the details had mentioned anything but I'd read somewhere else that there would be registration at 5:30 am on Friday. All we could do was head back to the sports centre the next morning and sort it out then. To cut a long story short, we got up at 5 am, spent a stressful hour or so being told various different things and eventually registered at 6:30 am after having got up an hour earlier than necessary, walked about for an hour with a full day on our feet ahead and consumed a lot of worry energy. It all worked out in the end but it wasn't what we needed before a big day out.

We headed to Courmayeur on one of the buses with the 1,900 other competitors. This is a massive race, the only bigger one I'd done at the time was the London Marathon. Ultras in the UK are generally limited to about 300 runners. The top priority here was to get through the toilet queues before the start, which is always the way at big races. The start itself was incredible. As there were so many runners, all heading onto a narrow trail after a few kilometres, the field was split into three and started at 9:00, 9:15 and 9:30 am, based on your predicted finish time. We were in the 9:30 am start. Timing was done by electronic chip on our rucksacks so we wouldn't lose those thirty minutes; our clock would start when we crossed the start line. There were 1,900 runners crammed into a narrow street, music was blaring, people were hanging off balconies, French, Swiss and Italian national anthems were played, poles were waved in the air. It was just fantastic.

As each third of the field were released we moved forward until we found ourselves one row from the front waiting for our start. More music, organisers dancing, crowds of supporters. It was the best race start I'd ever experienced, more of a party than a serious running event. Finally, we were off with a gentle run through the streets of Courmayeur, gradually climbing. Support was everywhere, with cowbells, horns, music and cheering. It was an incredible atmosphere to get us underway.

In the first few kilometres we bumped into Mark. He's a much faster runner than us and finished the Lakeland 100 the same year we had but five hours faster. We chatted and expected not to see him again until after the finish. The first nine kilometres were straight uphill, climbing 1,400 metres in one go. This is the equivalent of climbing Ben Nevis. Brandon and I stopped after a few kilometres to take a layer off, as we were getting hot. Just shorts and t-shirt were needed after the coolness of the early morning. Mark moved ahead here and all the way up the climb we could see his bright orange t-shirt a few minutes ahead of us. This climb was slow and tricky. It was nose-to-tail on a narrow trail and we all went up at the same pace. At times we had to stop and queue for rocky, technical parts but there was nothing that could be done. As we gained height, the views of the big mountains of the Mont Blanc Massif became spectacular and the air became noticeably thinner towards the top. A steady plod for just under three hours and we made the summit of Tete de la Tronche at 2,584 metres.

We then had a four-kilometre run down a ridge to Refuge Bertone which was absolutely spectacular. Mont Blanc was across the valley to our right, with a wall of snow, ice and glaciers descending from it. At times like this when it's easy running, warm weather and the views are incredible, you forget everything else and just enjoy it. This is what life is all about and times like this are very precious and make fantastic memories.

As we ran down here, all the runners were kicking up lots of dust due to the dry conditions. We were all getting filthy and I could feel it in my eyes, hair, teeth and everywhere else. We laughed that road runners would be horrified; we felt and looked like coal miners.

The race had a 26-hour time limit at the finish and cut-offs at various points en route. As we didn't know the terrain and hadn't recced it due to the location, we'd generated an arbitrary schedule to run on. Our initial estimate was 23 hours, which we revised to 25 hours when we got all the details through, almost the time for a standard 100-miler with all that climbing. The organisers had provided a fastest and slowest schedule based on previous years, so we took the slowest schedule of 26 hours, added rest time in and scaled it down to 25 hours. We'd know where we were against the overall time then. At Refuge Bertone we were eight minutes behind schedule after nearly four hours.

We refilled our water bottles, grabbed some cake and headed off. The next thirteen kilometres were along the side of the valley, gradually descending to the valley floor where at 26 kilometres was the first major checkpoint. There were lots of supporters here, cheering us through and we refilled bottles, grabbed bread, cheese, salami plus some chocolate and headed on. This formed a pattern; we found the checkpoints very hot and congested so went through them as quickly as we could. We were seven minutes ahead of our schedule at this point.

We then had five kilometres with 800 metres of ascent up to Grand Col Ferret at 2,537 metres. This is the equivalent of climbing Snowdon, in heat and at much higher altitude. We climbed strongly as the trail zig-zagged about but it became clear that others were suffering in the afternoon heat and after six hours or so of exertion. People were resting by the trail, some sitting down. One guy was heading back down. I saw someone bent double being sick, then a guy a few metres ahead of me stepped off the trail and vomited. Great stuff; big climbs always sort the men from the boys and we were strong up here. We caught up with two other British guys (we all had our national flags on our race numbers) and got chatting. Our conclusion was that these big climbs were tough but we were all going as well as anyone on this climb.

High up I could feel the thinness of the air. Everything felt harder than it normally would and I was slightly light-headed.

Brandon said he'd got a headache but nothing too bad. We were glad to reach the top which was also the Swiss border, not that I realised at the time. We had pulled a lot of time out of our schedule and were now 36 minutes ahead. Then it was a long, long descent down into a Swiss valley and the only valley running of the entire route. This was easy and straightforward, losing over 1,400 metres in height, a huge amount. It was hard on the legs though as downhills always give you a good pounding.

We lost ten minutes against the schedule on the downhill which set a precedent for the rest of the route. We'd gain huge amounts of time against the schedule on the climbs and lose most of it on the descents. This can happen when you run on someone else's schedule. As our schedule was taken from previous slow runner times, what it showed was that we were fast climbers but slow descenders. This was very visible as we shot up every climb but then had a lot of people come back past us on the descents. It doesn't really matter as everyone has different capabilities and I'd rather be a better climber as that's the mentally hard part.

While trotting down the valley, we came across Mark. This really surprised us as he should have been at least an hour or two ahead. When he saw us, he looked surprised too. We chatted, agreed how hard the two huge climbs had been and trotted along together until he moved slightly ahead again. We were heading towards a 500-metre climb up to Champex where the major halfway stop would be with some hot food. Neither Brandon nor I wanted to stay there for long but we both had sore feet and needed a sort out. We stopped in the valley on a bench overlooking an idyllic Swiss village and sorted our gear out, applied anti-chafe cream to feet and changed socks. I realised how dirty we were as my legs were black, with dirt ingrained into the creases in my arms, face and everywhere. This ten-minute stop was the only time I sat down in 24 hours and was worth its weight in gold. Fresh socks (brand new too) felt fantastic and we were both re-invigorated for the climb ahead.

We rocketed up to Champex, arriving as it was getting dark at about 9 pm. We saw Mark again here, who told us he was bailing out with the words, 'I can't take another twelve hours of this.'

Now this shows how much of a mental sport ultra running is. Mark is very, very fit. He's a much better runner than me and his race times are much faster. He finished the Lakeland 100 in 34 hours; I did 39. Today, for whatever reason, his mental strength was below par. The course was hard, he was slower than he expected and when he realised he'd be out for the best part of 24 hours he cracked. Physically, he could have finished the course, mentally he couldn't. Long ultras are incredibly hard like this. Running a road marathon, you're never more than a few hours from the finish and the suffering only reaches a certain level. On an ultra the time stretches endlessly in front of you, the suffering ratchets up and up, and if your determination drops even a few percentage points you'll drop out. It's no disgrace as just to start an event like this takes a whole lot of bottle, but today wasn't Mark's day and he knew it. He wished us well and off we went into the night, while he headed for a bus.

About a kilometre after Champex we stopped again to put on headtorches and thermal tops for the night. The weather had been perfect all day but running overnight always gets cold. Brandon then summed up the challenge ahead, 'Just three climbs of Snowdon to go.'

We were both tired, dirty, sore, with lots of aches and pains, and the finish seemed an immense distance away but we were in good spirits.

The first climb to Bovine was endless. We were in a train of people and just kept slogging up. It was dark so there were no reference points or things of interest to look at. It was just one foot after another, knowing it would take about two hours and watching my watch tick by as I went. All the overnight climbs were like this, endless route marches done at a decent pace in a train of others, following the feet in front. If we looked up,

185

we'd see headtorches endlessly above us on the switchbacks. When we felt we were much higher we'd look up again and they'd still be stretching way up above. When someone tired, they'd step out of the line and the rest would continue endlessly up. We never stepped out of line once on any climb; I'm very proud of this as in a world of tough little mountain climbers, I'm the toughest when it comes to grinding out a climb. Brandon too. When I was at the front, I'd be watching out for the reflective markers every 200 metres or so to check we were on track. This event is fully marked so navigation is not an issue. On the Lakeland 100, it's unmarked so you have to navigate yourself. This is one of the reasons why Lakeland 100 versus UTMB is debated as to which is the hardest.

The high meadow of the pass at Bovine was surreal. We could hear cowbells from a distance and just before the summit headed straight through a herd of cows. It was nearly midnight and we were meandering through them. Overnight ultras are always full of bizarre experiences.

The next descent to Trient was huge and never-ending in the dark. We could hear the Trient checkpoint from kilometres away. Blaring music, cowbells and cheers. We arrived at 1 am and a party was in full swing. The event buses spectators around to the various valleys and this village was rocking. There were cheers of 'Bravo! Bravo!' or 'Chapeau!' and once even 'Animaux!' All around us people were cheering and cowbells were ringing, before we headed into the calm of the checkpoint. There were at least two competitors throwing up outside and another throwing up inside the marquee. I've never seen so many people vomiting in one day before, which shows how hard the race is. Brandon commented that it was like a high school disco. The music was blaring and dazed competitors were sprawled about everywhere. We grabbed our usual bread, cheese, salami, chocolate and bananas and headed on.

Ten minutes later on the hillside above Trient, we could hear *Walk of Life* by Dire Straits blaring into the night. It was very apt and a crazy memory I'll remember forever. Then another massive climb in a train of feet. The guy in front of me had some music playing from somewhere which helped keep me focused. I followed his feet for about ninety minutes to the top. Then another huge descent and my legs were really tired by now as they'd had a huge pounding. My feet were incredibly sore and my rucksack was rubbing my back badly, but there was nothing I could do about any of this, apart from take painkillers and keep moving. The one guarantee about long ultras is that they pound you into the ground physically. It's a complete war of attrition on a decaying curve and if you're not mentally strong then you'll retire.

Vallorcine at 4:30 am was the same as the valley before with more music and support. I was feeling queasy here but knew I had to keep eating. The only thing I could face was bread so I took a few lumps of French bread and ate them as we headed off. We then had three kilometres up a decent track before the last major climb. This was easy ground and we didn't need to concentrate. The problem was we were both falling asleep on our feet as our brains weren't occupied. We were staggering around, crashing off each other and generally struggling badly. We knew that we just had to get along this track to enable us to snap out of it. It was only for about half an hour and when we got to the top of the section we stopped for caffeine tablets, gels and chocolate. We'd both been hallucinating too. I'd seen cats around the trail but it was just shadows moving in headtorch beams. Brandon had seen all kinds of nonsensical things, which kept us amused later on when he was telling me about them.

Then it was onto the final, big climb which was a never-ending monster. It was steep, narrow and, as it started to get light, I could see it winding between large crags on a very steep mountain-side. All tiredness was gone as we had to concentrate on moving up the winding trail. With tired legs it was ninety minutes of pure grind. However, the view from the top across Chamonix to Mont Blanc and the Mer De Glace glacier at first light was just breath-taking. From here it was across rough ground for a few kilometres and then a 1,000-metre descent to the finish in Chamonix.

Entering Chamonix, we were guided through the town by marshals and were cheered in all the way. This was an unbelievable experience after a night in the mountains. Music was blaring and the public address announcer hailed our arrival as we finished in 23 hours and 52 minutes. We were awarded our finishers' gilets, then sat on a kerb at the finish eating more bread, cheese and salami. We just enjoyed the moment, the sunshine, the mountains and the happiness of other finishers coming in behind us.

The French know how to do these things properly and they had beer and wine chilling in the fountain for finishers. My one regret from the weekend is I didn't have a beer sitting on that kerb at 9:30 am but you don't always make great decisions after missing a night's sleep and that amount of physical exertion. At one point, the public address announcer said, 'These finishers have run for 24 hours, over the Alps and through the night.' We'd done a good job.

We limped back to our hotel to assess the damage. I'd got very sore feet but only one blister, was stiff from head to toe but my biggest injury was my back. My rucksack had badly rubbed my lower back. Despite plenty of anti-chafe cream on the area to stop this, I had huge grazes which stung like mad. There wasn't much I could do about this, except wait a few days for them to heal.

After an hour's sleep in the hotel, we spent the day around Chamonix watching UTMB finishers come in. The atmosphere was incredible as we sat at a pavement cafe eating lunch with a beer and clapping them in. In the evening we ate at another square, sitting outside, and still the UTMB finishers were coming through. The next day after breakfast they were still coming in. That's the thing with big ultras, the field is spread over such impossibly huge distances that the finishing times are spread over many, many hours.

I'd rate the CCC as the second hardest thing I'd ever done.

The Lakeland 100 was the hardest by some margin but the CCC is comparable to other 100-mile races. It's arguably slightly harder because of the huge climbs but not by much. It's hard to judge these things.

So what did we conclude from the run? It confirmed something that we'd been talking about for a few months. We were ready to return to the Lakeland 100 for a second attempt. Entries opened while we were still in Chamonix and we both entered the 2014 race within the first few minutes of them going live.

I had said that I didn't need to do the Lakeland 100 again because I'd done it once before but, on reflection, I'd changed my mind. That event was absolute hell on earth and took me to my limit. It still makes the hairs on the back of my neck stand up when I think about it. I'd decided that I wanted to return, to take myself to that level again and test myself to my limit once more. If it went well, there would be only one place left to go.

The UTMB. It's hard to get an entry so might take a few years but it had a certain destiny about it. We now knew the event format and had recced the second half of the course. Would it be harder than the Lakeland 100? There would be only one way to find out.

1,910 started, 1,320 finished, I came 816th. The race had a 31% drop-out rate.

21   The Road to Hell

'Why couldn't Pheidippides have died at twenty miles?'
(Frank Shorter)

I've always said that I wanted to run a marathon. I said it when I was at school but I was too young. I said it again at university but I had too many other distractions. I said it again after I'd been working for a few years in my mid-twenties but I turned to the hills and spent my hours there bagging peaks. Running a marathon was a big target but I wondered if I would ever do it.

In November 2003, life changed when our first son, Kieran, was born. At first this didn't make too much difference to my activities, which were predominantly hill walking and cycling. However, slowly my available time to head off to the hills decreased and I was cycling or running more from home. While this wasn't a problem, it left me without any specific targets to chase, although I had an extra dimension to my life in terms of a busier family life. Then, completely unplanned and unknown, as with so many things in life, we stumbled across something that changed my focus.

In October 2005, when Kieran was just short of his second birthday, Clair and I left him with her parents and headed off to North Wales for a weekend away at a hotel. The plan was just to relax and have two nights away as a break. On the Sunday, we'd been out in Caernarfon and decided to drive the scenic route back through the mountains to return to pick Kieran up. As we drove through Llanberis, we were stopped to allow runners to cross the road. There was a big event taking place that had taken over the village. As we sat watching, we became aware that it was the Snowdonia Marathon, billed as the toughest road marathon in Britain. It's a 26.2-mile circuit around Snowdon, mostly on road but with some good track too. The big challenge is that it has nearly 3,000 feet of ascent on its route.

It was an epiphany. I loved the mountains. I loved Llanberis and Snowdon. I'd always wanted to run a marathon. I liked a challenge. Here was a marathon in the mountains, circling Snowdon, starting and finishing in Llanberis, that was Britain's toughest. Sitting there in the car, I had a calling. I knew that I would be running it the next year in 2006. It was as simple as that. I've never looked back since.

When we got home later that night, I looked the event up. I watched the website and found out when entries opened. In those days it was a form to fill in and post. Numbers were allocated on a first-entered basis. I posted my entry the day the form was available and received number 34. The first twenty numbers were reserved, so I was quick-off-the-mark and the fourteenth entry they received out of over 1,000.

I started marathon training on the 20th November 2005, eleven months ahead of the event. Effectively, I've been marathon training ever since.

Training for my first marathon was daunting. I'd done lots of big things before, particularly cycling. I'd had lots of big days out walking in the hills, including a number of days over twenty miles up to a maximum of thirty miles. A marathon, however, involved running for 26.2 miles, a non-stop, high-speed commitment to get to the finish. It was something new, something different and something completely energising to me. I threw myself into it 100% as I always do.

I started road running more than I was cycling. Only short distances of three or four miles but I was doing this four or five days a week. I was still hill walking and cycling but road running became something that I did religiously during the week. As with everything else I've ever applied myself to, naturally I overdid it.

I was slowly picking the distance up on the long runs in the early part of 2006. I also started fell running, which was as simple as converting my hill walking trips into ones where I ran the route rather than walking it. This is the classic route into fell running, where you build on a good, solid base of hill walking ability and mountain-craft skills, then start running on the fells in your mid-thirties, off the back of this firm foundation.

By June I was running distances of thirteen miles on the roads and similar on the fells without too much trouble. Then disaster struck. We were away on a family holiday in Devon and I was running and cycling while we were there when my right knee started getting painful. It became too painful to run on and I had to stick to the cycling. This was my first running over-use injury of which there'd be plenty more to follow in the years to come.

On returning home, I booked a physio appointment and it was confirmed that it was a re-occurrence of the problem I'd had before, when training to cycle from Lands End to John O'Groats. It was a cartilage problem in my right knee due to the running but was slightly different as it didn't stop me cycling this time. The recommendation was to switch to cycling which I duly did. With fourteen weeks to go, I cycled six times a week for the next eleven weeks in the build-up to the marathon and didn't run once. I then re-introduced the running and ramped up quickly. Within the space of five days I ran four, then eight and then sixteen miles, all of these runs at a sub-7:30 minutes per mile pace. I'm not sure how I did this after such a big lay-off and without years of running in my legs but I did. The training was unorthodox and most people wouldn't have run the race but I wasn't deterred and knew that I could do it. I was back and ready for the race.

My first marathon was probably similar to many other people's. It was all about getting round and chalking up the achievement of having run a marathon. I said that I might only ever run one, so this was my big day to achieve something that I'd always wanted to do. Due to the injury in the run up, I had no time target in my mind, although I knew that four hours was the standard good marathon target and would be an incredible time for a first marathon on such a hilly course.

I arrived very early on the day and was the first car in the car park. This is something that I still do at races today, arriving early so that I have no pressure from rushing there and then queuing for registration or toilets. Waiting at the start, I knew I was as well prepared as I could be, given the circumstances. I'd cycled the course twice in the run-up so knew it well. I knew exactly where all the drinks stations were and the distances at key points along the route. It amazed me to hear other runners talking about the event who clearly had no idea where the climbs were and what the course entailed, as it was far from flat. It was also along the quiet roads of Snowdonia where there would be minimal support. Mentally, I knew it inside-out and just wanted to be underway.

The event itself went well. My knee hurt slightly in the first mile but apart from that didn't cause me any problems. I ran steadily for the first half, up and over the Llanberis Pass, down the long descent to the valley and then along to Bedgellert. There's then a long climb from mile thirteen up to mile fifteen. This was a steady pull but my background in the hills served me well and I was overtaking others all the way up here. Then it was an undulating run all the way to mile 21, where the huge 1,000-feet climb up and over the shoulder of Moel Eilio begins. This was where the fatigue set in, but as I'd run comfortably for the first half and taken care to take energy gels every forty minutes or so, it was limited. I'd made good time all the way round and knew that I'd be able to finish in under four hours, although it would all depend on how much time I lost heading up this climb. The climb was tough after all those miles but I'd cycled it twice and also run up it before. Today I was down to a slow jog at times with some fast walking thrown in. I always knew how far up it I was because of the landmarks along the way, which was psychologically beneficial.

Once I was over the top, it was just a fast downhill back into Llanberis and a loop of the village. The course has changed in the last few years and this loop has been eliminated as it was a potential blow if you were unaware of it. I could hear the public address at the finish and almost see the finishing field but took

193

a right turn a few hundred metres short of it. I knew it was coming but two runners in front of me didn't. They both took the turn away from the finish and then slowed instantly to a walk as it dawned on them that there was still a mile to go. I overtook them and a few more on this final loop. This shows the importance of preparation and of knowing your event. Those that thought they were almost at the finish all took a big mental hit on this loop, while those that knew it was coming were prepared.

Snowdonia is a quiet marathon for crowds because the roads are only closed for the first four miles. There are always a few spectators at strategic places in the villages along the way but it's only at the finish where the crowds gather. The final run-in down the road and into the finishing field was fantastic with the crowds applauding at the barrier. Clair and her parents had come to see me finish and I picked them out as I ran in. It was an incredible feeling to know that I'd run all that way, especially after the injury and the severe lack of running in the build-up. My time of 3:44 was beyond anything that I could have expected too. It was something that I knew could never be taken away from me. I'd done it: I'd run a marathon and ticked that particular challenge off my list.

In the days after the marathon, I knew it wouldn't be my last. I'd enjoyed it and had put in a decent time for the course. While I wasn't really focused on time, I knew that I could do better if I did it again for a number of reasons. Firstly, I had trained in a completely unconventional way due to the knee injury. Secondly, I now knew the event and was completely familiar with it, so I'd be more comfortable knowing the routine next time. This was the first running race that I'd ever done so I now knew how they worked. Finally, and most importantly, was in my head. I knew that I could run a marathon. So any little doubts about my ability were removed. Next time I didn't need to worry about finishing because that would be a given. I could worry instead about pushing myself along towards a faster finishing time.

I entered the 2007 Snowdonia Marathon on the day the entry form came out. This time I took a different approach and trained just three to four days per week, mixing road running with fell running and cycling. This kept me injury free, motivated and is an approach that I've kept doing since. There were no issues or problems along the way and I improved my time by nine minutes to 3:35. A great result.

I was back at Snowdonia in 2008, now a veteran of two marathons, and I improved my time by another eight minutes to 3:27. I was over-the-moon with this because they say that Snowdonia's hills add about twenty minutes to your flat marathon time. In the years since I've confirmed this with the difference between my flat marathon best and Snowdonia best being 21 minutes. I knew that 3:27 would take some beating, as my focus was not chasing time on a road, although I needed to explore that concept a little further first.

With three hilly marathons under my belt, it was time to see what I could do on a flat marathon. I entered the 2009 Blackpool Marathon, which was the only flat road marathon in the North West at the time. I thought I might only ever try this once as I'm a mountain man, not a road runner. I stuck with my approach of training three to four times per week, mixing running with cycling and the gym. This was the only time in my life that I've had a gym membership, which I kept up for two years. I found that a good gym workout midweek, incorporating a spinning class worked well. However, I didn't go enough as I preferred to be outdoors, and the cost was averaging £18 per session so I certainly wasn't getting value for money and gave it up.

Blackpool is a strange town with its own unique style. A marathon comprising two laps of the seafront was always going to be a very different proposition to running a long loop around the beautiful roads of Snowdonia National Park. This marathon confirmed to me how one-dimensional road running is. I was there for one thing and one thing only: a fast time. I'd set two targets; my goal was to run 3:15 but I'd be happy with 3:20. I trained well through the winter and had good speed heading towards the race in April. Then I hit a problem that I had to endure for many races around this period: I caught a cold.

Our second son, Harry, was born in January 2007. Both Kieran and Harry were in full-time nursery and then school, so were exposed to the full range of diseases that small children spread. In 2009 the boys were aged five and two, so life was a perpetual cycle of colds and minor illnesses. I caught a cold ten days before what was potentially my one and only crack at a fast marathon time. All I could do was rest and try to recover, so I did no exercise for a full seven days prior to the start.

Conditions were perfect on the day, with cool temperatures and no wind. I wasn't fully over the cold but it could have been worse. I knew that it would affect me but hopefully it would just be in the last few miles and not have too much effect on my time. There were 634 starters which is a small field for a street marathon, where a town centre has been closed to traffic to allow the race to take place. At the start I was lined up one row from the front in the 3:15 to 3:30 start box. This was the first time that I realised that my marathon-running ability was actually quite good. If I could do sub-3:30 at Snowdonia and the start box for this time at Blackpool was right at the front, then I must be ok at this. This might sound naive but I'd not thought about it until that moment. I knew that I'd finished in the top 8% at Snowdonia but it was only when I stood on that start line at Blackpool that it struck me that there weren't many runners lined up in front of me.

This was where I went wrong and made the classic marathon-running error: I started too fast. The field was relatively small, I was still an inexperienced marathon runner, I was focused on getting a fast time and I was mixed in with runners capable of running times as fast as 2:40. It was inevitable that I'd get sucked along at a pace slightly too fast for me and I'd be unable to sustain it to the finish.

I set off at a pace of seven minutes per mile which I maintained for the first fifteen miles. I felt myself tiring after eleven miles but was running strongly with a group of about ten others so kept the pace up. This was where my inexperience caught me out. As the race was two loops of 13.1 miles, it was shared with a half marathon which started at the same time but did just one loop. Unknown to me, all the runners I was with were doing the half and not the full marathon. At thirteen miles they all peeled off into the finish while I was directed on. There was no one in sight in front of me and my motivation crashed as I realised that I had no one around me and was running too fast to maintain it. I'd gone through the halfway point in 1:33 but was definitely going to be slower for the second half.

I kept the pace until mile fifteen, then gradually slowed over the next seven miles to eight minutes per mile. Despite the cool start, it was now warm and I was hunting out shade to keep cool as I was working at my limit the entire time. Each mile became an endless slog against the clock, just counting the minutes down to the next mile marker. It was soul-destroying, ploughing away against a ticking clock which was the only measure of success in this flat race. There was no scenery, no hills, no variety in the terrain and no navigational challenges to broaden the experience. It was an awful experience, completely one-dimensional, me against the clock.

After 22 miles, I hit the wall. I was pushing and pushing but had nothing left to give. My pace slowed to nine minutes per mile and there was nothing I could do to improve it. I was calculating finishing times in my head but by now I didn't really care. It's a horrible experience to be chasing down a time when you're spent, the clock's ticking and you've got to keep pushing yourself, trying to speed up to get to the finish faster.

I gave it everything in those final miles as this would be my best marathon time and my only attempt at doing a fast, flat time. This game wasn't for me. I came into the finishing straight and saw Clair and the boys who'd arrived to see me finish. I crossed the line in 3:20 which was my secondary target. I was finished with flat marathons. I'd hated every minute.

As Clair drove me home, I sent Brandon a text with my

time. His reply congratulated me on a great time but then he summed up road running with an expression that I now repeat often, 'Chasing fast times on a road is just nonsense.'

How true.

I texted back to say, 'If I ever enter a flat marathon again, shoot me.'

I was done with flat road running and didn't think I'd ever run another one as the whole experience was awful. My time of 3:20 was an acceptable one to retire on and I was happy with it. I was slightly disappointed not to have run 3:15 because I'd started too fast and the cold must have been a factor, but I wasn't disappointed enough to enter another. I was wrong on it being my last but it would be three years before I hit the flat roads again.

I was back at Snowdonia in 2009 and 2010, running solid times of 3:35 and 3:30 respectively. I'd now run this race for five consecutive years, with my last four times grouped closely between 3:27 and 3:35. I was consistent over the tough course. I skipped Snowdonia in 2011 because it clashed with the OMM but would be back in 2012. Before that, I was back on the flat roads because I'd been successful in getting a London Marathon place.

Once I'd run a few marathons, a question I was frequently asked was, 'Have you run London?' While Blackpool told me that I wasn't interested in chasing flat marathon times, I realised that I'd like to run London once for the experience. London is hard to get an entry for because of the demand for the 40,000 places. I wasn't fast enough to qualify for a Good-for-Age entry at the time and charity places required fundraising of over £2,000, which I felt would require too much commitment to achieve. I wasn't a member of a running club, so a club entry wasn't an option. The other route was to enter the ballot for a place, with a one in seven chance of success. I was lucky and got a place through the ballot at my second attempt.

The build-up to London was problematic because I was suffering from pain in my left achilles tendon. I'd been running well through the winter but had done more running than cycling and had been pushing my speed. The result was that in the five weeks running up to the marathon, I only ran once and that was just six miles. Once again, I'd trained by cycling and took a full fortnight's rest before the day. With hindsight this was a blessing because it meant that I had no time expectations on the day. I was focused on enjoying the occasion and the atmosphere because it would be very different to the Snowdonia and Blackpool marathons that I'd experienced so far.

Brandon had got himself a place too, through his running club. There are multiple starts but we were both at the same start and in the same starting box as we have similar marathon times. Brandon had run the Brighton Marathon the weekend before in his fastest time of 3:22, so he was out to enjoy this one too. I met him on Greenwich Park beforehand and we lined up at the start together. The agreement was that we'd start together but there was no commitment to run together. We'd meet up after the finish.

It was a perfect day for running, a cool start but it would warm up as the race progressed. We ran together for the first fifteen miles before I faded and Brandon pressed on to finish in 3:27, while I came home seven minutes later in 3:34. Brandon had run two sub-3:30 marathons in a week, an incredible achievement. For me, time wasn't important on this day, as it was all about the experience and the memories.

If you're ever going to run just one marathon, then make it London. It's such a great day and worthy of its status as a special event on the UK's annual calendar. It involves more effort than a local marathon because you have to collect your race number the day before, so requires an overnight stay. It's worth it though as it's an incredible thing to be a part of.

Crowds line the entire route. They might be thin for the first few miles but the pavements soon pack out beyond that and the support is amazing. The crowds make a lot of noise and this really encourages you to keep smiling and just to enjoy the whole experience. Running through Greenwich and past the Cutty Sark with Brandon was a wall of noise and a brilliant experience. A few miles later we crossed Tower Bridge, passing the Tower of London and the experience was similar. To be running through these world-famous landmarks with Brandon, when we'd had so many days alone in the hills together, was such a contrast to our usual events and we both soaked it all up. Just before halfway we saw the leaders heading the other way through Shadwell. These were the best athletes in the world and they were flying. To be able to run in the same race as the best in the world and to see them en route is fairly unique in the sporting world.

Docklands was a mix of contrasts. Some sections were quiet as I ran around the bottom of the peninsula, but weaving through Canary Wharf was a cacophony of noise with the huge numbers of spectators here. Brandon was ahead by now and as I ran towards Billingsgate next to a giant banana, I came across a giant apple bent double, throwing up at the side of the road. The whole event is a bit mad. Clair, the boys, my sister and parents were all watching near here and I managed to spot them in the crowd from across the street. Brandon was more clued-up than me and had high-fived them all as he passed a few minutes earlier.

Running through Shadwell where the race doubles back on itself is a great section. Runners about seven miles behind me were heading the other way. Obviously these were slower runners and a lot were in fancy dress which London is renowned for. It also made me realise how big the event is because the road was packed in both directions with runners with widely different time expectations and this would be the case for a significant length of road.

Once you're back past the Tower of London for the second time, it feels like you're heading home. There's then an underpass that's very quiet with no spectators where you're all alone for a short while. As I ran through here, there was a runner on the ground, being attended to by St John's

Ambulance personnel. This distracted me with thoughts of his well-being as I emerged back into the bright sunshine onto the Embankment. The noise and brightness of the daylight took me completely by surprise. It was as if I'd emerged at Wembley stadium into the roar of the crowd. It was incredible, very moving and the closest I will ever come to experiencing the big match atmosphere that a professional athlete does. I wasn't expecting it and was in awe of the crowd, the bright light and the wall of sound that I'd suddenly burst into.

The run along the embankment was noisy all the way, quite an emotional and inspiring thing to be going through. Then the run-in to the finish is perfect, past the Houses of Parliament and through Parliament Square, down Birdcage Walk along the side of St James's Park and then turning in front of Buckingham Palace, past the Victoria Memorial and into the finish on the Mall. It's a very special run-in to finish off a very special race. It is as good as the hype and one not to be missed. I was pleased to have experienced it and have added it to my bank of memories.

Later that year, I was back at Snowdonia, running my course best time of 3:26, eight minutes faster than my flat London time. This seems illogical with the climb to deal with, but it was one of those days you occasionally get where everything drops into place and I flew round, never once in any trouble.

A year later in 2013, I was unable to run Snowdonia due to a family holiday. I decided to enter Chester instead, which was a relatively new race on the country lanes south of the city on the Welsh border. I did 3:25 and thoroughly enjoyed it. I'd matured as a runner since the hell of my first flat marathon at Blackpool, was less time-conscious but more focused on just putting in a good solid performance. This seemed to be an approach that suited me and made me keen to run a few more marathons around my ultras.

So in 2014, I ran five marathons, all in good, solid times and achieved two new personal bests amongst them. Manchester 3:12, Liverpool 3:21, Chester 3:11, Snowdonia 3:33, before finishing the year off with the Liverbird Marathon on New Year's Eve in 3:26. This last one was a lovely, small event, doing four laps of Otterspool Promenade on the River Mersey. There were only 140 runners but it was great running up and down, with high-fives and seeing the gaps to the front runners increasing and then lapping the tail-enders on the fourth circuit. It was a great day out, although I was too tired later to see the New Year in. Earlier in the year, Manchester was notable, not only in that it was my fastest marathon at the time, but it is the closest that I've come to running that holy grail of marathon running, a negative split. This means running the second half of the course faster than the first. I ran the second half just 53 seconds slower than the first, which pleased me as much as the time itself. The other key thing about this Manchester time was that it qualified me as Good-for-Age for London for the first time.

In 2015, I also ran five marathons. First up was Manchester, where I ran a personal best of 3:05 on a perfect day for marathon running. Then just seven days later I was at London again, this time starting from the small Green Start with the other Good-for-Age runners and the celebrities. It passed the time watching the celebrities being interviewed on television before the start, although the toilet queues were far worse than at the mass start I'd been at a few years before. I ran 3:13, with my standard London fan club of Clair, the boys, my sister and parents, who I managed to spot on the first pass of Shadwell. Clair has a bright pink coat which is easy to spot in crowds and this is the key to seeing your supporters, something bright and distinctive that you can spot from a distance. I didn't realise it at the time but I was in the form of my life and these two back-to-back marathons will stand as my greatest pure athletic achievement. I ran both races in a completely laid back way, put no pressure on myself and I just flowed through both of them. I'll never repeat it. It was one of those times where everything aligned and I was flying without trying. The day before London, I'd been to Portman Road on a corporate ticket to be wined and dined and watch Ipswich Town play Nottingham Forest. The evening before both races I'd drunk half a bottle of red wine to relax. I think this proves that if you relax and slow down, you will actually go faster. I'm not sure that alcohol is recommended in many marathon training books but it's an approach that seems to work for me.

After my greatest athletic achievement in April, the rest of 2015 was then ruined by injury. I had a summer with almost zero road running, so ran a personal worst at Great Langdale of 3:53 in September. This is a lovely race, one to rival Snowdonia with its scenery and amount of climbing. It's two loops of the Great and Little Langdale valleys and was the smallest field of any marathon I've run with only 85 starters. There's a half marathon that starts simultaneously, so it's a true race of two halves, the first being with plenty of other runners who are running the half. Then for the second loop you're mostly alone and just have the glorious Lakeland scenery for company. I loved it, despite the worst time, which didn't detract from a fantastic day out.

I then regained some road running speed and put in a solid 3:22 at Chester, before rounding the year off with another personal worst at Snowdonia a few weeks later of 4:00. It had been a roller coaster of a year on the marathons. A personal best and two personal worsts but what a rich learning experience, going through both the highs and the lows. I became mentally stronger for it. It amazes me when runners are always expecting a personal best at every race. How can this be? If you've reached your full potential then you shouldn't ever be able to get near it, unless everything falls into place as it had with me on a number of my marathons.

I won't ever beat my 3:05, even though it dangles precariously close to that magic three-hour mark. I'm happy with that time and even happier that I consolidated it at London a week later. I doubt it's down to pure athletic ability but more likely it's down to my unusual methods and the relaxed way in which I approached both races. I know that 3:05

is good because other runners have asked for my training methods, been jealous or reacted as a Chinese business colleague did, with the words, 'You must be professional athlete.'

However, a 3:05 marathon time doesn't define me. I'm an ultra runner, I care not for times. I was perfectly happy with my long-time marathon best of 3:20. Don't get me wrong, I'm very proud of my 3:05, but I'm more proud of the fact that I can run 100 miles, no matter what the finishing time.

Marathon running has proved a useful distraction to me, but I'm a mountain man and I love the hills. The thought of pounding the streets, chasing the clock over 26.2 featureless miles, is abhorrent to me but I'm good at it. In many ways I wish I wasn't because I've suffered a lot of injuries in the process. I think I've given it a good shot, knocked out some half-decent times and experienced the big city marathon on a number of occasions which is the draw of all club runners. I've always said that, given a choice, I'd pack road running in tomorrow if it jeopardises what I want to do in the hills, whether that be running ultras, fell races or just trotting about bagging peaks. I didn't think it would ever come to this but effectively it has. Since that glorious week in April 2015, when I ran those awesome Manchester and London times, I've suffered a series of debilitating injuries. The speed and the pounding caught up with me in the end and so, for that reason, I'm out. I will no longer chase fast times over 26.2 miles of featureless tarmac because I keep hurting myself. On the one hand, it's a decision taken with sadness. On the other, it's an easy choice to make as I've achieved what I wanted to at this discipline.

Brandon sums up marathon running the best. 'It's just training for bigger things,' he says.

'Chasing fast times on a road is just nonsense,' should be a quote that he becomes famous for.

Personally, I see it as a necessary evil, as the easiest way to run is on a road. For me though, there's no getting away from it, road running is one-dimensional, tedious, boring and drives me to injury. In a strange way, I've enjoyed having a good crack at marathon running and think it's the one discipline where I've come closest to achieving my true potential. If I was results-driven, then it's the area on which I should focus above all others. In other ways, I hate it for what it is and the way it draws everyone in. The hills are my true love and the ultras are my true calling, so that's what I'm going to focus on.

The marathon is nothing but the road to hell.

22   Grind: Fellsman *(April 2014)*

'When you're going through hell, keep going.'
(Winston Churchill)

Events don't get any better than the Fellsman. They say ultras are just, 'Eating and drinking contests with a bit of scenery and running thrown in.' Nowhere is this more apt than at this race. The organisers even send a menu as part of the pre-race pack and describe the event as, 'One long picnic.' If you don't mind a bit of hardship, it's worth entering for the food alone.

2014 was my fourth time at the Fellsman. It's a circular route through the Yorkshire Dales, starting at Ingleton and looping around to finish at Threshfield. It takes in two of the famous Yorkshire Three Peaks, as well as multiple other peaks along the way. It covers 61 miles with 11,000 feet of climbing, a lot of that over pathless moorland and at high-level. It's tough underfoot, requires good navigation as it's unmarked and is very exposed to the weather. It's a classic, old-school event without any of the frills of more modern ultras. It's very tough but also very rewarding.

The route starts and finishes in different locations. As the event centre is located at the finish, the organisers bus all competitors over to the start. This makes for an early rise, as we needed to register by 5:30 am, before catching our bus. Brandon stayed at my house on Friday evening and we were up at 3 am on Saturday morning to drive over to Yorkshire. This wasn't ideal when we'd be out running all night but was better than trying to sleep at the event centre or any other logistical arrangements.

Unfortunately, I had a terrible night's sleep beforehand. Even though I'd done the event three times before and should have been relaxed, for some reason I just couldn't sleep. This is often the case with big events or challenges as the excitement beforehand stops your brain from switching off. There's not much that can be done apart from trying to relax and rest, without getting stressed over it. I didn't doze off until about 2 am so didn't get much more than an hour's sleep. At least I'd been lying down and resting so I was physically rested even if not mentally so.

After the bus delivered us to Ingleton, we had the kit check to get through. This is a very strict affair, as is the case with many of the big mountain ultras. The kit list is very specific and every item is checked. There's always a lot of debate as to why items are required, how to cut corners and how to minimise weight. My view is that if it's on the list, then just pack it. Anyone with mountain experience is used to carrying a rucksack so a few extra grams of weight shouldn't be an issue.

Then there's the relaxing part of the Fellsman: hanging around in the hall, waiting for the start. Inevitably we'll see a few people that we know and it's a good time to catch up. A couple of cups of tea and then out onto the field for the pre-race briefing and we were away at 9 am.

Nearly 400 runners swarmed across the field towards two exits onto the road. It felt like the charge of the infantry as we all spread out across the breadth of the grass, a shambles of bodies released after hours pent up on buses and in a hall. We squeezed onto the road and started climbing out of the village, heading onto the trail towards our first objective, Ingleborough. This is a fine peak, the best in Yorkshire and many people's favourite anywhere. The approach from the south is a decent trek in, with a stiff climb up the rocky front to the summit. It took precisely an hour in the rain, with mist clouding the top and a cold wind blowing. We were wrapped up warmly and the forecast promised improved weather as we headed through the morning.

A trot across the rocky top and we descended down the very steep path to the flatter ground below. This part of the race is always frantic, with lots of runners together racing across and down. It's a false economy as there are another 55 miles beyond this and the risks of a fast descent could easily write the day off with a slip on steep ground. One or two runners were impatiently barging past on the path or careering down, just off to the side. We just patiently trundled down with the majority. It might cost a few minutes but what's that when spread over a full day?

At the bottom, we didn't stop at the checkpoint, except to clip our Tallies. The Fellsman Tally is a collector's item. It's a thin plastic disc, about six inches in diameter, with all the checkpoints around the outside, mileages, heights and a schematic of the peaks in the middle. I was carrying it around my neck on a length of string, stuffed down my top. At each checkpoint I'll fish it out and the marshal clips the relevant box on it, much as a train conductor clips a train ticket. After the event, it's posted back to you, effectively as a finisher's medal. In 2013, we ran overnight with a triathlete who'd completed three Ironman triathlons. He regaled us with stories of chipping ice off Salford docks so they could train and other great tales of his triathlon sufferings. In the early hours, with us all struggling, he turned to me and said, 'When I get home, my Ironman medals are coming off the mantelpiece and this Tally is taking pride of place instead.' High praise for the event indeed when coming from a multiple Ironman finisher.

We climbed up onto Whernside where the wind was screaming into our faces. This peak is always windy but it was only a quick out-and-back to the summit, before heading down into Kingsdale. We grabbed flapjack and biscuits here, then were subjected to a random kit check. This was a nuisance as it meant unpacking my rucksack to root out the items that they wanted to see. The rules are the rules though and it was the same for everyone.

The weather was definitely improving now as we climbed roughly up the open hillside to the next peak of Gragereth, to be followed by a long, exposed run northwards along the ridge, eventually dropping across rough footing into the beautiful village of Dent. This was the first checkpoint with proper food and we enjoyed warm sausage rolls, beans, bread and butter, washed down with a cup of tea. Everyone carries a mug and a spoon. There's a certain amount of cross-contamination goes on, as the mug gets used for everything, in this instance baked beans and then tea. It's all part of the fun and the tea tasted great.

It was 2:30 pm and we'd covered twenty miles. On any other day, this would be a big day out already but we were only a third of the way. The valley was sheltered and the sun had now come out, so we ran on and headed up the long, steady climb onto Blea Moor. Once on the moor, you have to leave the good footing of the track and head straight across tussocky ground. The cloud had lifted so we could see across and navigation was straightforward. We hit the checkpoint then headed off into the valley for pasta and sauce, with bread, butter and cheese, finished off with cake and of course tea. This is arguably the day of the year when you drink the most cups of tea, as it's on tap at every checkpoint.

Then it was a big climb and a demoralising out-and-back onto the peak of Great Knoutberry, followed by another off-path trot around to the road at Redshaw for hotdogs with onions, tomato soup, banana and more tea. I don't ever need to eat much of my own food on the Fellsman as we get so well fed.

We were over halfway but the tough terrain was taking its toll and my legs were heavy. At least the weather was settled, still cool, but the wind had dropped and it was going to be a dry night. We navigated the next few sections across two more peaks to arrive at the road at Fleet Moss just before 8 pm. This is my favourite food stop with stew, rice pudding and fruit salad.

We were grouped here. This is a peculiarity to the Fellsman that some love and some hate. For the overnight section, you're grouped with a minimum of three other runners for safety. The second half of the course has some difficult and indistinct sections to navigate, where solo runners who are not good navigators could get into serious difficulties on very exposed ground in the dark, hence the grouping. Your group must stay together until you're released at a later checkpoint once it gets light again. There are time cut-offs at each checkpoint in the evening and, as they come into effect, all runners afterwards must be grouped. Grouping isn't a problem in my experience, as the runners around you are about the same pace, so hopefully you should all travel through the night at a similar speed.

As we prepared to leave the checkpoint, the marshals gathered up two other runners for us, George and Ben. We were given a grouping card that had to be submitted at each checkpoint until we were ungrouped in the morning. We left the marquee and made our introductions as we headed off into the night with two strangers. What became clear over the next hour was that Brandon and I were the strong navigators and had the knowledge of having done the race before, while the other two were less so and didn't have the local knowledge of the ground. George was the stronger runner and Ben was a steady and reliable team-mate who could keep up easily and was good to chat to.

We headed onto the most feared section of the route in the last hour of daylight. This is Fleet Moss which is notoriously boggy and awful to cross. However, we knew that if we headed south for a quarter of a mile, we could pick up a wall and skirt the edge of the boggy area, although we'd have to pick up a bit of height again as we got further along. George was trying to push the pace along from the outset, which I didn't like, as we had a myriad of walls and pathless ground to navigate across and speed would only cause us to make a potentially serious error. At one point, he was in front and had stopped for me to catch up, with Brandon and Ben following up the rear. As I drew up to him, he asked where we were heading to next. I pointed ahead and said that we were heading over the brow of that hill, half a mile ahead, where you could just see another pair going over it. He replied, 'Ok,' and set off at ninety degrees from where I was looking. He'd been looking at the opposite side of the valley to where I'd been pointing. This was worrying.

As we headed towards the end of daylight, George and Ben

got ahead of us and I quietly said to Brandon that we needed to be very careful with the navigation and not let George lead us astray. Brandon agreed as he'd also observed worrying signs. Shortly after this we let our guard down and had a major crisis on our hands.

Brandon and I had navigated us through the series of walls onto the edge of the moor using map and compass. It had got dark as we'd come through here, so we'd all now got our headtorches on. We left the last wall and contoured around the hillside to an obvious stream. At this point we knew exactly where we were and needed to navigate approximately three-quarters of a mile south across the open moor to the next checkpoint, which would be two marshals in a small tent who would be difficult to see until close by, although they'd have a light with them.

As we emerged onto the moor, both George and Ben whipped out GPS units and said they'd get us to the checkpoint. GPS is banned at many races but not here. Neither Brandon nor I use it as we're both competent map and compass navigators but it does have its uses, especially on indistinct open moorland in mist or darkness, like we had now. I was getting really tired already and was pleased for someone else to take over. As George led the way with his GPS in hand, all seemed fine. Ben was having trouble with his and put it away. We moved slowly across the rough ground with George calling out distances to go. It should have taken about twenty minutes to reach the checkpoint but time seemed to be dragging on. George was saying that it was 400 metres to go but seemed perplexed that we weren't getting any closer. It always seemed to be 400 metres to go. It then dawned on me that we were on the top of the moor, when we should have been skirting the edge of it and so should have been able to see the lights of isolated farms down in the valley to our right. We couldn't. I realised that we were out of position but I hadn't been paying attention to my map or a compass bearing, so I had no idea where we were.

We were completely reliant on George and his GPS which was still reading 400 metres to go. Ben got his GPS out but confessed that he didn't really know how it worked. All we could do was keep going. I was fully alert now but getting really frustrated as we were wasting time and I was too tired to be adding extra distance tonight. As we headed on through the darkness I was wondering how we were going to relocate ourselves as it was a pretty featureless moor.

Then we got lucky and hit a wall. If we'd have been a few hundred metres to our left, we'd have missed the end of it and kept going miles off course. I instantly found the wall on the map and could tell where we were within a few hundred metres from the flatness of the ground against the contours on the map. We were about half a mile past the checkpoint. I took a compass bearing for it and we started backtracking, knowing that we should see the headtorches of other groups coming straight towards us. True enough, after five minutes or so we saw a group and ten minutes later we were at the checkpoint.

We'd recovered the situation but had added a mile and lost about half an hour in time. It could have been a lot worse if we'd have missed that wall. It soon became apparent what had happened. We'd been moving past the checkpoint a quarter of a mile to the left of it. The GPS was reading correctly that there was constantly 400 metres to go because we were sailing straight past, with it 400 metres to our right. I learnt a valuable lesson from this: don't trust anyone else's navigation but my own. In reality I knew this from my experience on mountain marathons and fell races where following others can lead you off course but in my fatigue had failed to apply it tonight.

Now we had the toughest section of navigation of the whole route. Two miles straight across the moor on a compass bearing, picking up a wall halfway. Brandon and I were now attentive and in charge of the navigation. The terrain got significantly worse, with deep peat groughs to drop in and out of. Brandon, Ben and I were sticking closely together but George was always at the limit of our vision and we had to trust that he was still with us. It was worrying but we eventually all came back together and the ground improved.

I could see lights miles off in the distance but my vision was blurring them. I thought they must be a TV mast or something similar but I didn't remember seeing them on previous races. Eventually my vision refocused and I realised it was the checkpoint lights only a few hundred metres ahead. It was such a relief to have crossed this difficult section and now have a good path from here to the next major checkpoint at Cray, where we arrived at 11 pm. We had vegetable soup with bread, butter and tea. This warmed us ready for the real night-time running.

The next section over Buckden Pike was fairly straight-forward, navigating our way on small tracks and all keeping closely together, to arrive at the next road checkpoint at 2 am. Hot chocolate was gratefully received before pressing on to the final climb of Great Whernside. As we headed up towards the top of the climb we got into the cloud, with visibility down to a few metres. The top is flat and indistinct with no paths, so we were relieved to find the marshals on the top without any problem. A bit of confusion and miscommunication then saw us very nearly head off the top at ninety degrees from where we wanted to go, but luckily we caught it before we'd gone more than a few metres. Sheer tiredness was affecting my ability to navigate clearly but we were heading towards easier ground and daylight was only a few hours away.

After running along the top, we had some indecision again before finding the right fence to drop off the moor on. As we headed down the long, easy descent, I was struggling badly with fatigue and was lagging a long way behind the others. I was dozing off on my feet and stumbling about on the tussocky grass. I just couldn't snap out of it and couldn't get going with any speed. I'd had enough by now, with the navigation difficulties, the mist and my poor night's sleep from yesterday all catching up with me. It really didn't help that the other three were all trucking along nicely.

We eventually hit the path at the bottom and the last seven

miles to the finish would all be on paths now. It was getting light but I just couldn't wake up. Brandon and George were running ahead and I was following with Ben. He was great, he just kept pushing me along with a hand on my back to keep waking me up and steadying me as I fell asleep and wobbled about. He was amazed that anyone could fall asleep while running as he'd never seen it before. I was all over the place and going through hell but I'd been in similar situations before and knew that I'd eventually snap out of it. If Ben wasn't there, I think I'd have taken a nasty tumble somewhere as my eyes were closing for long periods on the easy track. It was the worst sleeping episode I've ever had but eventually I got through it as we headed into the final checkpoint where we'd be ungrouped.

My legs were agony and I was struggling to move very well but we all left here with no commitment to stay together. George strode on ahead; Brandon, Ben and I trundled along until Ben told us to go ahead as he needed to slow down. The pain in my legs was unbearable as we descended the road but there wasn't far to go now. Down to the bottom and up the other side into Threshfield and the school where the event is based. It was 5:41 am and the only people who saw us finish were the two marshals manning the finishing table. We'd finished in a time of 20 hours and 41 minutes. We were relieved of our Tallies, congratulated and given a token for breakfast. A completely understated finish for one of the toughest events in the country but that's all part of its appeal and what makes it special. I was shattered and barely able to move.

We hobbled to the car, hobbled to the showers, hobbled back to the car and then hobbled in to get breakfast. Everything was 100 times the effort it should have been. I was like a zombie at breakfast and could hardly talk. I'd run further before but this had really taken it out of me today.

Despite this, I needed to drive us home. The event specifically asks that you don't do this as it's so dangerous. However, there's no other option unless you involve other people. We returned to the car, wound the front seats back and slept for an hour or so, right there on the main road. I've done this many times and keep airline eye-masks in the glove box of my car for this very purpose.

The drive home was only ninety minutes but I was still tired. We stopped three times to break it up, walk around, get some fresh air, eat some chocolate and get home safely.

By mid-morning I'd dropped Brandon at the train station and was tucked up in bed for a few hours' sleep, as I was absolutely good-for-nothing otherwise.

The Fellsman is an awesome event. It has none of the razzamatazz of other more modern races but stays true to its long history and is, quite simply, a very, very hard slog over a significant distance. I love it.

383 started, 285 finished, I came 178th. The race had a 26% drop-out rate.

23   A Marathon's a Sprint

'Everything in moderation and nothing in excess. Except ultra running, which by its very definition must be in excess.'
(Anon)

Although I do a lot of running, I don't see myself as a runner. I see myself as a mountain man. Others find this strange because I'm known to friends and family as Martin-the-Runner, Marathon Man, or similar but it's not the running as such that I enjoy the most. It's being out in the hills and moving efficiently across them.

I've never run any of the traditional road races that regular runners have and most running club members will have racked up many times before. I've not done the standard 5k, 10k or half marathon races. This often amazes people as much as some of the tales of my longer distances. I'm often asked, 'How can you run a marathon without running a half?'

I'm just not interested in running road races over short distances. I've come into the sport through hill walking and cycling, with running being added as another element. I would give up all running on roads to enable me to cycle and go to the hills. It's just not where my focus is or where my passion lies. I know that I will never run a half marathon or a 10k. They're just not on my agenda.

So when talking about running to non-ultra runners, I can have some odd conversations where the other person looks at me as if I'm daft. This is all down to perspective because unfortunately I can be quite blase about distances and the time I'm out for. I always describe a marathon as a sprint to the amusement of others. I've done events that last through two nights while a marathon takes less than four hours, so you can see that it's down to perspective.

To try and understand this, you can look at the data from my races. If I take every race that I've ever run (I haven't skipped any to make it look better) then I've run seventy races, at an average distance of 43.4 miles, with an average climb of 7,771 feet, an average finishing time of 12 hours and 21 minutes and an average pace of 17:06 minutes per mile.

Compare this to a flat marathon of 26.2 miles with zero climb, with my average finishing time of 3 hours and 19 minutes and an average pace of 7:35 minutes per mile.

While running a marathon, my heart rate monitor estimates that I've burnt off 2,300 calories with an average heart rate above 160 beats per minute. On the Lakeland 100, that same heart rate monitor estimates that I've burnt off 16,000 calories, seven times as many, with an average heart rate of less than 110 beats per minute.

This is why I call a marathon a sprint. It's relatively short and the pace is flat-out, more than double the speed of my average race pace. So, for me, it's akin to a sprint, an eyeballs-out effort from gun to tape, for a relatively short period of time.

While I know that 26.2 miles is a long way to run and I wouldn't ever dismiss or belittle it, I'm just looking at it from the opposite direction to most runners. Most runners will have an average race distance substantially less than 26.2 miles. Their average race pace will be faster than their marathon pace due to the shorter distance. For me, my average race distance and pace are significantly longer and slower than for a marathon. So I have the opposite viewpoint and my race data shows that.

My approach to a marathon is completely different from my approach to an ultra. I'll focus on a big ultra for months ahead, knowing that I have to get myself completely ready for it: logistically, mentally and physically. I'll have planned my schedule and booked any travel arrangements a long time in advance. I'll have packed all my food and gear about a week in advance. I'll be reviewing maps and race details constantly in the week running up to the event. I'll be going to bed early and relaxing consciously in the last few days as I head towards it. This is to give myself the best possible chance of completing the event. This whole process involves getting myself mentally ready, completely focused and in-the-zone. When the week of the race arrives, I have tunnel vision because ultras need that level of focus.

For a marathon, the process is different. There's no gear to prepare in advance as it's just running kit plus a few energy gels in a bumbag. There's no race route or time schedule to review and logistics are typically much easier because they are usually local. There's no sleep deprivation to deal with and no concerns about driving afterwards as you don't get that exhausted. So the build-up process for me only really starts a few days beforehand. My laid-back approach to them also means that I'm not getting myself mentally prepared for them in the same way as I do for an ultra.

The best example of how committed I am mentally to an ultra is the 2016 High Peak Marathon. I'd done my usual preparation and was well organised with a week to go. All arrangements were made, my gear was packed and I spent the final week reviewing the route to re-familiarise myself with it as it was two years since I'd last done it. The weather forecast was for cold weather and the possibility of some snow. I was prepared for that, with plenty of warm clothes packed, over-mitts and ski goggles too. The event starts at 10 pm on Friday night. By Thursday, the forecast was for snow in the North of England during Friday. The weather deteriorated on Thursday evening with a significant amount of sleet and rain at low level in the North West. On Friday morning, it was snowing and the roads were treacherous. I heard on the travel news that the Snake Pass in the Peak District was closed due to snow. This is the main road through the centre of the event's 42-mile circuit and the access route for the marshals to the checkpoints. It is also the only means of exit in the event of an emergency. At 10 am, the event organiser gave the heads-up that they were assessing the situation, that there was a significant risk of cancellation and it would depend on the roads. At midday, the event was cancelled as it would be unsafe to proceed because it was still snowing heavily in the Peak District and there was no chance of the Snake Pass being re-opened to traffic that day.

All the way up until the final cancellation, I was mentally committed to the event. Even when the heads-up was given that they were assessing the situation and it was likely to be cancelled, I was still 100% committed to the race. In my mind, I have to be. There's no other way. I'm doing it 100% up until the point where it's called off, because if it were to go ahead I need to be in the right frame of mind. The result of this was that when it was cancelled, I was floored. I'd focused on this race all winter as my first of 2016. I'd got myself prepared for it and committed to it, even if conditions were going to be extremely testing with poor weather. When it was cancelled, it was as if a rug had been pulled from underneath me. It felt as if I'd failed, which might seem illogical given that it was outside of my control. Suddenly, the thing that I'd built-up to and was about to start, was gone. I didn't know what to do and found myself at a loose end. It surprised me how down I felt that afternoon. My reason for being that day had been taken away from me and it was a very strange feeling. To have committed so much mental energy to that race and then have an eleventh hour cancellation was far tougher than I could ever have imagined.

I know that I wasn't alone in being knocked down by this cancellation. All logic would say that we should be pleased that a race that was going to be run in horrific conditions would not go ahead. John sent a text that said simply, 'HPM cancelled. Damn.'

Brandon sent a text that said, 'In London with a big bag of winter kit and non-refundable train tickets. Gutted.'

We had all built up to it and been flattened by the decision to cancel it.

I've skipped races before due to injury but that's been my decision and means that I haven't committed to the mental build-up. While disappointing, this doesn't flatten me in the way this did. I've had to run a shortened course at the Mountain Trial in 2011, due to very bad weather. This was disappointing but at least we ran something and it's a smaller event anyway.

The cancellation of the 2016 High Peak Marathon was a big blow that day. If it had been a marathon, then I'd just consider going out for a decent length training run instead. However, this was a fifteen-hour, overnight commitment. Instead, I went for a short forty-minute run just to get some fresh air and that was it. I'd got no energy or enthusiasm to do anything more. That night I slept for nine hours straight through. Considering I was supposed to be awake all night running, this seems crazy. I think my mind was geared towards the event and then sub-consciously switched off and needed to rest.

This is where I think there's a big difference between road running and ultras. Ultras require a much broader focus, more preparation and a far greater commitment in the lead-up. There's no hiding from the challenge and a turn-up-and-run mentality would leave you very exposed to not making the finish. You can get away with it on road runs but ultras can bite back if you're not well enough prepared.

An interesting area where perspective plays a part is back in daily life, when some fairly frequently-heard expressions are used. For example, you will often hear someone say, 'My feet are killing me.' What I say next might sound unkind but until you've run ultra distances, then you've not experienced foot pain. A race that takes nearly forty hours requires you to be standing upright for almost the entirety of that duration. Blisters and chafing will make the problem worse. Feet that shoot pain on every footstep, that feel like they're on fire or that feel like you're walking on razor blades, could possibly be described as killing you. An afternoon round the shops is unlikely to get you to that level. Another common expression is, 'I'm shattered.' Again, at the risk of sounding unkind, ultra running raises the bar somewhat. Try two nights with no sleep. I've been awake for over fifty hours straight on four separate occasions. Being shattered is when you're so tired that you can literally fall asleep while running or standing up, being so tired that you're hallucinating or simply so tired that you could cry. It's another level and beyond anything that you'll ever experience in the normal day-to-day world. This is part of what I love about ultra running, taking myself to the limits of what my body can endure because everything else in life seems tame and less of an issue by comparison.

I'm often referred to as an ultra runner but what's the definition of an ultra run and who can label themselves an ultra runner? The definition of what defines an ultra runner can be debated for many hours. If I had to define an ultra, then I wouldn't just define it on the standard definition of being more than 26.2 miles. I know this is the accepted definition and it needs to remain that way as it's unambiguous. However, I find it very one dimensional and races as short as 27 miles on roads are technically ultras. While this is ok to the letter of the definition, it doesn't embody the spirit and ethos of ultra running which has a different mindset and outlook to running sub-marathon distances. I would add to the definition that it has to be run on trails, include hills and involve night running because this adds the variety that makes it into an adventure, rather than just a running race. I've been told that this is an extreme view but it's how I personally think of ultra running through my experiences and therefore how I would define it. For me, it's an adventure in the hills where I'm self-sufficient, that lasts through the night, with all the challenges and experiences that this brings.

I think that anyone who has run an ultra of any distance has achieved something incredible because I know first-hand how hard ultras are. However, at what point do you become an ultra runner rather than just a runner? Personally I think that it's mindset, rather than down to any hard-and-fast definition. So if you've run ultra distances multiple times and your focus is on covering long distances in the great outdoors, rather than hitting fast times on the roads, then that's good enough in my book.

With an average race distance of over 43 miles, average finishing time of over 12 hours, running over harsh terrain, mountains and having completed 24 overnight runs, I think I'm justified in calling myself an ultra runner. For that reason I will always look on marathons as sprints but that's simply about perspective.

24   Once More: Lakeland 100 *(July 2014)*

*'The event requires competitors to be experienced ultra
distance runners with excellent navigation skills. Before
considering an entry, consider the preparation, consider the
hours and consider what it takes to complete the Lakeland 100.
If it was easy, it wouldn't be an achievement.'*
(Race Organiser)

I have a rule when finishing a tough physical challenge: never
say, 'Never again.' When I finished the Lakeland 100 in 2012 I
broke that rule and said, 'Never again.' It took me to my
absolute limit and tested me to destruction but I came through
it to finish. The pain and suffering of the event were immense.
Then physical recovery saw legs still swollen two weeks later,
shooting pains in my left shin for three weeks and it was six
weeks before I could run again. Mentally, it took about a year
to have any fond memories of it. So why attempt it again?

Simple. I needed a big challenge. Why not take the hardest
challenge I'd ever completed and do it again? Knowing how
horrific it was would drive me to train harder and prepare even
more thoroughly than the first time. Unfortunately, that's how
my brain works.

This was also the acid test for whether I should enter the
UTMB. If the Lakeland 100 destroyed me once again, then
maybe I should keep my limit here. If not, then the UTMB
would be the next logical step. It was an important weekend
and I was ready for it.

Once again, I found myself in Coniston on a hot, sunny
afternoon, chilling out with Brandon and attempting to keep in
the shade out of the sun. The forecast was for temperatures in
the high twenties, so it was going to be a testing weekend. We
spent the afternoon relaxing before the pre-race briefing,
conserving as much energy as possible, before assembling for
the singing of *Nessum Dorma* by an opera singer at the start
line. At 6 pm we were off.

We started close to the back of the field and had a slow run through Coniston to the cheers of the crowd. This was a strange experience because it was exciting, but we knew that it would be two days until we returned again on Sunday morning, a very sobering thought. We both just remained very calm and didn't get carried away by any hype.

As usual, we had a schedule to monitor our progress, based on the split times that we achieved in 2012. We would monitor how we were doing against the time cut-offs en route and against our previous finishing time of 38 hours and 47 minutes as we progressed around the route.

The first seven-mile leg over to the Duddon valley was straightforward, although a decent climb of nearly 2,000 feet. It was hot but we just took it steadily. I had three water bottles with me but had only filled two before starting as water is heavy to carry. I drank most of it before the checkpoint as we were sweating loads. We lost seven minutes versus 2012 due to the heat but at least it was evening and surely it had to start cooling down. At the first checkpoint I drank a load of water, refilled the two bottles, took some biscuits and moved on.

The next leg was seven miles through plantations and open fell, over the shoulder of Harter Fell and into Eskdale. This section is notorious for being wet and boggy. This is not an issue on a short day out but on a long event wet feet gives trench foot after many hours and your feet then blister horribly. However, we had two things that went in our favour here: the critical forest section had been recently felled, then the recent warm weather had allowed the newly exposed ground to dry out. With some careful picking around any wet patches we kept our feet dry. This gave us a massive lift, although the heat was still a problem and we were losing lots of fluid through sweating. My two bottles were dry by the checkpoint. It was now nearly 10 pm but it wasn't cooling off much. I drank another load of water, refilled the two bottles again, ate some cake and off we went.

The next leg was over to Wasdale past the notoriously boggy

Burnmoor Tarn. It got dark soon into this leg, so we donned headtorches and were chatting to two Geordie lads we'd met at a few events before. They'd done the event the year before but had bailed out at 89 miles in bad weather; they were determined to finish second time round. Our luck continued on this leg as the bogs were dry and we managed to pick our way around them and not get wet feet. This was looking good, although we were now seventeen minutes down due to the heat.

From this point onwards, I carried three full water bottles out of every checkpoint, as I knew I needed to be drinking a lot. From Wasdale, there were the two large passes over into Ennerdale and then Buttermere. Headtorches were strung out into the distance and high above us on Black Sail Pass as we headed upwards, a spectacular sight with the stars above. As we climbed, a theme started becoming apparent; I was feeling queasy and many people around us were too. We caught up with two runners who we'd met at another recent event. They weren't feeling too good and were struggling. It was apparent that everyone was finding it very heavy going due to the heat. It was past midnight but we were all in shorts, t-shirts and sweating loads. I knew my queasiness was due to dehydration, as I'd not taken a pee for a few hours. I focused on drinking every few minutes and replenished two bottles from a stream high up on the pass. By taking some gels, eating salty nuts, a salt sachet and drinking five bottles of water, I was feeling much better by the time we got to Buttermere. It was clear that I'd only get through this heat by working very hard on keeping hydrated.

At 2 am, I thought I was losing the plot when I could see two vehicles with yellow flashing lights across the valley in Buttermere. I was trying to work out what they were and asked Brandon, 'Are those gritters on the road?'

He'd been watching them too and replied, 'Yes, they must be gritting the road to stop it melting.'

Things were clearly serious, as councils very rarely do this and only ever in the hottest weather. It showed how hot it was and worried us for the huge duration that remained, confirming that keeping hydrated needed to be our top priority. At least I was peeing again, although I was still dehydrated from the colour. This is the only measurement system to judge whether you're drinking enough in the heat.

Heading out of Buttermere was the long climb up to Sail Pass. I was leading the way but had a train of headtorches strung out behind me. There were a couple of people throwing up on this section and one guy who was retching continuously. Thoughts were turning to survival now, as it was still only the first night and all the signs confirmed that the heat was starting to take its toll on our fellow competitors. My focus was just to keep drinking as these guys wouldn't be going too much further.

Part of the challenge of the Lakeland 100 is the navigation. I knew the course well from the previous time, as well as many recces and the Lakeland 50 sister race. I can navigate any sections I'm not sure about using the map and road book they provide but others are less prepared. As we dropped over the col, there were lights up on the fells above. At first I thought they were stars but then realised they were headtorches. I said to Brandon that it must be a group of six people not related to our event as they were well off course and going the wrong way. He commented, 'Who else would be up here at 3 am?' This was a good point. As we descended the other side, two runners dropped down to the track just ahead of us. They'd got lost and had simply gone much too high up.

It was now getting light and we dropped down to the next checkpoint at Braithwaite, stopping to change socks on a bench in the village before heading into the checkpoint. We had a nice surprise here as John was helping and was really pleased to see us. We had pasta, rice pudding, a chat with John and then were off again.

The next two sections were uneventful around to Dockray where we were four minutes behind schedule after 49 miles.

Mark, who'd been on the CCC with us, was watching here with his daughter as he was on holiday in the Lakes. He'd completed in 2012 so knew what we were going through. This was another mental boost, although I apologised for being four minutes late. Then we were off to the midway point at Dalemain where we had our drop bags and another friend, who'd also finished in 2012, was helping out. John was here now as well and they both commented how fresh we were looking. John was superb, running around after us, getting food, filling bottles and keeping us motivated. I had a full change of shorts, t-shirt, socks and shoes here to freshen up, as well as replenishing food into my rucksack. It was baking hot but off we set for the back half of the course.

The first troubles started soon after. We had a hot climb up from Pooley Bridge. Due to the slow pace and the heat, we both started falling asleep even though it was only 2 pm. If anyone had seen us, they'd have thought we were drunk, staggering about and bumping into each other. We were all over the place on this climb, really struggling and neither of us was mentally with it at all. The only option was to keep plodding up until we could start to run again to wake ourselves up. As soon as we crested the top, we managed to get moving more efficiently and became wide awake once more.

The next problem started showing soon afterwards. My stomach was churning due to the effects of drinking so much water, eating high energy food and constantly moving. This was unpleasant but there was very little I could do about it, apart from soldier on. My feet were getting sore too so I'd started taking painkillers to take the edge off. On long ultras, the suffering always ratchets up but all you can do is keep moving and keep managing yourself. They say, 'One doubt and you're out,' which is completely true. If any one of these things get on top of you and starts playing with your mind, then you won't finish. It's essential that you blank them out and do whatever you can to turn the negative thoughts into positive ones. This is easier said than done but demonstrates why ultra running requires so much mental strength, as well as the physical ability to simply run the course.

We ran all afternoon and evening through Fusedale, Mardale, Longsleddale and into Kentmere just after dark. The heat remained all day until evening when it started raining. A tired body is very susceptible to temperature changes and we were instantly cold and had to put waterproofs on. We were veering from one extreme to the other due to sheer fatigue. We were trying to ensure that we kept moving and didn't let discomfort factors like this get to us which is not easy when you're so tired. At Kentmere we had a good sort out to revive ourselves and set ourselves up for the second night, including some hot food and smoothies. There were some runners on the fifty-mile course retiring here and one looked very bemused as she watched me take two ibuprofen, two paracetamol and four caffeine tablets. The look on her face was a picture.

We headed off into the second night with another runner, who kept us company until Ambleside. As we climbed up the rocky Garburn pass, I was navigating and leading the way but in the small pools of our headlight torches, there wasn't much to keep the brain occupied and we all started dozing off. All we could do was try to keep talking to keep ourselves stimulated and get to the top. We woke up on the run down the other side to Troutbeck. We stopped in a doorway here so I could change headtorch batteries and Brandon could repair some blisters on his feet. It was 1 am and the residents were blissfully unaware of the activity occurring on their doorstep.

Then it was another small climb and descent into Ambleside at 2 am, where John was waiting for us again. We questioned whether he ever slept as he was appearing at all times of the day and night. This checkpoint was very hot and we just slumped down shattered. John got us soup and bread, filled water bottles and offered encouragement. There were people crashed out asleep everywhere, some retiring but others napping before proceeding. It was like a war zone. It didn't look like any of our fellow competitors would be leaving here anytime soon but we were ready for the final push. We'd completed 89 miles with sixteen remaining, only another eight hours to go.

We then had another climb over Loughrigg Fell and into Langdale. We were getting closer to the end now but the pain in my feet from blisters was increasing and we were both shattered. The army say, 'No one's ever died from blisters,' although I think I've pushed my luck over the years. My entire body hurt: I'd got some large grazes from my rucksack rubbing, all my muscles were sore and every movement was getting increasingly more painful. However, we were still moving at a reasonable pace and certainly in far better condition than we had been on our previous Lakeland 100.

Brandon navigated this section and I struggled to recognise it, even though I'd recced it only a few weeks before. I knew which section of the race we were on but I had absolutely no idea whereabouts we were on that section as I didn't recognise any of the details. Such are the effects of extreme fatigue and darkness. This also shows how easy it is to make a navigational error on the second night as your brain just isn't functioning correctly.

We then dropped onto a flat section of easy path that was awful. We were both constantly falling asleep while moving. Brandon suggested finding a bench for a sleep, which seemed a good idea when we were simply dead on our feet. In reality, this was a very bad idea but neither of us had the mental capability to think correctly. I saw a bench instantly but it was just a hallucination from the bracken and torchlight. As we moved along, all I could see on both sides of the path were benches and patio furniture, loungers, chimineas and parasols. It was as if I was running through the furniture section of a garden centre, with comfortable chairs and other outdoor items everywhere. Later on I kept seeing cartwheels and gates, then animals moving about, especially frogs, mice and snakes on the path and people hunched over at the side. These hallucinations seemed very real at the time but didn't really worry me:

cartwheels and gates were just bushes, frogs and mice were leaves, snakes were sticks, people were large rocks. Brandon mainly saw people sitting there, although he mentioned a roast dinner somewhere too. It's another world when you're deep into a long ultra, your vision is going, your brain is sparking incorrectly and the fatigue is causing havoc with the messages going from your eyes to your head. You really have to experience it to believe it. Someone once said that, 'When you are 99 miles into a 100-mile running race, your brain is not the same brain you started with.' It's very true.

Onwards we staggered, day broke again and we reached the penultimate checkpoint at Chapel Stile at 94 miles. This was a large marquee with sofas, a big fire going and music playing. It was very welcoming and it was all real, not a hallucination this time. We slumped down, had soup and tea and rested for ten minutes. There were a few others in a bad state here but we wished them well and headed off for the final push.

We headed on through Langdale, a blur of foot pain and fatigue but every step got us closer to the end. We were down to the last few hours of pain but my stomach kept churning away and I'd given up eating anything between checkpoints as I couldn't stomach any energy food, although I was still drinking. At 7 am we reached the final checkpoint at Tilberthwaite at 102 miles. There was just the final climb up, then the rocky descent into Coniston. We could still run, although it was agony by now and we just needed to be finished. We ran through the village and down to the school. We passed another runner here and slapped him on the back in congratulation. We shook hands between ourselves on the run-in and I could feel the emotion welling up in me. A year's work and I was going to deliver the result. Then the icing on the cake: we turned into the finish line and there was John with camera poised as we crossed. Amazing. He was so pleased for us, he shook our hands and congratulated us. He said he never had any doubt about us completing it again. We'd finished in 38 hours and 26 minutes.

A marshal took us into the hall, announcing, '100 finishers.' There was huge applause, to which I gave a sheepish wave, then received my medal, t-shirt and a till receipt of split times. We slumped into two chairs utterly drained. I looked at the receipt and couldn't read it as my vision was so blurred. I just thought, 'So this is what it's like if you need glasses.'

If I looked at a solid object, it appeared to be shrinking. The whole world was on the verge of spinning and I was unable to focus on anything. To say that I was exhausted is a gross understatement. I was beyond shattered. Someone I knew came across to congratulate us and shake hands. Ten minutes later, two more that we knew finished, more hugs and handshakes. Everyone was just pleased to be done with it.

Then the evidence of how mental a sport ultra running is. Despite having run into the finish strongly, I could hardly get out of the chair. All life had exited my body because I no longer had any reason to keep going. I'd spent hours mentally pushing a physically battered body along but when the goal had been completed I was spent. Hobbling to the tent took ages. Removing clothes and getting showered was a slow, painful process. Then into a sleeping bag for ninety minutes' sleep. I woke up feeling fantastic as I was no longer feeling sick for the first time in about twenty hours. I could hardly move but that was the price to pay for a hard job done well.

I'd coped well with the Lakeland 100 this time. The conditions had been good underfoot but the heat had added a different challenge to overcome. I had drunk about 30 litres of water on the race, a quite incredible volume, but it had been essential to keep myself hydrated. I'd coped well with the long course and had never struggled to the same level as I had on my first completion. This confirmed that I was competent operating at this level, on a race requiring a double overnight. I'd become comfortable with the awesome size of the challenge and was ready to continue.

A decision was made there and then: the UTMB beckoned. I wasn't done with this game by a long shot.

306 started, 192 finished, I came 139th. The race had a 37% drop-out rate.

25   An Occupational Hazard

'Tough times don't last but tough people do.' (Anon)

One of the unfortunate aspects of most sports is that you get injured occasionally. With running this can happen frequently, with statistics saying that 70% of club runners will pick up an injury each year. I've had my fair share of injuries over the years and every time it's an incredibly frustrating and potentially depressing period because it stops you doing what you love.

In my experience, injuries fall into one of three categories, based on their cause. These are overuse injury, trauma injury or event injury. However, whatever the cause, they all have the same effect of stopping or reducing my ability to run and get out into the hills.

The first type of injury, overuse injuries, are the common running complaints that are well documented everywhere and common language at running clubs the world over. They are caused by the repetitive action of running and a particular part of your anatomy telling you that it's had enough for now. They appear out of nowhere with a few warning signs that you never see at the time, become niggles which you ignore and then, before you know it, you're injured. I've had quite a few in my time, including stress fracture, shin splints, tendinitis and joint and muscle pain. For me, they usually occur after sustained periods of road running, when pushing the pace, as I do when training for a road marathon.

My theory is that trail and fell running might appear to be more severe on the body but they are actually less so. This is because the terrain is mixed, the pace varies and it includes uphill, flat and downhill. This results in the whole body working, feet hitting the ground at different angles and the varying pace giving variety to the load being put through the legs. For road running, the opposite is the case. Every foot strike is the same, the pace is fast and the resulting load through the body is high. This eventually catches up with me and results in an overuse injury.

My three worst overuse injuries and their causes are:

1: Stress fracture of lower fibula in 2015, caused by road training for autumn marathons.
2: Achilles tendinitis in 2012, caused by road training for the London Marathon.
3: Inflamed knee in 2006, caused by road training for the Snowdonia Marathon.

So the pattern for my overuse injuries is clearly road running, focused on maintaining a fast pace during marathon training.

The second type of injury, trauma injuries, are those caused by an accident or mishap. The main difference with trauma injuries from overuse injuries is that you know you've done them immediately. If you've fallen and had an impact which is causing pain, then you obviously know that you've done something to yourself. Trauma injuries typically cause swelling, bruising, cuts, grazes and other visible signs of the injury. While they can be quite debilitating in the short-term, if they are only superficial injuries then recovery can be in days rather than weeks.

My three worst trauma injuries and their causes are:

1: Knee and shoulder injuries in 2015, caused by a bike crash on a road.
2: Knee and elbow injuries in 2009, caused by a trip while running fast downhill during the Snowdon fell race.
3: Shoulder injury in 2010, caused by a heavy fall during the Saunders Lakeland Mountain Marathon.

The theme for my trauma injuries is a fall onto hard ground, with the parts of the body that have taken the impact sustaining the injuries. What is also different from other running injuries is that the injuries can be sustained to the upper body rather than the legs, due to your arms being used to break the fall.

The third type of injury, event injuries, are those that occur during a race and that you would normally stop running on to prevent them getting worse. However, as you're focused on completing the event, you continue to the finishing line, making the injury worse. In my experience they are overuse injuries that surface during a long event, typically as pain and swelling and that you have to cope with to complete the event. They could be considered a combination of overuse and trauma. Although the root cause is typically an overuse injury that was unknown to you, they become visible during an event in the way a trauma injury does, so you are in no doubt that you have the injury.

My three worst event injuries are:

1: Severe shin pain and muscle bruising in 2012, sustained during the Lakeland 100.

2: Severe shin pain in 2015, sustained during the South Downs Way 100.

3: Inflamed tibialis anterior tendon on the top of my right foot in 2013, sustained during the Thames Path 100.

For all three of these injuries, the recovery method and period was the same. They were all sustained during 100-mile races, so I was expecting a fortnight afterwards with no running to recover, even without an injury. This meant that as soon as the injury was sustained, I rested immediately because I was expecting to. I then just had to extend this rest period further. For all three I rested for six weeks and then was ok to run again.

For the most common running injuries, which are overuse injuries, I find that I go through five stages from the start of the injury to full recovery.

Stage 1: Denial. As a person who has always run, walked or cycled long distances, I've always suffered from niggles. These are little aches and pains that come and go: stiffness, soreness, tweaks, twinges, things that hurt at times. It's never enough to stop me doing anything but enough to feel it and wonder what's going on in that part of my anatomy. A fellow ultra runner summed it up to me once by saying that ultra runners will always have niggles. The difficulty then comes in knowing when a niggle is a niggle or when it's something slightly more serious that you should be paying attention to and correcting. So the first sign of an injury normally results in denial that anything is actually wrong as I always think it's just another niggle.

Stage 2: Acceptance. When a niggle becomes a bit more persistent, then at some point I will cross over the line into accepting that I've got an injury. I find that I start to reduce my training, slow the pace down or take a rest from running. At this point I will be trying to identify the problem through my own research or past experience. This stage is frustrating because I've accepted that there's a problem but have not yet identified how to deal with it and get back to normality. The point at which I finally accept that I have an injury is on a run where I effectively take the view that it's kill or cure time. I'm not sure if this is the best method but it's the point in my mind where I know that if the run doesn't go well, then I'll move onto the next stage. I've learnt that the key is to move through this whole stage as quickly as I can as it's the most demoralising. In this phase, I can see no end to the problem and have no plan to recover. Generally, the best way to do this is to seek the professional advice of a physiotherapist.

Stage 3: Diagnosis. If I've had an injury before, then I may be able to self-diagnose the problem. If not, then self-research and the advice of others is easily available but can often be misleading. A physio appointment is worth its weight in gold here. I will get a diagnosis of the problem, advice on recovery and an approximate timeline for the recovery period. I've seen a lot of different physios over the years and have always found them to be good at diagnosing injuries and setting me on the path to recovery. So my view is that as soon as I know I've got a problem then I'll see a physio.

Stage 4: Recovery. This is the turn-around point in any injury. Once I have a diagnosis, then I'll have some method of rehabilitation and advice on how to recover it, plus some timescales. Generally, it will involve reducing or eliminating any running, as well as some rehabilitation exercises to stretch and strengthen the relevant parts of the anatomy. While still

236

frustrating, at least I am now working on recovering from the injury and can constructively work on getting back to running fitness. I usually do a lot of cycling during the early recovery phase to maintain my fitness, while avoiding all running and concentrating on the rehabilitation exercises. Once progress is made, then I'll gradually reintroduce some running, slowly and carefully. I'll do an initial test run of about twenty minutes at a slow pace. Then I'll leave it a few days and repeat, building the time up to an hour but always at a slow pace. Dependent on the nature of the injury and how I feel, this can be quite a quick process of sometimes only a couple of weeks. The key is that I've always maintained my aerobic fitness through cycling, so simply need to get my legs back to running again, rather than starting from a low fitness position.

Stage 5: Normality. Once I've done a few runs of an hour or so, then I'll know that I'm effectively recovered. I find that I lose two things with an injury: some speed and the ability to recover from big runs quickly. In my experience, these both come back fairly quickly as I continue training. I find that my ability to run long distances is generally unaffected and that I can step straight back into long training runs or events without any difficulties. I will have just lost some pace and be stiff afterwards. Once I'm recovered and running again, the final worry I have is about whether I'm doing too much too soon or anything that will aggravate the condition. I'll be constantly looking for pains and twinges in the affected area and be very conscious of it. The point at which I finally know that I'm injury free is when I'm no longer worrying and at some point have a realisation that I've not thought about it for a while.

For a relatively minor injury, the recovery period tends to be a few weeks and the time of worry and stress is fairly short. For a more serious injury, however, weeks can turn into months and the mental test is much greater. My greatest test was the stress fracture of my right leg. In total it was a five-month recovery, the only positive being that it was through winter so didn't stop me doing any of my larger focus races.

Injury is always a very testing time. Personally I find the early stages the hardest and most frustrating because it's unknown as to exactly what is wrong, how serious it is and how long it will take to recover. Essentially I don't feel in control of the situation. Once I have a diagnosis then my confidence starts to grow as I feel that I'm back in control, know what to do and have an approximate timescale to recovery.

Throughout the whole period, I always maintain a vision of what I want to get back to. This tends to be a successful race finish in the future or the achievement of some other goal but I don't have a timescale-driven plan to get to it. Sometimes a timescale might be involved because the event is already entered but I don't set targets along the way. My experience tells me that this is dangerous and pushes me to attempt to achieve the targets which can be detrimental if the recovery is taking longer. So I hold a vision of where I want to get to but do not pressure myself to build towards it. In essence I allow my recovery to progress at its own pace, even if there's a jump required at the end when time runs short. I've run marathons without any structured build-up and run a 100-miler with absolutely no running for six weeks beforehand. While nonconformist by any standard methodology, this works for me and ultra running is by its very definition an unconventional and extreme sport.

My final advice on injury is not to panic and to keep a long-term view. Keep that vision in your head of where you're heading back to, but don't panic about rushing back there. The recovery will come but it's important to keep your motivation up, think long-term and tell yourself that in six months' time you'll look back and wonder what all the fuss was about.

*'You've got to want this one 100%. If you only want it 99.9%
then you'll fail.' (Lakeland 100 finisher)*

Brandon and I entered the UTMB in 2015 but failed to get a
place.

There are two phases to the UTMB entry. The first is that
you have to accumulate sufficient points from qualifying races.
Some ultras offer points based on their severity but they have
to pay for the privilege of being a UTMB qualifier. They use
this as a marketing tool to promote their own race. The longer
and harder the race, the more points it awards. However, a lot
of races are now refusing to pay and so no longer award points.
The Lakeland 100 no longer does, as it considers itself its own
race, not a qualifier for someone else's. While I completely
agree with this, the result is that it's getting harder to accrue the
necessary UTMB qualification points. Despite this, I already
had sufficient points for entries in both 2015 and 2016.

The second phase of the process is a ballot. In the first year
of applying, you get a single entry in the ballot with odds of
slightly under 50% of getting a place. If you fail and have
enough points to enter again the next year, you get two entries
in the ballot so your chances are about 90% of getting a place.
Failing that, with sufficient points again, your entry is
guaranteed in year three.

You can link entries together as a pair or small group, so that
you either all gain a place or not. Brandon and I had done this
and so both got rejected. Our chances would now double in
2016 but first we needed a big challenge in 2015 to keep us
ticking over.

So it was back to the awesome Lakeland 100.

This time would be a real test as I was carrying an injury. In
May I picked up an innocuous shin niggle while road running.
It was one of those niggles that I get a lot but that usually go
away. This one became worse so I rested up for a few weeks

before running the South Downs Way 100 in June. I finished that race but it blew the niggle into a full-blown injury just six weeks before the Lakeland 100. I had shooting pain up my leg and couldn't put any weight on it. After a fortnight the pain was less but I was still limping badly and unable to push up on my left ankle. I saw a physio who didn't rule out the Lakeland 100 but recommended getting it checked out properly as it could be a stress fracture. An A&E physio gave the same diagnosis but an x-ray proved it to be soft tissue damage only. Rest and more rest was prescribed. It was another two weeks until I could walk without limping, leaving just two weeks until the race.

During this period, I cycled a lot to keep my fitness up but took a full two weeks' absolute rest before the event. In the eleven weeks running up to the Lakeland 100, I'd run just once and that was another 100-mile race. The lack of running didn't worry me too much as ultra running is an unusual sport. What did worry me though, was my ability to carry a recovering injury through such a hard event. The South Downs Way 100 had been very painful but that was twelve hours shorter. I knew I'd probably damage it badly again and need a lengthy lay-off, but I'd accept that outcome just to be able to finish. Couple this with my record of finishing every event that I'd started. This is very rare for an ultra runner but something I'm incredibly proud of. The day I don't finish an event I'll be devastated. So taking an injury into the UK's hardest single-stage race with a 100% determination to finish is not a good combination for a healthy outcome. However, not once did I ever think about skipping the race. My mindset was simple: it was the Lakeland 100. I'd be starting. I'd be finishing. There was no other possible outcome.

At 6 pm on a Friday evening in July, Brandon and I lined up in the starting pen with 300 other runners. The event anthem *Nessun Dorma*, aptly translated, 'None shall sleep,' was sung by an opera singer and then we were off. A slow jog through Coniston with crowds cheering and we were rolling.

The important thing about ultras is not to think too far ahead. Especially on a long one like this; the time involved is too daunting to be able to deal with. Run for say six hours on any day and you'll be shattered. If you think about the 33 hours still to go, you'll collapse mentally. You have to deal with the time stretching in front of you by ignoring it or it'll weigh you down.

The first section over the Walna Scar road to Seathwaite in the Duddon valley took less than two hours. This was taken at an easy jog for the flat sections and a brisk walk on the uphill sections. We just chatted to a few people and enjoyed the evening, getting the first 2,000 feet of climb completed and the first few hours out of the way. I could feel my shin straight away which was a worry for later but it wasn't restricting anything. We arrived five minutes ahead of schedule due to the good conditions.

We then headed over to Eskdale, which is a rough section, although a lot of recent track improvements helped. We knew the route well and were very careful to pick our way round boggy sections to minimise getting our feet wet. On a normal run we wouldn't worry but we were keen to avoid any problems with trench foot on such a long one. The weather was cool and perfect so we arrived ahead of schedule, refilled water bottles, grabbed cake and headed on.

Next was a short six miles over to Wasdale Head. It got dark on this section so we donned headtorches and picked our way around the boggiest patches. There was half a moon so we could make out the outlines of the mountains around. It was fantastic scenery but a pity to be doing it without views. We gained slightly on this section and arrived in Wasdale fourteen minutes ahead of schedule after five hours of running. It was a good start. We had soup and a sandwich, then headed off into the night.

We now had the three big passes to climb, all on rocky tracks: Black Sail Pass to Eskdale, Scarth Gap to Buttermere and finally Sail Pass to Braithwaite. It was 4,500 feet of climbing by headtorch. On all these climbs we could see the lights of other runners stretched out above and below us, plus the stars above. This was an awesome sight in the dead of night. Descending a steep section from Black Sail Pass, Brandon slipped on a rock and fell heavily on his hip. There was no harm done but it was a reminder of the risks of overnight running on rough ground when you're tired. As little as one wrong foot on the rough ground and your race could be over.

After hotdogs in Buttermere at 2 am, we had the long slog up Sail Pass on a small path. I was leading the way and navigating but my batteries were fading. There was one point where I lost confidence as I'd passed a path heading off to my right which I thought was wrongly placed. I couldn't find the features I was looking for to confirm we were heading the right way. In my faded torchlight I couldn't see far enough to reassure us easily but after a few minutes it became clear. These little things play on your brain, as a navigation error is very easy to make in the dark when tired. I didn't bother changing batteries as the spares were in the bottom of my rucksack and it would be light within an hour.

As we headed up towards the col, I started dozing off on my feet due to fatigue. I'd also got pain in my foot as I could feel the first blister forming. We'd been underway for nine hours and already little stress factors were building up, each small and insignificant but at 3 am and with another thirty hours to go these things can soon get on top of you. As we summited the col, I fished my poles out of my bag and used these to stabilise myself on the long descent, to stop me staggering about when falling asleep and prevent further aggravating the blister.

It got light on the way down and Keswick was below with the mighty Skiddaw and Blencathra across the valley. We would be heading that way next. We stopped to change socks on a bench before heading into the checkpoint at Braithwaite. The blister on my foot was surprisingly big and I was going to have to run over seventy miles on it. I drained and taped it, re-applied plenty of anti-chafe cream and we headed into the village. We ate pasta and rice pudding and pressed on. We'd lost time on this section against the schedule and were now slightly behind. This wasn't a worry but more a comparison that we were running close to our last year's times and a 38 to 39 hour finishing time. It was 5 am and we'd completed the first major milestone by clearing the big mountain climbs and the first night.

We ran round Keswick and climbed up Latrigg, heading towards Blencathra. This climb is steep and as we were walking we both started falling asleep. I was really struggling, staggering about like I'd lost all control of my legs, until I could snap awake again. This continues to happen to me on most overnight runs and I'm used to it now, but it's never a pleasant experience. After half an hour or so I tend to recover and, sure enough, on the faster section around Lonscale Fell I was fine. We arrived at the Blencathra Centre at 7:30 am with 41 miles done. We buzzed through quickly, filling bottles and grabbing cake and biscuits but there were a lot of dead bodies here. The night had taken its toll and the retirement rate was starting to mount.

Next stop was Dockray after another two hours or so. Jon, who we'd run a couple of High Peak Marathons with, was sat here in a chair, retiring as he was recovering from a virus and couldn't go on. Jon's a top ultra runner and event organiser and has completed this race a few times before. He asked us, 'Why did I enter the 100? Why didn't I just enter the fifty?'

A good question Jon and one we've been asking ourselves. He wished us well and we pressed on to the midway checkpoint at Dalemain where our drop bags were. Our schedule had us arriving at 1 pm; we arrived three minutes early so were bang on our previous year's pace.

As in 2014, John was knocking about here, as were two of the event organisers. The checkpoint was quiet so we had a good chat to them while sorting ourselves out. They were all great and said we looked fresh which always helps. There were a few bodies in a right state lying around us but we just concentrated on the job in hand. We had a complete change of running gear, including shoes and re-supply of food into rucksacks. They brought us stew, pudding with custard, cups of tea and made sure we were refreshed and ready for the back half of the course.

It was then into a long afternoon and evening, running down to Ullswater, over to Howtown, through Fusedale and over High Kop, endlessly down the side of Haweswater to Mardale Head, over Gatescarth Pass into Longsleddale and finally over the pass to Kentmere. It was dark as we ran into the Kentmere valley but we had enough night vision to cope without headtorches until we reached the checkpoint. We were within ten minutes of our previous year's times all the way which gave us a massive boost. My feet were sore with multiple blisters, muscles were hurting, legs stiff and everything was really painful. I was taking painkillers every four hours but we were in relatively good shape.

We had soup and smoothies in Kentmere, put an extra layer on and headed off into the second night. A big climb up the Garburn Pass was tricky with tired legs on unstable rocks but I was leading the way and using my poles for stability. Brandon was starting to fall asleep again but I was ok and another competitor was with us so we did our best to keep chatting to stay awake. The descent into Troutbeck was absolutely endless and I suffered a loss of confidence near the bottom when I thought I'd missed the track we needed to take. I hadn't missed it, but in the darkness and with such fatigue little things get magnified massively.

From Troutbeck, we headed over to Ambleside on a section that I always struggle with. It's straightforward but on both previous events I'd had massive low points here as I'd struggled with fatigue. I had no trouble this year as I navigated and was very attentive, although I had another major wobble when there was a left-right decision to make. I was reading the course notes but in my fatigue I just couldn't make them out. There were four other runners with me, who just stood around like zombies and were no help at all. I needed Brandon to catch me up, which he shortly did, and he soon confirmed my thinking to solve the problem.

John was at Ambleside again at 2 am. This was a massive boost to us as we ran in and he told us we looked great, while he described most coming through as, 'The walking dead.' Soup, sandwiches, yet more foot repairs, clean socks and we were off into the night again. It had got cold now so we'd got fleeces, jackets and hats on. When you're so tired you feel the cold badly. Heading up onto Loughrigg we passed another runner who was bent over a fence looking at the ground.

'Have you seen my mate?' he asked us.

'Is that Joe?' Brandon asked.

'Yeah.'

We hadn't seen him and he didn't seem too worried. He kept leaning on the fence as we headed off. Under any other circumstances at 2:30 am it would be bizarre. On an ultra, it's just normal. The great thing is you all have your names on your rucksack in large letters and become soul-mates on such an epic journey. These two finished a few minutes ahead of us in the end.

Climbing over Loughrigg wasn't a problem but then we had a mile or so of straight, easy track towards Elterwater. This was where the fun started. Brandon started falling asleep and bumping into me. Then I lost it too and was sleeping and staggering. It had got freezing cold and I was shivering because we'd slowed down. There was a mist which was playing tricks with my brain. I'd see the mist in my headtorch and it would come down like a curtain and the lights would go out as I fell asleep. Then I'd jerk awake. I was hallucinating too. There were snakes, frogs and mice everywhere I looked on the path. Bizarre dancing shapes to the side. Small screens playing videos on the floor too. It was a wonderland of colourful madness. Snakes were sticks, frogs and mice were leaves, dancing shapes were bushes and the screens were puddles reflecting torchlight. Brandon had a severe pain in his kidney and was hunched over. He kept stopping to double over and relieve it. We were both gone.

We eventually emerged after 94 miles at Chapel Stile at 4:30 am to a roaring fire and music. I'd snapped back out of it with daylight emerging but was worried about Brandon and his kidney. He was in a lot of pain and I thought he might need an ambulance. It seemed to be a serious problem as he'd been hunched over for a while and all his movements were very awkward. I was mentally preparing myself that he'd have to make a big decision to retire and I'd press on alone. We'd often talked about the fact that one day one of us would have to retire from a race, but neither of us had ever had to make that decision before. With the amount of pain that Brandon was in, it was clear that he was going to have to cross that bridge in the next few minutes.

I grabbed stew and bread while he headed slowly to the loo. A few minutes later he emerged, rubbing his hands, a huge grin on his face and a spring in his step.

'That's shifted it. The kidney's sorted. What is there to eat?'

This is one of the funniest things I've ever seen in my life: he was too far gone to realise he just needed a massive poo after 34 hours of running and eating. If I hadn't been so exhausted I'd have rolled on the floor laughing.

Onto the final push. Just eleven miles to go. We'd lost a lot of time on that last section and had a slight concern over the finish cut-off. We had five hours to get there and had taken four the year before. However, we knew that we'd been running well that year towards the end. So I set the pace and we pushed on as fast as we could to minimise the risk. I was in agony, my whole body hurt and my legs weren't working as they should. They'd be fine going uphill but as soon as I crested a rise or headed down they'd just not work in a coordinated way and screamed pain until they got used to the motion again. My feet were wrecked with blisters and sore all over. Every footstep hurt. We were on the death march but we were getting there.

We headed over the pass to Blea Tarn and the final checkpoint at Tilberthwaite. We'd matched last year's time for this section so the pressure was off for the finish cut-off but we needed to be done with it. The final climb over the Yewdale fells led into an agonising, rocky descent into the valley. A mile of downhill road running and, once again, I could feel the emotion welling up in me. We shook hands on the final road and dibbed in at the finish for the last time. John was there shaking us by the hands and slapping our backs. We'd done it.

We were led into the hall and announced as, '100 finishers,' once again. We were handed a finisher's medal, t-shirt and the till receipt of spilt times. It all felt very familiar but I was too tired to care. We slumped in a couple of chairs, utterly drained. After 38 hours and 54 minutes of running, we were done. Literally. I could hardly move.

A shower, the greatest bacon butty and cup of tea in my life, an hour's sleep and I was able to function again, although with the body of a ninety-year-old.

While driving home I stopped at the motorway services. I was wearing my finisher's t-shirt. As I was hobbling at snail's pace across the car park, an unknown guy came up to me, patted me on the back, pointed to my t-shirt and said, 'You're a legend. No one here knows what you've done, but I do. You're an absolute legend.'

I had tears in my eyes.

I'd had no contact with anyone outside the event since starting, except a quick text to Clair after finishing to say I was safe. She was in the USA so I couldn't ring due to the time difference. On both my previous finishes, I was in tears when ringing her. At home I switched my IPad on and it went mad with notifications from the running club. I couldn't believe that so many people had been looking out for me. I cried again. I'm not an emotional guy but these big ones properly destroy you, not just physically but mentally and emotionally too. They strip you bare and let you find out what you're really made of. I've never come across anything else in life that does that to me.

To show how wrecked I was, I went to bed at 6:30 pm. I woke at 2 am to find the bedside light still on. I must have passed out the second I climbed in without switching it off.

What a journey that race is. It's preposterous. In my head I can't actually see it as one race; it's more a series of disjointed memories spread across three days and two nights, with a whole host of backdrops in the glorious Lakes. At times the views were fantastic and the climbing was easy. At others I'd hit the depths of despair and struggle to keep moving, struggle to keep eating, drinking and navigating and knowing what on earth I was doing. It's like a surreal experience that didn't happen, something I dreamed, the very best of life and the absolute worst, all rolled into one agonisingly painful experience. It takes time to come down again and get it back in perspective and to actually enjoy and appreciate what I did.

As for the shin and what so often happens with these things: I didn't notice it. It ached all the way round but I was in so much pain in my lower legs that I didn't really notice it after the first night. My legs were very swollen for a few days afterwards, with incredibly sore feet, but that's always the way and it settled within a week. A fortnight later I was running again, only slowly, but the pain in my shin was not an issue any more.

The big, bad Lakeland 100. I'd now entered three times and finished three times. There are only a handful of people who can say that. Should I leave it at that? Retire on a high? Not risk that 100% finish rate? No. Absolutely not. I knew that I'd definitely be back. It's the most horrific experience I've ever been through but also the greatest.

The only thing that could top the Lakeland 100 would be to run the UTMB. In 2016 I would be entering both.

305 started, 209 finished, I came 189th. The race had a 31% drop-out rate.

27 Stress Fracture

'Mess with the ultras and they'll mess with you.' (Anon)

2015 was a testing year for injury. Pain in my left shin had stopped me running in May and I'd run just twice all summer. These runs were both 100 miles, the South Downs Way 100 in June, which made the problem far worse and then the Lakeland 100 in July. I'd cycled for a period of thirteen weeks with no running apart from these two races. I'd spent the whole period limping with the discomfort in my leg. After a fortnight's recovery from the second race, the pain had largely gone so I started running again in mid-August, focused on getting back to a reasonable pace for the Chester Marathon in early October. After a slow start, largely due to ongoing fatigue from the Lakeland 100, my speed came back fairly quickly and I used the Great Langdale Marathon in mid-September for my only significant long run. The week before Chester I came down with a heavy cold, so I wasn't expecting too great a time but went into the race just aiming for a solid finish of sub-3:30.

Chester Marathon was a fairly uneventful race, with cool weather giving perfect marathon running conditions. My pace wasn't affected much by my cold in the first half but I knew that it would probably slow me down later on. This happened in fairly spectacular fashion at twenty miles where I hit the wall harder than I ever had in a marathon before, with a sudden and catastrophic drop in pace of two minutes per mile. I felt this coming on and recovered it within five minutes by eating a couple of gels and drinking well. I finished in 3:22 which I was very pleased with given the lack of running all summer and having to run with a cold.

I hadn't felt any problems during the race but as soon as I walked away from the finish I could feel a sharp pain in the outside of my lower right leg. I didn't think anything of it, assuming it to be a tweaked muscle or similar due to the fast running and something that would settle in a few days. I was limping around on it but this is nothing unusual for me after a race. I was so pleased to be back at a decent marathon pace after such a frustrating summer without running, that the day after Chester I entered two additional races a month later. That was how certain I was that I'd just got a short-term problem that would recover quickly. How wrong I was.

Four days after Chester, I was still limping but went for a slow four mile run. I could run ok, although still with pain. I still wasn't moving too well from stiffness from the marathon so didn't think too much about the pain. I left it another four days and ran gently again. This time all stiffness from the marathon had gone but the pain was still in my leg. I rested again and decided that I'd run one last time before seeking advice. This run was with the running club so a bit faster and further but the result was the same, pain in the outside of my right leg. I had incredible soreness to touch just above my ankle, on the outer of the two bones of my leg. I also had a burning pain higher up on the outside of that lower leg. I booked a physio appointment to get it looked at. The diagnosis was a tendon problem in my ankle. I was given some exercises to do and told to rest. I'd got a marathon five days later and I asked whether I should be running or not. It was recommended that I didn't but if I chose to run then it shouldn't do any long-term damage; it would just set my recovery time back. With my mindset, naturally I went ahead and ran the marathon. Big mistake.

Snowdonia Marathon is the race that I've run the most times and this was my eighth time on the course. I was still limping with the pain in my ankle on the morning of the race. With hindsight, I wonder why I didn't question what I was doing attempting the marathon. I can only explain it by my single-minded focus in everything that I do. This was my favourite marathon and it never even entered my head that I shouldn't run it. For a clever and well-educated guy, I can be pretty stupid sometimes because of my obsessive personality.

As soon as I started, I could feel pain in my leg but I'd run races on injuries before so thought I'd just go slowly and get round. Snowdonia is a very hilly course with a climb up the Llanberis pass to the youth hostel at Pen-y-Pass in the first four miles. Although I could feel my leg injury, I ran this section ok but found that I was very slow on the long descent down into the valley that followed, with loads of runners coming past me. This was unusual as I can normally hold my own down this descent but my leg was so uncomfortable that my speed was limited. I then ran reasonably strongly through the valley and had a strong climb from mile thirteen to fifteen, up the second major climb, overtaking most runners around me. There is then six miles along the valley to Waun Fawr which rolls along. My leg was getting progressively worse along here and I was gradually slowing down. By mile seventeen I'd lost a significant amount of pace and had pain shooting all the way up the back of my leg. My leg felt like it was going to collapse underneath me. It was the only time I've ever considered walking in a marathon and the only time I've seriously wondered if I was going to finish or not. I just kept trundling along, ignoring all the other runners who were by now flowing past me. At mile nineteen a runner in a 100 Marathon Club t-shirt went past me who I've seen at events before. I thought that if I could catch him and get chatting then I'd progress more quickly and get my mind off the pain. So I made an effort to catch up and ran with him for the next few miles until we hit the major climb from mile 22 to 24. I struggled badly up the climb but at least everyone was struggling up here and I wasn't any slower than others around me. Then the final big descent into Llanberis for the last two miles was awful, with severe pain shooting all the way up my leg on every footstep. I knew that it was only for a short time and would all be over once I was into Llanberis high street at the bottom. I finished in my slowest ever marathon time of 4:00 and was just really pleased to have got round.

The pain in my leg was intense and, as I limped back to the car from the finish, I knew that the races I'd just entered over the next few weeks were definitely off. Something was seriously wrong as I hadn't expected that level of pain for what was a short race for me, on a supposedly minor tendon injury. I went for a pint with Greg afterwards, who had finished thirty minutes ahead of me. My leg was agony and I was limping badly with the pain. The only consolation was that it was late October so if I'd got a bad injury then it was the right time of year to get it.

Over the next few days, I applied the usual RICE (Rest Ice Compression Elevation) techniques to try and calm the injury but it was having no effect. The pain on the bone was far worse and less localised than it was before, with severe tenderness when touching the outside of my ankle and front of the outer leg bone. The burning sensation all the way up the outside of my calf had got worse too. As well as this, my ankle was swollen. I was hobbling badly which I seem to have spent far too much of my life doing. In fact, in the preceding six months, I'd spent three-quarters of the time limping due to injury, which is not good for a supposedly fit guy in his mid-forties.

At this point, I thought I'd need a good period of rest and aim to get myself back for the Tour de Helvellyn race, which was eight weeks away in late December. I was incredibly frustrated, having been injured all summer. Eight weeks would be enough time to get back from any injury I'd ever had before, so it seemed a sensible aim. After a fortnight of complete rest there was absolutely no improvement in any area and my ankle was still constantly swollen. Something was wrong and it definitely wasn't the tendon problem that I'd been diagnosed with. I assumed this was a misdiagnosis, so I booked an appointment with a different physio to get a fresh look.

My first session with this physio was great. He very quickly diagnosed that I'd got a serious imbalance in my hips which was loading my legs asymmetrically and could well be the root cause of my recurrent problems. He also diagnosed that I'd torn the peroneal muscle on the outside of my right leg, which may or may not be related to the pain lower down. This was great to hear and he did some work to reset the balance of my hips.

He thought that I should be well on my way to recovery within a few weeks.

Over the next few weeks, I tried some test cycle rides on my turbo trainer. These were only ten minutes and very gentle, but they would cause my ankle to swell up worse than it already was. This was very frustrating and demoralising. I'd never had an injury that I couldn't cycle with before. Was this really just a muscle tear? I had another physio appointment where he diagnosed that the muscle tear was healing but he was confused by the swelling and the lack of general progress in my recovery. His view was that there was another problem in my ankle but he couldn't diagnose it as he didn't have access to scans. His recommendation was that I get myself a hospital appointment for an MRI scan and a proper diagnosis.

I visited my GP and outlined the problem. He confirmed my physio's recommendation that I see an osteopath to get a proper diagnosis. I'm lucky to have private medical cover through work so this happened very quickly and two days later I had an appointment at the Spire Hospital in Cheshire to see a specialist. My foot and leg were examined and x-rayed. The x-ray picked up an abnormality on the outside of my right fibula, just above my ankle, exactly where the worst pain was. It was recommended that I return for an MRI scan to examine it properly. A few days later, I returned for the scan which was one of the most surreal experiences of my life. After leaving all metal objects and valuables in a locker, I was laid down and my foot wedged into a holder so that it couldn't move. I was given headphones and asked what radio station I wanted to listen to for the duration. Then I was manoeuvred so that my leg was inside the scanner, which is a giant donut-shaped machine. The scan took about forty minutes, the duration of which I just had to lie completely still and listen to the radio. The machine itself is noisy, with various vibrations and rumblings being emitted as it goes through its process. The only way to track the passing of time was by thinking how long I'd been listening to the radio and counting songs. It felt like my foot was twitching as I was concentrating on keeping it very still. This was imaginary but it was a very strange experience. Once the scan was done, I returned a day later to see the osteopathic surgeon.

Once it came, the diagnosis was crystal clear and everything fell into place.

'Mr Thomerson, we've found your problem. You've got a fracture of your lower fibula.'

The surgeon had the scan on his computer screen which clearly showed a v-shaped crack through the bone, just above my ankle. This was exactly the place where I'd had the severe and sharp pain to touch on the outside of the bone.

He added, 'Basically, you've broken your leg, but don't worry about it, it'll sort itself out.'

A stress fracture is the worst injury that a runner can get. They say it's the only injury that will actually stop you running. So you'd expect that when diagnosed with one, you'd be devastated. Not so for me. It was two months since I'd suffered the injury and that entire period I'd had no path to recovery and no end to it. I'd spent the whole time limping and unable to put all my weight on my leg. I'd had my leg constantly in a tubigrip bandage and had barely exercised because just ten minutes on a bike would cause swelling. It's the only injury I've ever had where I was losing fitness because I wasn't cycling to keep fit.

So when I got the news, I was relieved. It was known, it was bad, but it was straightforward and not as complicated as some of the things that were being mentioned. I'd also been walking around on a broken leg for over two months, so was over the worst. There wasn't anything that needed doing as I'd been walking on it for so long and the bone was already healing. The time for being in a boot to support it was long gone. It just needed rest from running for another month.

Running the Snowdonia Marathon on it was, with hindsight, an incredibly bad decision. The diagnosis explained the pain and how hard that marathon was. That was effectively the start date for my recovery and I'd rested from running since then. The standard recovery time to begin load-bearing exercise is six to eight weeks and I'd almost served that time when I had it diagnosed. Stress fractures often don't show up on x-rays but mine did. This was because the healing process was well underway and the x-ray picked up the calcium deposits being laid down around the injury. The MRI scan then confirmed it by showing the fracture itself.

As I drove home, I knew that I'd turned a massive corner. There was still a long way to go until I could run again but the surgeon had said that I could cycle as much as I wanted, even if my ankle was swelling. The fibula is the smaller of the two bones in the leg and isn't the main load-bearing one so cycling wouldn't hinder the recovery process. I knew that the Tour de Helvellyn race in December was off but my focus now shifted to the High Peak Marathon in early March. That was three months away and a viable target for my return. I knew I could spend a month getting my fitness back on a bike and then start running again in mid-January. I had a plan to get myself back.

The other thought in my mind as I drove home was simple, 'If I can run a marathon on a fractured leg then I can do anything.'

Once again, I'd taken myself to a new limit and set myself a benchmark position in enduring pain that would be a useful tool to use in the future. There are always positives in negative situations and this was a good example. This was the worst injury that I'd ever had and I'd run a marathon on it. Nothing could hurt as much as that, no matter what I attempted in the future. In my mind, I'd earned my stripes as an ultra runner with that one.

I was about to enter the UTMB in the next few days and knew that this was another stepping stone along the way. It was a low point but one from which I'd recover and one from which I could draw strength. If I could finish one of the toughest marathons in the country on a fractured leg, then once again I'd proven to myself the level of pain and suffering that I could endure without quitting. Ultra running requires mental strength and I was getting stronger.

I tried cycling on the turbo the next day and did thirty minutes. I had some slight swelling in my ankle. I repeated it again two days later and this time the swelling was minimal. I then started cycling on the turbo every day and was getting no swelling at all. The timing was incredible because within days of getting a proper diagnosis, I was also free of the swelling and most of the pain. The fortunate thing was that I wasn't tempted to run because I knew what the injury was. If I hadn't known it was a fracture, then I would have been tempted to run again at this point and may well have suffered a set-back. This shows the importance of getting injuries diagnosed properly.

I built up to doing an hour a day on the turbo during the week and a few rides on my road bike at weekends. I could feel my general fitness rapidly improving and I was gaining in confidence again. Over Christmas we were away at Clair's parents in North Wales. I hadn't got space to take a bike with me but I borrowed my father-in-law's mountain bike so I could continue to train for an hour a day on that. We had very heavy rainfall overnight on Christmas Day and it was still raining heavily on Boxing Day morning when I went out for a ride. There was a strong wind along the coast and water everywhere, with flooding on the roads and local rivers had burst their banks. I was cycling down the promenade at Colwyn Bay with the wind behind me, doing approximately 25 mph. All the manhole covers had water pouring from them as water ran off the hills. As I flew down the seafront, I suddenly saw a raised manhole cover directly in front of me. Water was flowing from underneath it and the force had raised it up like a ramp. I saw it too late to avoid it and was going too fast to even touch the brakes. I managed to hop the front wheel over the cover but took off when the rear wheel hit it. As soon as I landed I lost control and crashed off sideways onto the tarmac, landing heavily on my right leg and taking a big impact on my right arm.

As I landed the only thing that went through my mind was that I'd written the whole year off and that the UTMB was gone. Logical or otherwise, that's what I thought in that split second. I lay on the ground and could feel pain in my right leg, arm and shoulder. I just felt like crying as this wasn't supposed to happen. I was really worried about my leg because obviously I was cycling to protect a fracture and had landed heavily on that side. I dragged myself out from under the bike and rolled over onto my front, then with difficulty got myself upright. I realised that my leg couldn't be too bad, although there was blood and a large rip in my cycling tights. My knee had taken the impact and was badly grazed but nothing was broken. My elbow was sore and I couldn't move my shoulder very well as my collarbone had taken the full force of the landing.

This all happened quite quickly on the seafront road, which was deserted due to it being such awful weather and early on Boxing Day morning. As I fished the bike up off the ground, a car pulled up, with the windows wound down and three people open-mouthed looking at me, asking if I was ok. It was a picture that I'll remember for a long time as they looked totally shocked. I explained that I was ok and they watched me hop on the bike and ride off. They'd obviously seen me at a distance riding and then suddenly vanishing as I crashed onto the ground.

The fall-out from the crash was a swollen, grazed, very sore knee and a very sore collarbone. I could hardly bend my knee for a few days due to the swelling, although it would get moving enough to cycle each day. It was badly grazed too. It was so sore that I had to wear shorts for a few days, as long trousers were painful to wear. My collarbone didn't feel broken but I couldn't lift my arm as it was sore at the joint under my neck. Both injuries took about three weeks to recover, although I still have a large scar on my right knee to remind me of this low point.

This was a testing time because it really felt like being kicked when I was down. It was just a freak cycling accident that I couldn't avoid. In thirty years of cycling, it was the worst crash I've ever had, coming at a time when I was trying to look after an injured leg. The timing was impeccable. In the end, no long-term harm was done but I really did think things were stacked against me.

A fortnight after the crash, I tried my first run of twenty minutes. This was fine with no pain but resulted in a lot of aching at the fracture point over the next few days. I decided to delay the running another fortnight but started walking instead. At first just for thirty minutes, building quickly up to an hour's walking every day, with some longer walks of two hours thrown in at weekends. This was a great way to get confidence back in putting weight onto my leg. I then introduced the running through five minute jogs as part of the walks and finally did a few twenty minute runs again. Through this whole period my ankle ached and twinged a lot. This was very disconcerting and different to any other injury that I've ever had. Normally, once I start to run again there are no issues. With this injury though, it just ached constantly, questioning whether I was doing the right thing by doing these walks and small runs. I was only running once a week but very quickly could add distance and managed twenty miles within five weeks of the first test run. I then backed off the distance and increased the frequency to run three times a week but over shorter distances.

In total, it took five months from suffering the stress fracture to considering myself recovered. This was the longest and most demoralising injury I've ever had because for a long time there was no end to it and no clear path to being recovered. I eventually got through it though and it's made me stronger for the experience. I also know that I will never suffer an injury as bad as this one again, a simple yardstick to measure future injuries by. To add insult to injury, I suffered my worst ever bike crash during the recovery period. I hit rock bottom when that happened and seriously questioned whether I'd ever run big distances again. Injuries seemed to be stacking on injuries, I'd spent months limping about and I'd almost had enough.

However, 2016 beckoned and I had a dual focus. I had an entry for the Lakeland 100, the hardest thing I've ever done in my life, attempting to go for a very hard four finishes from four starts. I'd also entered the race which has been my destiny for a few years now, the UTMB. The ballot results would be announced in January 2016 and there was nothing that could be done apart from await the outcome.

This was a high risk plan. In all the races I'd ever done until this point, I'd still finished every one I'd started, with not a single DNF (Did Not Finish). The drop-out rate on marathons is very low at about 2%, so the average runner would expect to run fifty marathons before not finishing one. However, the average drop-out rate on the ultras and fell races I'd done was 21%, so the average runner would run just five before not finishing one. By these odds, an average runner would not have finished nine of the ultras or fell races I'd run. Based on these high drop-out rates, the odds of me finishing every race that I'd started was incredibly small at 0.001%, odds of only 1 in 100,000. That's how hard ultra running is and how determined I'd had to be to finish every race that I'd done. I'm incredibly proud of this record but I was risking it all heading into 2016.

Given the low point that I found myself in at the end of 2015, the plan for 2016 was very risky. I would never consider not entering something because it risked my 100% finish rate. However, it was going to be a challenge to get myself back to the level, both physically and mentally, that I was used to and to pitch the odds back in my favour of finishing both the Lakeland 100 and the UTMB.

Would I get an entry to the UTMB? Could I emerge from the worst period of injury in my life and get myself to the start line of that awesome event? Better than that, could I complete the course and finish? It was time to find out.

28   The Big One: Ultra Trail du Mont Blanc
(August 2016)

'We do these things not because they are easy but because they are hard.' (JFK)

At 9:18 am on 13th January 2016, I received a text from Brandon that simply said, 'We're in.'

The UTMB was finally on.

I was still recovering from the stress fracture and this gave me a massive boost, with a long-term goal to focus on. It was just what I needed. Brandon and I already had a ramp-up plan in place, with some very hard races along the way to provide the necessary training for the Alps. I had a huge focus and a plan of action to get myself there.

First up was the High Peak Marathon at the start of March. This was to be my come-back race after my enforced winter lay-off. Unfortunately, this was cancelled at the last minute due to heavy snow. While this was incredibly frustrating at the time, it gave me more time to become comfortable with running on my leg again. I was only just ready for this race physically, but mentally I still wasn't fully confident running on it. This proved to be an example of how there's always a positive to be found in negative situations as it bought me extra time.

I found recovering from the fracture to be quite a mental challenge, as well as a physical one. I was acutely aware of the need to ramp up slowly and not to put too much pressure onto my leg, with constant aching a daily reminder of this. However, I overcame this in typically unconventional style. Despite a low running mileage as I slowly ramped up, I started getting a lot of pain on the instep of my right foot, just before I was due to run the High Peak Marathon. A physio appointment diagnosed a tendon problem which was yet another injury to add to my recent list, but the aching in my ankle stopped at the same time. I think there's a lot of truth in the link between your thought processes and physical injuries. Once I had the pain in my foot, all aching from the fracture disappeared almost instantly. My only explanation is that my sub-conscious was finally switched off from the fracture and focused on this new injury instead.

I now had time to re-group and re-focus myself on my next race. This was the Manchester Marathon, which I'd entered before I'd suffered the fracture. I had subsequently said that I'd just saunter round to bank some miles. However, I quickly realised that this was a very bad option as my body really did not need a pounding over 26.2 miles of tarmac, even at a slow speed. It would be a recipe for disaster and a potential serious set-back on the road to the UTMB. I pulled out a few weeks before the start.

My come-back race now moved onto the Fellsman. What an awesome event to use to return from a bad injury, one of my favourites and a long, slow run over relatively soft, forgiving ground. This was a far better proposition than a road marathon.

The tendon problem had responded to treatment and was now a nagging niggle, rather than a painful injury. I avoided road running as far as possible but spent as much time heading out to the hills as I could, to run and rack up some large amounts of ascent. The winter was not kind in assisting as snow lingered into late spring and I was constantly running in arctic conditions. My mini crampons were used more than in any previous winter. As a result, I was in good shape to jump back into the ultras with Brandon when the Fellsman arrived in late April.

The Fellsman turned out to be an epic. It had been very wet in the lead-up, so the Yorkshire Dales were as water-logged as I've ever experienced them. The going was very heavy due to the amount of water on the hills, turning everything into boggy ground. This sapped the energy of all competitors and we constantly lost time against the schedule we were using from our previous slowest finish. Then overnight, the temperature plunged to a significant minus number, freezing everything solid. It became very treacherous, with ice on all rocky surfaces, the bogs freezing up, steep grass frozen into slippery slopes and stiles coated in ice. Again, this slowed us down considerably as care was needed not to have an accident under these testing conditions. It was a beautiful night to be out though, with the stars and moon crystal clear above us, but another night where our water bottles froze and we were forced to drink slush. We finished in 22 hours and 26 minutes, our slowest ever. However, the race winner was an hour slower than the year before, which would translate into us being two hours slower than expected. Our finishing time was respectable when taking this into consideration.

I'd banked over 22 hours of continuous running on the Fellsman, a significant start to my UTMB build-up. More than that though, I'd banished the demons of the winter and a major line had been crossed. In my head I had exited my injury phase and was now officially on the UTMB ramp-up. It was as if a switch had been flicked mentally and I now had the tunnel vision required to progress towards the Alps. Finally, after almost a year of injuries, I was away and on a build-up to something I was desperate to achieve.

Next up was another old favourite, the Old County Tops fell race in May. Once again I was running with Greg, who had also had a winter of injury to contend with. This was a key race for both of us, to prove that we'd each recovered our fitness. Like the Fellsman, conditions were wet underfoot which slowed the pace down generally as the ground was boggy. We ran a solid race, finishing in 10 hours and 57 minutes, a finishing time right in the middle of all my previous times for the course. However, it was another confidence booster and confirmed that I'd put the injuries behind me.

In June, I ran the South Downs Way 100 with Brandon as a very long build-up race before the Lakeland 100 and UTMB. It was a very warm and humid weekend so we were battling dehydration as we ran, with sweat constantly pouring off us. We just concentrated on drinking well and maintaining a steady pace. When we arrived at Southease at 83 miles, we were eleven minutes behind our best time which we'd set in 2015.

From here on, we were both very strong and had our best finish to a 100-miler, taking 25 minutes out of our previous fastest time to finish with a new 100-mile personal best of 26 hours and 7 minutes. My recovery from this race was very pleasing too; after a full week's rest, I was cycling strongly and then running without any issues from the race. My confidence was building, as I was getting better at dealing with the problematic last twenty miles on the 100-milers and my speedy recovery showed that I was in good physical shape.

The decks were now cleared and I was back on form ahead of the two big ones.

The Lakeland 100 in July was a fantastic journey as always, made all the more special because Greg was running it as his first 100-miler. While I prepared in my usual meticulous manner, Greg had been unable to recce any of the course, then picked up a knee injury the week before, forcing him to make a last-minute decision whether to run or not. On the day of the event, he got stuck in traffic and arrived at the start just fifteen minutes before registration closed. It really was an approach at the opposite end of the spectrum to mine. The weather was perfect all weekend, although boggy conditions in the first third of the race resulted in the on-set of trench foot by mile thirty, which I managed to recover by a change of socks, followed later by a change of shoes at the 56-mile checkpoint. My experience at managing significant issues during a race was showing. However, I suffered a lot of dozing issues on the second night, twice falling asleep standing upright and only being saved by stumbling onto my poles on one occasion and having my arm grabbed by another competitor on the other. Brandon, Greg and I stuck together all the way round to finish in 38 hours and 42 minutes, completing my tenth 100-miler and Greg's first. It was a special weekend, with the three of us running together to keep motivated. Greg showed that a lack of planning can be outweighed by sheer determination in wanting to finish.

I'd run just four races in 2016 but they had set me up perfectly for the UTMB. I'd maintained my 100% finishing rate and run two 100-mile build-up races. I was as prepared physically and mentally as I possibly could be for the trip to the Alps.

I recovered quickly from the Lakeland 100, with a full week's rest and then a week where I was cycling strongly. I did some short runs in the fortnight leading up to the UTMB but nothing significant. I was focused on arriving at the start line as rested and relaxed as possible, ahead of such a big challenge.

Two days before flying to Chamonix, I received an email from the event organiser warning that the temperature was forecast to be over thirty degrees during the race. Competitors were requested to increase their water-carrying ability to two litres and to take caps and sunscreen. This was a serious concern because this race was going to be hard enough to complete in cool conditions, let alone with the added difficulty of high temperatures. As I went through my final mental preparations, I thought positively about previous events that I'd completed in heat: I'd finished the Old County Tops fell race in very testing conditions and the 10 Peaks had been a big day out in hot weather. In 2014, I'd had my fastest finish of the Lakeland 100, when temperatures were in the high twenties. A significant part of the UTMB would be at altitude and at night which should lessen the effects too. All I could do was keep positive and embrace the conditions that we'd encounter.

I flew to Geneva on Thursday afternoon to be hit by a wall of heat at the airport. Conditions really were suffocating. I had a bus transfer to Chamonix, where I arrived in plenty of time to register a day ahead of the race start, which was on Friday evening. I met up with Brandon and we had a pleasant evening soaking up the unique UTMB atmosphere, with pizza and a beer or two to relax.

Friday was spent around Chamonix, enjoying the mountain scenery while walking slowly to conserve energy. I had a siesta after lunch to avoid the heat, where I lay down on my bed but knew that I wouldn't be able to sleep; I was already well-rested and my mind had too much excitement from the anticipation of the start. I spent an hour or so in a very relaxed state, calmly reliving memories of all the big races and challenges that I'd completed, visualising my success in them all. I also walked my way round the entire CCC course in my mind, which would comprise the last 57 miles of the UTMB. The final thing I did was to read all the messages I'd had from well-wishers. I felt relaxed, positive and ready for action.

At 5:30 pm, we assembled in the village square with the other 2,500 runners. Everyone looked fit and focused, with an air of nervous energy and excitement ahead of the start. The atmosphere was unique, with music blaring, commentary in multiple languages, people waving from balconies and flags of different nations being flown. Just standing there and being part of such a high-level race, with other like-minded people from 87 different nations, was an amazing experience. Just before 6 pm, the event's anthem, *Conquest of Paradise* by Vangelis, started up and then we were away. The first ten minutes were very slow, through the narrow, crowd-lined streets of Chamonix. The music continued and the crowds were almost on top of us all. It felt like the intensity of a big Tour de France climb, with spectators crowded tightly onto the road and us all slowly making our way between them. It was an emotional and moving beginning to an epic journey, the greatest start to any race that I've ever experienced, topping even the start of the CCC in 2013. Never again will I hear *Conquest of Paradise* without the hairs on the back of my neck standing up and thinking of the UTMB. The same happens when I hear *Nessun Dorma*, which reminds me instantly of the Lakeland 100.

The first eight kilometres were along the valley to the next village of Les Houches. This was taken at a gentle jog and took us an hour, in a constant stream of other runners. There were plenty of supporters along this section and any British ones shouted our names out, which were on our race numbers along with a Union Jack. Despite being evening, it was hot from the outset. All runners were drenched in sweat and were glistening in the sunlight, an ominous sign with so many hours stretching ahead of us.

At Les Houches, we refilled our water bottles and headed onto the winding path of the first climb up to the pass of Le Delevret. This was a decent climb of 800 metres and had us working hard. The sweat continued to pour off us but all we could do was keep moving upwards and keep drinking from our water bottles. I was carrying three full bottles, with a fourth available in my rucksack to be used later in the race, during the day-time heat of Saturday. I was drinking fairly constantly, as well as wiping the sweat from my eyes as it streamed continuously off my forehead. We just hoped that it would cool down as we headed into the night.

The views on this climb were spectacular, with the southern edge of the Mont Blanc massif visible, as well as views back down into the Chamonix valley. After eighty minutes, we crested the col slightly ahead of our schedule and descended down the ski slopes towards Saint-Gervais. For this race, I'd put together a schedule based on the event's published times for previous slowest finishers. I'd added time for stops, adjusted splits in the second half against our previous CCC timings and scaled the whole schedule to give a 44-hour finishing time. This gave us two and a half hour's margin of safety against a 46 hour and 30 minute final cut-off time. This seemed reasonable, especially as we knew that Lakeland 100 finishers typically took a few hours longer to finish the UTMB, so we should expect a finish somewhere under 45 hours.

It got dark on the way down to Saint-Gervais, so we put our headtorches on. All the way down this descent, we had a constant stream of runners coming past us. This happened on the CCC too, confirming that both Brandon and I are slow descenders versus other runners. Arriving at the checkpoint, we'd lost a small amount of time against our schedule but nothing to unduly worry about after 21 kilometres and three and a half hours of running. We refilled our bottles quickly and moved on.

266

We now had ten kilometres of valley running to the first major checkpoint at Les Contamines. Not far into this section, we came across an ultra running friend, Nick. He was bent over, tying a shoelace, and we very nearly ran straight past him in the dark. Nick is a very experienced ultra runner, having done over 200 ultras, including many very hard ones. He's finished the Lakeland 100 five times and this was his fourth time at the UTMB. His first two attempts ended in retirement but he completed the course in 2013, which he always says is his greatest ever achievement. Nick is our sanity check for the UTMB and Brandon has often said to me, 'Remember, it took Nick three attempts before he finished.'

We had a very sweaty group hug as we were all pleased to see each other. We ran along together but Nick was not in high spirits. He was struggling badly and already considering retiring. This really was out-of-character for such a proven ultra runner. Brandon and I encouraged him and chatted, with Nick eventually moving slowly ahead of us on the trail.

All the way along this relatively easy section, it became apparent that lots of runners were struggling. We constantly passed people who were sitting down or simply taking a few minutes' rest. There were a few people retching and I passed someone vomiting by the trail. This was very early in the race to be seeing such things but the heat was clearly affecting a lot of our fellow competitors.

We arrived at Les Contamines at 11:30 pm to a scene of devastation. We were only thirty kilometres into a 170-kilometre route but this checkpoint was carnage. There were dead bodies everywhere and many looked like their race was done. It was a scene you'd expect at an eighty-mile checkpoint, not at the first one with less than 20% of the race completed. I've never seen such a big fall-out so early on a race before. Given that the qualification criteria for the UTMB is so high, this was incredible. I'd run two 100-milers and the CCC for my qualification points; there should be no inexperienced ultra runners and no shirkers on this race. We would later discover that 159 runners retired in these first thirty kilometres.

We just refilled our bottles and grabbed a few biscuits to eat, before heading quickly on. We passed Nick here to gain a few minutes on him. We continued along the valley, where the support was incredible, even though it was past midnight. Both Saint-Gervais and Les Contamines had been rocking with music, supporters, flags, cheering and children high-fiving us all. This continued through the valley and is all part of the UTMB experience; a quite incredible race atmosphere that I've never experienced anywhere else. Big city marathons, such as London, can have a lot of noise but this was different. It's far more personal and more intimate, with the feeling that every supporter knows you personally and is willing you to get round. As we approached a small lake at Parc de Loisirs, music was thumping and it was clear there was a party going on. As we turned the corner, there was a bar with a disco outside, with the DJ on a jetty over the lake with his record decks. The race literally ran through the middle of his dance floor. It was just unbelievable and shows how the French have really made this race unique.

We were making a long, steady climb through the valley and up to the Col du Bonhomme; three hours of climbing, requiring us to gain 1,600 metres of altitude. We overtook lots of runners up here, as we just steadily ground out the climb. Everyone was struggling by now. The air was noticeably thinner at altitude, making all our efforts harder still. On one of the steeper sections, I heard Nick's cheery voice behind me as he'd caught us up again. We continued trudging upwards, chatting away, all of us still with sweat pouring from us, despite it being the early hours of the morning. I was soaking wet; I was only wearing shorts and a t-shirt but they were sodden. This was the same for everyone. It was still hot and humid, even at altitude and in the dead of night. We knew it would get a lot worse when the sun rose later on.

Nick moved ahead of us at the top and we wouldn't see him again. This was a pity because talking to others is a great form of motivation and makes the hours pass more quickly. On a UK race, everyone speaks English so it's easy. However, there are so many nationalities and languages on this race that it's not easy to talk to others as you go.

At the Col du Bonhomme, we were three minutes behind our schedule after eight and a half hours of running. We were in a good position but I knew that we'd been working hard in the heat and would lose time on the descent. We headed across the hillside on a rough track to the top of the climb, Croix du Bonhomme at 2,439 metres. This next descent and the huge climb that followed would complete the night section but I knew they'd be critical to us in terms of time against the schedule. In the first half of the race, we had less than an hour's buffer to the cut-offs and it wouldn't take much for that to be eaten away.

We lost twenty minutes on the descent and another ten in the checkpoint at Les Chapieux. This left us with less than a thirty-minute margin to the cut-off. We were both very tired after over ten hours of running, so changed socks here to give us a new lease of life. We also had salty noodle soup which was perfect for trying to recover ourselves and replace the huge amounts of salt that we'd been losing through sweat. The checkpoint was a scene of devastation again, with the number of runners retiring now up to 277.

I knew that we now faced a problem with the cut-offs on the course. It would all depend on the next leg, a huge 1,000-metre climb up to the Col de la Seigne, which would take about three hours. I thought that our only chance was to recover some time on this climb which seemed reasonable given our performance on the two previous climbs. I thought we could possibly pull back twenty minutes which would restore a healthy buffer again.

As we headed along the valley in the dark, our headtorches kept picking out runners asleep to the side. I've seen runners asleep many times but this was very strange as there were loads of them. As we jogged along, they were every few hundred metres, just asleep in amongst the rocks on the hillside. I started dozing off on my feet along here, with the effects of working so hard against the heat catching up on me. I then started hallucinating, seeing animals in the rocks, interspersed with people. I saw zebras, giraffes, cattle, buffalo, monkeys and snakes, sometimes with people draped over them. Some of the people were hallucinations of rock shapes but others were actual runners asleep. It was a crazy hour or so where I was at a very low ebb and was not in control of myself, although we were still moving along, which was far better than all those asleep at the side of the trail. There must have been thirty to forty bodies strewn along this section, showing how much toll this race was taking out of everyone.

This climb was murder. We were slow and the rigours of the long, hot night were catching up on us. My feet and legs were hurting but I couldn't take any painkillers because it's very dangerous when you're so dehydrated. I hadn't taken a pee for about five hours, despite drinking bottle after bottle of water en route and glugging huge quantities at the checkpoints. I was calculating times to cut-offs, how far we'd come, how much longer was left and processing everything. Normally, I'll only focus on one section at a time and ignore the enormity of what lies ahead. However, cut-off times were going to be critical and I needed to review the ones in the mid-section of the race to see where we'd be against them. It didn't look good. I also knew how hard the second half of the course would be, as I'd covered it all on the CCC previously. I thought we might be ok except for one thing: it was getting light and once the sun cleared the mountains then the temperature was going to soar.

As we headed towards the top of the col, with the early morning sunshine lighting the fantastic mountain scenery around us, I knew that the attempt was doomed. We hadn't gained any time and I could see that we'd actually lost more. We had a very rough section next, which would be slow, and we'd then lose further time on the long descent that followed to Lac Combal. In my mind, I just wanted to clear that cut-off and see where it left us. Beyond that, I knew that we had a race to each cut-off for the rest of the route and it was inevitable we'd get timed out somewhere; we had no margin of error left and another 110 kilometres to cover. This wasn't negative thinking but just the harsh reality of our situation.

Brandon had been making the same calculations. We've done a lot of big challenges together over the years and I've seen him endure some very tough times. High up on the col, he turned to me and simply asked, 'Can you take another thirty-odd hours of this?'

He looked as drained as I've ever seen him. We'd been going for nearly fourteen hours and both knew this battle against the heat and the mountains wasn't sustainable, as we'd only covered a third of the course. He'd confirmed all my thoughts and calculations in one simple question.

I replied, 'No. Let's just see if we can get halfway. I'll be happy to get to Courmayeur and complete the loop to the CCC start point.'

This was the first time in any race or challenge that I knew I wouldn't complete it. I was disappointed but knew that I'd done everything I could. There was no point beating myself up over it; I simply hadn't got the ability on this course in these conditions to get to the finish.

We headed slowly over the col at 2,502 metres and confirmed that we'd lost a further ten minutes against our schedule. It looked like we might not even make it through the next cut-off, let alone get to Courmayeur. As we reviewed the land ahead, we could see that we were high above the cloud down in the valley below. Snow and glaciers were to our left and the sky was a pure blue, without a cloud to be seen. It was going to be another beautiful day but would be far too hot for an epic run in the mountains.

We dropped 300 metres in height before climbing over small snow fields and the boulders of glacial moraines up to the Col des Pyramides Calcaires at 2,563 metres. The views were stunning as we picked our way slowly across the very rough and tiring ground, then all the way down to the checkpoint at Lac Combal. We were losing time consistently now but were still at 2,000 metres of altitude, so enjoyed the mountain scenery while refuelling with more noodle soup, bread, cheese and salty sausage.

We departed the checkpoint just two minutes ahead of the 10 am cut-off, knowing the next climb would be done in the full heat of the day and we had no chance of beating the cut-off at Courmayeur in the valley beyond. We headed up what would be the final climb for us, a 500 metre ascent to Arete du Mont-Favre at 2,435m. The sun was fully on us and this climb was very hot, with sweat streaming into our eyes once more. Others were stopping on the ascent but we just trundled up, soaking our hats in every stream to cool our heads. A television helicopter was buzzing up and down the valley filming, then flew in to film some close-ups of a string of us labouring our way up the mountainside.

It took ninety minutes to reach the top, where the marshals were enjoying a fantastic view across to Mont Blanc and its glaciers. One marshal told me to remove my cap and brace myself, as he tipped ice-cold water over my head and down my back. It was a shock to the system but very welcome. A lot of runners were sitting around here, enjoying the views because we all knew our race was done now, as the Courmayeur cut-off time was fast approaching. We trotted a few miles across the side of the mountain with incredible views of the snow and ice on the other side of the valley. We dropped to the cable car station above Courmayeur, then headed steeply down a tiny path clinging to the steep hillside, kicking great clouds of dust up as we descended. After an eternity, we emerged from the trees into the baking heat of the valley, with a gentle jog through the village streets and into the checkpoint. Our race chips were scanned for a final time, the barcodes were un-ceremoniously cut from our race numbers and we were timed-out.

We'd run eighty kilometres and climbed nearly 5,000 metres

in a twenty-hour overnight run over five mountain passes, with a significant amount of time spent above 2,000 metres. We had only made it halfway round the route but it had been an epic run in anyone's book. We were shattered. We caught an event bus back to Chamonix and both fell asleep instantly for the full duration of the ride back through the Mont Blanc tunnel. Our work here had finished prematurely but we were done.

After a few beers and a good night's sleep in Chamonix, we took the cable car up to the final checkpoint at La Flegere on Sunday morning and watched runners coming through. We walked along the side of the valley for three miles, before sitting with a beer and admiring the views of Mont Blanc, its glaciers and the paragliders in front of the Aiguille du Midi. We then descended back into Chamonix on another cable car and watched the final hour of the race, cheering the final finishers home after more than 46 hours in the mountains. The atmosphere was incredible and it was an emotional experience to see some of the runners who we'd been running with the night before come home. We bumped into Nick too, who confirmed that he'd also been timed-out at Courmayeur, but was enjoying every minute of the unique UTMB experience that Chamonix offers. We had another group hug, though less sweaty this time. I learnt a lot this weekend and had finally discovered that there is life after a DNF, which I'd never believed possible previously.

The UTMB was my seventieth running race and all of them have been tough ones. This was my first experience of not finishing one. I'd always thought I'd be devastated when this happened but this wasn't the case. I knew that I'd prepared as thoroughly as I could for the race. I'd got good physical fitness and had arrived in Chamonix well-rested and in a positive frame-of-mind. The course was always going to test me but I went into it with my eyes wide-open as to how difficult it would be, having completed the CCC previously and also with multiple Lakeland 100 finishes under my belt. Our schedule only gave us a 5% margin of error from the cut-offs and temperatures in the thirties were the critical factor in eliminating this margin. The inevitable result was being timed-out on the course which is exactly what happened.

I'm not disappointed but very pleased to have got halfway round a brutal course in testing conditions. Of those that started, 1,087 dropped-out. This is incredible considering the qualification criteria and therefore the high-calibre of the starting line-up. To lose nearly half the field in such a high-level race shows how difficult it is.

Ultimately, we ran fifty miles in stunning mountains which is what I love doing most in life. We also completed the first half of the course to link up to the start point of the CCC. This means I've now run 100 miles all the way round Mont Blanc in two sections, which is a significant achievement in itself.

After falling short on a challenge, there's always talk of 'unfinished business' and the need to return to conquer it at the next attempt. However, I don't feel like this with the UTMB. This surprises me because, prior to the event, I thought if I failed then I'd feel the need to return to put it to bed, but I honestly don't. I focused on this race for five years, building up through many other very hard races. I know within myself that I did everything I possibly could to prepare myself physically, mentally and logistically, and then made sensible decisions on the run itself. I don't see how I could prepare differently to ensure a successful outcome. This then leaves it to a lottery of the weather, underfoot conditions and how it would pan out as I ran. This would essentially mean relying on an element of good luck to hold that 5% margin of error from the cut-offs open for me. The UTMB is too big a commitment in mental and emotional energy, focus and time for this to appeal to me.

However, saying that, I have no doubt that I will be back one day. The atmosphere is too good and Chamonix has a setting in the mountains that I'll never tire of. I'd love to finish the race to crown my ultra running exploits but I have no expectation that I ever will. I certainly won't dwell on it and definitely won't put pressure on myself to do it; these huge double-overnight races take too much out of me mentally. I feel that I've reached the pinnacle of my ability just by being a part of the UTMB. To actually finish the race dangles right on the very limit of what I could achieve and I'm just not interested in dedicating potentially years of my life to doing it. I've got other things I want to do.

My mindset has changed through not finishing this race. I've recognised what I always knew about myself but had never admitted before: I enjoy the process more than the result. That is, I love running in the mountains more than I need the ability to say, 'I finished the UTMB.' The only person I need to impress is myself and I do not need the badge of achievement to do that. When I come back, I'll be focused on the run itself and not have a desperate need to finish the thing. It's too hard for that. The whole UTMB experience and my first DNF has rounded me off nicely and given me something that I didn't have before: I feel at peace with what I've achieved and that makes me feel more confident and content with my ability and what I've done. I didn't ever expect failure to feel like this.

I'm happy that I achieved as much as I did here. Just to qualify and start the UTMB, to experience the atmosphere and to complete the first half of the course is enough for me. I feel I've been a success to get to this level and to achieve this much. Having completed the full loop of Mont Blanc in two runs, half-a-UTMB and the CCC, is the icing on the cake.

My work here is done.

2,555 started, 1,468 finished, I recorded my first ever DNF. The race had a 43% drop-out rate.

29   Why?

'I could arrange for a few lads to give you a good hiding. It would have the same end result and save you a lot of bother.'
(Work Colleague)

Ultra running is alien to most of the population who just don't understand it. Therefore, it generates a lot of questions and comments in day-to-day life, some relevant, some hilarious, some annoying but always a talking point with ultra runners and non-ultra runners alike.

The best reactions I've ever experienced are when someone is completely shocked by what I've done. I've had people do a complete double-take or mutter profanities when they've heard the distance I've run. A taxi driver who was driving me to the station for a race once enquired where I was going with my rucksacks. I told him that I was off to do a running race and he then asked how long the race was.

When I said, 'One hundred miles,' he re-clarified his question.

'How far will you run, not how far away is the race?'

He was open-mouthed in the rear-view mirror when he realised the run was 100 miles, rather than the train journey.

Generally, comments are positive but I always enjoy it when normal day-to-day logic is applied to ultra running and suddenly it seems easy. A few times I've had someone calculate that if it's 100 miles in thirty hours, then that's about three miles per hour, which is walking pace. I wish I could walk that fast for that long. It's definitely running, although slow and with walking sections and breaks. Brandon has a good way of getting this over to someone. He says that 100 miles is basically four marathons. Four hours is a good marathon time on the flat, so it might take five hours off-road with hills. If you ran another one straight after then you'd be slower, say, six hours. The next one would be slower again, say, seven hours. The last one, slower again, say, eight hours. Add an hour for stops and it comes to 27 hours. You can see how the time builds up to nearly thirty hours.

A question linked to this is, 'Do you run the whole way?' Naturally the answer is, 'No,' to which the other person always looks disappointed, I always feel like a fraud and sometimes the comment then comes that, 'It's not really running then, is it?' Unfortunately, there's not really an answer to this one. All I know is that you are running and can't cover the distance in that time if you were to walk. Everyone thinks that walking pace is four miles per hour, while the reality is that walking pace is a lot slower than that if you're covering long distances on ground that isn't perfectly flat.

Greg and I heard a great comment as we headed across Broad Crag on the Old County Tops fell race one year, after five hours of very hard work on tough ground. This is a section of big boulders that you need to pick your way across carefully. A guy was walking the other way with cigarette in hand muttering to his friends, 'There's not much running going on.' It made our day and gets repeated often.

On many an overnight run when we're shattered or going through a tough time, Brandon and I will joke that, 'I don't know what all the fuss is about. It's not really running is it?' or 'Three miles per hour? It's just a walk.' These silly comments are a shared form of motivation that keep us going when times are tough.

A very common question is, 'Have you done that one in the desert?' referring to the Marathon des Sables. I've been asked this question so many times, as it's the only long-distance race that most people have heard of. I always politely say that I have no interest in doing it as it's a stage race which isn't what I do, it's in the desert rather than the mountains and in my view is over-hyped and over-priced. My respect goes to anyone who does complete it though because it's a very tough challenge but it's just not my type of event.

Then there's always the comment, 'My friend's done...' followed by an event. If I've done the event or know of it then

I'll be able to comment on it, but I always feel that the other person is trying to impress me with the achievements of their friend, which they don't need to do. I'll always compliment anyone who's got themselves motivated to do anything physical, whether it be a 5k race, hill walk, marathon, ultra or any other challenge that they've had to commit themselves to train for. We're all different and what challenges each of us varies greatly on our background, physical make-up and experience. I happen to like endurance events. However, the commitment for a physically inactive person to run any distance or for someone fitter to achieve a target fast time in a race are just as impressive in my book.

Post-race comments that I always get are, 'Have you been running again?', 'What have you done this time?', 'You're not a good advert for running', 'You're not walking very well', 'It's time you packed that in', 'Do you want a race?' or many similar variants. I've lost count of the number of times that I've been told, 'You're not right in the head', 'You're not getting any younger' or 'Your knees won't last.' I'm so used to these that I can downplay them easily but they still always make me smile.

I get some fantastic comments on occasion when I'm out running in the hills. Many times as I've been running uphill, I've had comments made about fitness, speed, commitment, inspiration or any number of other things. This only happens when I'm on a busy peak with lots of tourists climbing but it always makes me feel good. The best comment I've had was on an ascent of Snowdon. I passed three lads in their twenties who were walking up quickly. One was talking on his phone and after I passed I heard him say, 'We're going up fast but just been left for dead by this guy. He must be some kind of gladiator.'

The big question that everyone asks though is, 'Why do you do it?'

I've been asked this so many times and I still don't have an answer because I honestly don't know. If the stories that I've told sound bad, then that's because they often are. The last twenty miles of a 100-miler are always hell on earth. Running up hills is downright hard work. A lot of running in the hills and towards the end of ultras is very painful. So how can it be enjoyable? There's an old fell running saying that, 'We do it because it feels so good when you stop.' I would agree with this and sum it up by saying that some things are enjoyable while you're doing them, while others are not so enjoyable at the time but you gain enjoyment from them afterwards. Fell and ultra running definitely fall into the latter group.

Something else that you have to experience to believe is the myth that there's an elation at the finish: there isn't. There's hardly anyone there as the field is so spread out and all you want is the pain to stop, a shower and sleep. You're as tired as you can get, you can hardly walk and you just don't care. So I don't do it for an immediate reward at the finish because there isn't one.

A long ultra hits your body very, very hard; physically, mentally and emotionally. It's impossible to describe because I've never known anything else like it. Imagine the most tired you've ever been after staying up all night. Imagine a bad hangover. Imagine being run over by a bus. Imagine the happiest you've ever been and also the saddest. Now multiply them all by two and have them all happen simultaneously. You're not even close. It's like a weird out-of-body experience. You feel detached from the world and you have absolutely no concept of what time of day it is. It's just utter madness. Everyone always asks about the physical side of things but it's the mental and emotional roller coaster that really screws you up. It takes a few days to come back down again which can be difficult when you need to fit back into the normal world immediately afterwards.

Going back to the question, 'Why do you do it?'

I can't answer it as I honestly don't know why. It's unexplainable. It's insane to want to do these things. It's daft. It's absolutely bonkers. So I just don't know why. However, I'm drawn to it and maybe there are some reasons deep down as to why I do it. Because my brain's not wired straight. Because I can. Because others can't. Because it's something that makes me feel different. Because it makes me feel like superman. Because it's exciting to run at night when others sleep. Because there's no finer sight than sunrise after you've run all night. Because I love the hills. Because it's an adventure and modern life doesn't have many adventures. Because it makes me feel alive. Because to experience being at your lowest ebb puts the rest of life's problems into perspective. Because it's there. I honestly don't know.

All I know is that I've run 100 miles ten times and have some incredible memories from a lifetime on the hills. For some crazy, mixed-up reason, this is very, very important to me.

30   Past, Present and Future

'My Mama always said, "You've got to put the past behind you before you can move on."' (Forrest Gump)

I've dedicated a lot of my life to running, cycling and walking in the great outdoors. Not only the thousands of hours that I've spent outside exercising but also the hours travelling, planning, organising and just thinking about it. This has been the biggest constant in my life, always there, always a distraction from other stresses and always something that I've derived great pleasure from. When I look back on what I've done, I gain great satisfaction in knowing that I set myself some hard targets, achieved some great things, made the most of the ability I was given and, above all, enjoyed it.

I've endured a lot of hardship along the way, whether that be through extremes of weather, pain from events and injuries, or the stress of battling hard times under enduring conditions. When all's said and done, I've definitely applied myself to something that has made me very happy, very proud and has made me a better and more rounded individual.

I've got so many memories of good times and bad, memories tinged with emotion, memories of great happiness, great relief or, at times, downright despair. They're all precious to me and I think that part of what I'm proudest of is that I'm not a specialist in one arena but rather a jack-of-all-trades and arguably a master-of-none. So when asked, 'What is your biggest achievement?' it's hard to isolate. If I really, really had to select my favourites and rank things, then I'd have to go with these ones:

1: I've completed ten 100-mile races. This doesn't need justifying. Even I can't believe it. It's ludicrous.
2: I'm the first person to have climbed all the 2,000-feet high Nuttall mountains of England and Wales twice and all Wainwright's Lakeland Fells twice. Only two others have now achieved this: they are John and Anne Nuttall, the

couple who catalogued the 2,000-feet mountains in the first place, so I'm in good company. This took me thirteen years to complete. There is nothing else in my life that took this long to achieve, nothing else that took as much planning and nothing else that required the same level of commitment to keep getting out and nibbling away at the target. I'm particularly proud of this one.

3: I've cycled 230 miles in a day. I've never met anyone else who's done this, even though I know a lot of very keen cyclists. I didn't realise it at the time but this was a massive, massive achievement.

4: I've climbed Snowdon more than 100 times. It's my favourite mountain and I'll never tire of climbing it, whether running or walking, in summer or winter, alone or with company. It's a great achievement every time and I'll never get bored of it.

5: My marathon personal best of 3:05, achieved at Manchester in 2015, followed by running 3:13 at London just seven days later. This was my finest hour as a time-chasing athlete and proves that I had some ability at pure road running. I'm told that I could have achieved a far faster marathon time but my heart was never in it and I'm more than happy with my best time.

I've stopped at five but there are others that come close, such as finishing the OMM Elite, cycling Lands End to John O'Groats, or running seventy tough races before recording my first DNF. The list of five has a nice balance about it, with long ultras, peak bagging, a huge bike ride, my favourite mountain and some fast running included. That probably sums me up as a person.

So what's next? What does the future hold? I plan to just keep going. My target is to run my 100th marathon to become a member of the 100 Marathon Club. However, this is really just about racking numbers up and I'm not going to chase it. I'd like to go back to doing more fell racing, hard but straightforward days on the fells that I love. I'm also going to complete a third round of both the 2,000-feet mountains and the Wainwrights, which will involve lots of planning, driving and exploring but brings a huge breadth and variety to what I'm doing.

Further off, I have a few plans for retirement, when I'll have the time to do more multi-day challenges. I'd like to walk the Pennine Way, 270 miles up the spine of England, but I'd like to enjoy it and savour it by doing it in daylight, with pub stops each night for a decent meal and a few pints of beer. I'd like to walk the Mont Blanc Trail over a leisurely ten days, savouring the incredible scenery in daylight, rather than attempting to run it in one go with large sections covered in darkness. I'd also like to do a round of the Wainwrights in a calendar month which should be achievable and good fun, requiring a bit of planning and a lot of back-to-back days on the Lakeland fells.

More than anything, I want to back myself off from chasing targets. I'll still run long ultras and push myself to my limits, but I want to enjoy what I do and let the targets rack themselves up with time, enjoy the scenery and spend as much time as possible out in the hills. After all, that's what I love most in life and I'd be out on the fells every day if I could.

I'm not a runner. I never have been. I've run a lot of miles in my time but my mindset is all wrong. I hope I've explained my thinking over the course of this book.

In many years' time, when I'm running the Great Fell Race in the Sky, I want to be remembered as a mountain man who never stopped, who pushed his limits, who maximised his brief time here and they'll simply sum me up by saying:

'It kept him off the streets.'

Acknowledgements

Firstly, thanks to Clair, Mum and Brandon for the hours of proof-reading they've all put in to add the final polish to this project. It really is much appreciated.

This book would not have been possible without the partners who were daft enough to accompany me on my adventures. Without them, I wouldn't have started these journeys, let alone finished them.

Dan and Guy were both awesome on the cycling trips, dragging me along during some of my lowest ebbs.

Greg has been fantastic company on many days in the hills, as well as on some epic fell races. He's the most determined person I've ever met.

John is rock solid, a real inspiration to me. He's achieved far more than I ever will and is the most supportive and encouraging influence to all around him.

Brandon is the most reliable, influential and dependable of them all. We've experienced so much in the hills together including some incredibly tough times and huge amounts of pain. However, this has easily been outweighed by so many highs and incredible experiences. Many of my greatest memories are shared with him. We've been through more together than most married couples and every second has been a pleasure.

Finally, to Clair, Kieran and Harry who have always supported me in everything I've wanted to do. I've had more than my fair share of pass-outs over the years. From the first mention of another escapade, to the time away from them and then returning dead-on-my-feet, they've never questioned it.

I've had a great time, so thank you all.

About the Author

Martin Thomerson has been running, walking and cycling in the hills of England and Wales for the last 25 years. He has never run a race less than a marathon or category A fell race. He is the first person to have climbed all Wainwright's Lakeland Fells twice and all the 2,000-feet mountains of England and Wales twice. His current goal is to become a member of the 100 Marathon Club. He lives in Warrington with his wife, Clair, and two children, Kieran and Harry.

Appendix: List of Races

Ultras and Fell Races – in order of distance:

- Ultra Trail du Mont Blanc (106 miles, 33,000 feet) 2016 (DNF: timed-out at 49 miles)
- Lakeland 100 (105 miles, 23,000 feet) 2012, 2014, 2015, 2016 (best time 38:26:26)
- South Downs Way Race (103 miles, 13,000 feet) 2010 (29:01:01)
- Thames Path 100 (102 miles, 2,000 feet) 2013 (27:23:22)
- South Downs Way 100 (100 miles, 13,000 feet) 2012, 2013, 2015, 2016 (best time 26:07:01)
- Courmayeur Champex Chamonix (63 miles, 20,000 feet) 2013 (23:52:23)
- Three Rings of Shap (62 miles, 8,000 feet) 2014 (18:47:00)
- Fellsman (61 miles, 11,000 feet) 2010, 2011, 2013, 2014, 2016 (best time 19:48:00)
- Lakeland 50 (50 miles, 10,000 feet) 2011 (13:47:19)
- 10 Peaks (45 miles, 18,000 feet) 2011 (19:51:00)
- High Peak Marathon (42 miles, 7,000 feet) 2013, 2014 (best time 13:53:57)
- Tour de Helvellyn (38 miles, 7,000 feet) 2011, 2012, 2013, 2014 (best time 9:08:51)
- Old County Tops (37 miles, 10,000 feet) 2009, 2010, 2011, 2012, 2013, 2014, 2016 (best time 10:16:33)
- Hawarth Hobble (32 miles, 4,000 feet) 2015 (6:01:10)
- Yorkshire Three Peaks (24 miles, 5,000 feet) 2011 (4:17:23)
- Welsh 1,000-metre Peaks (22 miles, 8,000 feet) 2009, 2010 (best time 5:54:12)
- Edale Skyline (21 miles, 4,000 feet) 2010, 2011 (best time 3:41:58)
- International Snowdon Race (10 miles, 3,000 feet) 2008, 2009, 2010, 2013 (best time 1:39:43)

Navigational Fell Races – in order of distance:
  (location and route different each year)
- Original Mountain Marathon 'Elite' (53 miles, 14,000 feet) 2011 (20:37:57)
- Saunders Lakeland Mountain Marathon 'Scafell' (38 miles, 12,000 feet) 2009 (14:57:27)
- Saunders Lakeland Mountain Marathon 'Scafell' (38 miles, 10,000 feet) 2010 (14:24:28)
- Saunders Lakeland Mountain Marathon 'Kirkfell' (33 miles, 8,000 feet) 2007 (11:19:54)
- Saunders Lakeland Mountain Marathon 'Bowfell' (29 miles, 10,000 feet) 2008 (11:29:12)
- Karrimor International Mountain Marathon 'C' (26 miles, 6,000 feet) 1993 (10:53:37)
- Lake District Mountain Trial (25 miles, 7,000 feet) 2009 (7:28:06)
- Lake District Mountain Trial (20 miles, 7,000 feet) 2011 (5:45:48)

Road Races – in order of fastest time:
- Greater Manchester Marathon (26.2 miles, flat) 2014, 2015 (best time 3:05:21)
- Chester Marathon (26.2 miles, flat) 2013, 2014, 2015 (best time 3:10:38)
- London Marathon (26.2 miles, flat) 2012, 2015 (best time 3:13:13)
- Blackpool Marathon (26.2 miles, flat) 2009 (3:20:06)
- Liverpool Rock n Roll Marathon (26.2 miles, flat) 2014 (3:20:47)
- Snowdonia Marathon (26.2 miles, 3,000 feet) 2006, 2007, 2008, 2009, 2010, 2012, 2014, 2015 (best time 3:25:48)
- Liverbird Marathon (26.2 miles, flat) 2014 (3:26:23)
- Great Langdale Marathon (26.2 miles, 3,000 feet) 2015 (3:53:21)